Walking the Camino de

Walking the Camino de Santiago

*Essays on Pilgrimage
in the Twenty-First Century*

Edited by
Tiffany Gagliardi Trotman

McFarland & Company, Inc., Publishers
Jefferson, North Carolina

Library of Congress Cataloguing-in-Publication Data

Names: Trotman, Tiffany Gagliardi, editor.
Title: Walking the Camino de Santiago : essays on pilgrimage
in the twenty-first century / edited by Tiffany Gagliardi Trotman.
Description: Jefferson, North Carolina : McFarland & Company, Inc.,
Publishers, 2021 | Includes bibliographical references and index.
Identifiers: LCCN 2021022867 | ISBN 9781476680132 (paperback : acid free paper) ∞
ISBN 9781476642147 (ebook)
Subjects: LCSH: Christian pilgrims and pilgrimages—Spain—
Santiago de Compostela. | Camino de Santiago de Compostela. |
Pilgrims and pilgrimages in literature. | Tourism—Religious aspects. |
BISAC: RELIGION / Biblical Studies / History & Culture |
HISTORY / Europe / Spain & Portugal
Classification: LCC BX2321.S3 W35 2021 | DDC 263/.0424611—dc23
LC record available at https://lccn.loc.gov/2021022867

British Library cataloguing data are available

ISBN (print) 978-1-4766-8013-2
ISBN (ebook) 978-1-4766-4214-7

Front cover image © 2021 77pixels/Shutterstock

Printed in the United States of America

*McFarland & Company, Inc., Publishers
Box 611, Jefferson, North Carolina 28640
www.mcfarlandpub.com*

In loving memory of James (Jerry) Gagliardi.
The Camino's yellow arrows pointed me toward Santiago de
Compostela. My Dad was called James. And so,
in his name, to Saint James I traveled.

Table of Contents

Part Two: Experiencing the Camino

Introduction

Beyond Pilgrimage

Tiffany Gagliardi Trotman

The Camino de Santiago, "that pilgrimage route in Northern Spain," is building a 21st century identity. Due to a boom in cultural depictions of the Camino that have been distributed world-wide and translated into many languages, the obscurity of the route is rapidly fading. Popularized through film, narrative, social media, graphic novels and travelogues, the Camino has been discovered. Every day new pilgrims set off to experience all that it offers.

Each pilgrim brings their own motivations to the Camino. Some seek purely to engage in adventure travel along a well-accommodated route; some are looking for answers, personal or spiritual. There are those aware of the Catholic faith's promise that completing the pilgrimage can absolve them of one-third of their sins (or the entirety if it's a Holy Year). Many have heard the call to the Camino, but are uncertain as to why. In the end, the Camino pilgrimage is unique to each individual. Indeed, pilgrims are often reminded that "[t]his is your Camino." There is no right way, no specific start or end point. The contemporary Camino is a personal journey that has moved beyond pilgrimage.

What could possibly be the draw of a medieval pilgrimage when we are living in a hypermobile, hyperconnected world in which convenience directs and facilitates our every move? In fact, the very nature of today's society is the reason why individuals are setting off on pilgrimage. Human nature does not thrive within the Western culture that we have created. In fact, our modern ways have bred isolation and loneliness due to a lack of community. Consequently, a return to an easier way that allows individuals to move at a natural pace, to connect, to share, to commune is attractive, if not luxurious. The popularization of the Camino is due to at least two factors, an increased understanding and awareness of the route through cultural texts, and the societal pressures of modern life which push individuals to seek a release in the form of pilgrimage.

The aim of this book is twofold: firstly, to recognize the influence of a body of contemporary cultural works that is affecting the growth and popularization of the Camino, and secondly to understand the experiences of scholars studying and walking the pilgrimage.

Before we set off too far down this path, however, it is important to recognize how this all started, which brings us to the Camino and the Legend of Saint James. The Camino, or the Way of Saint James, is not a single path, but a network of routes spread across Western Europe, all of which traverse through France and Spain ending in the autonomous region of Galicia at the Cathedral of Saint James in Santiago de Compostela. Pilgrims travel to this site as the relics of Saint James the Greater are believed to be held within. Saint James, the patron saint of Spain, is believed to have traveled to Iberia to preach Christianity. Upon his return to Jerusalem, he was martyred at the hands of King Herod Agrippa in 44 CE. According to legend, Saint James' body was sailed to Galicia in a boat without a sail or rudder by his disciples. He was buried and the tomb site was forgotten. In 813 CE, however, a hermit named Pelayo had a vision of a bright star in the sky which led him to a field with a burial site. The body within was declared to be that of Saint James. This site was later named, Santiago de Compostela—Saint James of the Field of Stars. By the mid–10th century, tens of thousands of pilgrims were walking the paths to Santiago de Compostela each year with the significance of the site within the Christian world equivalent to that of Rome and Jerusalem. Between the 12th and 14th centuries up to half a million pilgrims traveled each year. As is the case today, there were various motivations for the Camino. In the Middle Ages most pilgrims walked for religious reasons, for purification or salvation. Saint James has been credited with divine intervention in the Spanish Reconquest against the Moors as well as personal miracles for those walking the pilgrimage.

Contemporary pilgrims walk in the footsteps of those who have made the journey for hundreds of years. The Camino has a timelessness about it, a consistency, that connects with each individual pilgrim, regardless of the historical and social circumstances from which they have come. This timeless nature is ineffable and hence, those that experience it find it difficult to relate it to those who have not. Humanity, however, has tools to express the inexpressible. Poetry, cinema, theater, all forms of artistic production, can, when well-conceived, transmit the emotion of human experience.

Walking the Camino de Santiago: Essays on Pilgrimage in the Twenty-First Century is divided into two parts, Part One: "Contemporary Culture and the Camino de Santiago" and Part Two: "Experiencing the Camino." Part One focuses principally on reflections and interpretations of a growing body of cultural representations of the pilgrimage. These essays reflect on the meaning transmitted through cultural works and ultimately the impact that they have had upon the pilgrimage. Part Two consists of both the personal reflections of scholars and the reflections of other pilgrims as they travel the Camino, as well as the "Caminoization" effect on pilgrimage traditions beyond Spain and France.

In "Onward and Inward: The Changing Destination of the Camino de Santiago," Maryjane Dunn reflects on the changing perspectives of pilgrims through an invaluable survey of narratives from the late 20th century to the early 21st century. She traces the transformation of these narratives from tales of grand adventures reliving a medieval quest and guide books providing information about accommodation, weather and trail conditions in narratives from the 1980s to 21st century narratives that capture the personal transformation and spiritual reflections of pilgrims focused on the metaphysical nature of the route. Her summary of the evolution of Camino narratives, as well her detailed chronology of these works, serves as a meaningful tool for future pilgrims preparing themselves for The Way as well as researchers interested in the renovation and redefining of the pilgrimage.

Anne McConnell explores the search for meaning in Anne Carson's essay "The Kinds of Water: An Essay on the Road to Compostela" from her collection of writing entitled "The Anthropology of Water." The essay serves as a travel journal that documents the narrator's experience, as she attempts to find answers to simple questions. Anne McConnell's analysis of the essay highlights the modern pilgrim's search for answers along the Camino, and the challenges that unfold as the narrator grapples with the slippery nature of answer-seeking through pilgrimage.

Annie Hesp's analysis of the "*Río Salado* incident" and its interjection into Camino narratives highlights the intertextual nature of contemporary first-person travelogues. In tracing this specific incident first mentioned in the medieval *Codex Calixtinus* (ca. 1170), specifically its fifth book, the *Liber Peregrinationis* (*The Pilgrim's Guide*), Hesp identifies a common trend to contextualize contemporary pilgrimages through references to previous texts that provide historical, cultural and mythological meanings. Through this intertextuality pilgrim authors establish a link to pilgrims over hundreds of years and, in so doing, create a sense of timelessness and community in their writing.

Emilio Estevez's film *The Way* (2010) has been credited with popularizing the Camino de Santiago, particularly in North America, but also globally through its distribution. Javier Torre Aguado's essay explores several contributing factors that led to the creation of the film including Estevez's family ties to Galicia and Spain, literary and filmic texts that influenced character development and also an engagement with cultural identities in the work. The essay contributes to a greater understanding of the director's ambitions and achievements through the film.

"Screening the Camino de Santiago: Suffering and *Communitas* in *The Way* and *I'll Push You*" examines Estevez's *The Way* (2010) and the documentary film *I'll Push You* (2016) to explain the transformative power of the Camino. Using Victor and Edith Turner's theory of liminality, born out of their anthropological research into rites of passage, Tiffany Gagliardi Trotman analyzes the character development that occurs in large part due to liminal suffering and *communitas*, a unique sense of community, on the Camino.

Part One concludes with Danielle Terceiro's exploration of two distinct graphic memoirs, *Pelgrim of niet? Een voetocht naar Santiago* [*Pilgrim or Not? A Walk to Santiago*] and *On the Camino*, as they represent the contemporary pilgrim experience. Her analysis of the memoirs' different graphic formats, characters and artistic portrayals offers a window into the storytelling possibilities that arise from pilgrimage.

Part Two, "Experiencing the Camino," consists of essays from contemporary pilgrims who are engaging in new ways with the Camino. José Domínguez-Búrdalo's essay provides insights into the learning outcomes from an experiential course he developed and led entitled "The Way," offered by Miami University of Ohio's "Miami in Spain" program. Using a survey administered to students upon completion of the course, Domínguez-Búrdalo analyzes the student pilgrims' perspectives in terms of what they learned culturally as well as their own personal growth. The Camino is considered as an academic tool to foster the teaching and learning of global perspectives.

"Paradoxical Pilgrims: Remaking Religion for the Modern World" is a reflexive auto-ethnography in which Joanne Benham Rennick offers a personal reflection on her 2010 Camino experience and, in particular, its resonance beyond the pilgrimage itself. She explains the struggles of modern pilgrims and how the Camino, a route established out of faith, paradoxically appeals to contemporary secular pilgrims.

Kip Redick, in his essay, looks at the process of meaning-making among contemporary pilgrims. Using a phenomenological and hermeneutical approach, he explains the process by which today's pilgrims forge meaning out of their experiences. Redick describes the pilgrimage as an "ever-evolving intertextual journey" in which pilgrims wrestle with preconceived ideas about their Camino as they travel and how these ideas transform into meaningful understandings within the "Camino cauldron." This process is facilitated by liminality, embodied rituals, experiencing cultural texts, personal reflection on experiences and engagement with the myths of the Camino. The interaction between pilgrims is seen as an integral element in each pilgrim's process of meaning-making. Redick discusses the interpretation of texts as both icon and idol along the pilgrimage.

In "Women Walking: Purpose and the Poetics of Life Along the Camino de Santiago," Nicol Nixon Augusté relates the experiences and motivations of *peregrinas* [female pilgrims] and draws conclusions about what brings women to the Camino in the 21st century. She marries the voices of these women with the words of the Galician poetess, Rosalía de Castro. Nixon Augusté defines the primary reason behind women's pilgrimage as relationship in the form of communion with God, communion with self, and/or communion with others.

Terry Inglese's discussion of the training process for pilgrim guides in the essay "Designing Pilgrim Guide Training in a Secular Time: A Case Study from Switzerland" offers a view of the Camino from a Swiss perspective. This essay looks at the motivations behind 21st century pilgrimage and explains how the spirit of the Camino has transcended national boundaries through a process of "Caminoization." This has led to the replication of Camino-like pilgrimages in other places as evidenced by the first "Swiss Pilgrimage Day" in 2017 which involved a training program for pilgrim guides. Inglese defines guides as "spiritual bricoleurs" as he analyzes the types of activities that guides incorporated into the Swiss Pilgrimage Day.

Nataša Rogelja Caf and Špela Ledink Lozej extend the footprint of the Camino to Slovenia in the final essay. "Footprints of the Camino in Slovenia: Three Ethnographic Vignettes" briefly explains the history of pilgrimage in Slovenia and then, through three vignettes explores the Camino's impact on contemporary Slovenian culture. Rogelja Caf and Ledink Lozej identify the presence of the pilgrimage to Santiago de Compostela in toponyms, folk songs, literature and sacred sites in Slovenia linked to Saint James. The essay discusses the development of the Society of Friends of the Way of Saint James in Slovenia and efforts to revive the tradition of pilgrimage in Slovenia. Finally, the essay examines the proliferation of books, films and Facebook pages that provide information about the Camino in Slovenian.

It has been my sincere pleasure to work with a group of pilgrim-writers in the creation of this book. Many of them have walked the Camino de Santiago and have first-hand experience of what the Camino offers to pilgrims, religious and secular alike. To those who have not yet traveled The Way, my hope is that you too will be called to the Camino. *¡Ultreya!*

PART ONE

Contemporary Culture and the Camino de Santiago

Onward and Inward

The Changing Destination of the Camino de Santiago

Maryjane Dunn

"*¡Ultreya!*" "Onward!" This medieval call urged pilgrims to continue their journey, inspired them in their struggles, and gave them hope in reaching their goal—be it Santiago de Compostela, Jerusalem, or Rome. These days, townsfolk still call out "*¡Ultreya!*" to encourage pilgrims traveling the routes to Compostela. But onward to where? The original, medieval destination—the tomb of Saint James in the Cathedral of Santiago de Compostela—has become secondary to the journey, the Camino itself. The burial site of Saint James is no longer the longed-for destination as it was for countless pilgrims of the Middle Ages. The popular revival of the *Camino francés* (French Route) which began in the 1960s conceived and described it as a re-creation of the medieval Catholic pilgrimage to Santiago, linking the past and the present. Since then, as the numbers of pilgrims increased, the conception of, and inspiration for making the pilgrimage has changed. It may be undertaken for many reasons: an adventure vacation, an escape from the mundane, a personal quest, or a trip of spiritual discovery. For many of today's pilgrims who travel to Compostela the goal is not necessarily the arrival at an outward destination but rather to an inward state of being: one of self-love, courage, freedom, or wholeness. Pilgrims' travel narratives have a symbiotic relationship with the contemporary development of the Camino de Santiago. Personal pilgrimage accounts describe changes in perspective, experiences, and motivations and show a trajectory of popularization and commercialization that mimics the realities of the Santiago pilgrimage throughout the past sixty years.

Whether traveling the route to Santiago de Compostela, or arriving at the tomb of Saint James makes one a pilgrim has long been debated. The word pilgrim derives from the Latin *peregrinus*, from *peregrē* "abroad," which, in turn, comes from *per* "through" + *ager* "field." Perhaps Dante got it right when he said that the only true pilgrims are those who travel to Santiago de Compostela: "they are called *pilgrims* if they travel to the home of Galicia, since the tomb of Saint James was farther from his homeland than that of any other apostle" (*Vita nuova*, ch.29). Eighteen of twenty-two miracles collected in Book II (*The Miracles of Saint James*) of the twelfth-century *Codex Calixtinus* occur in places far away from his tomb in the cathedral in Compostela. Although the *Pilgrims' Guide* (Book V of the *Codex Calixtinus*) is a gazetteer rather than a travel narrative, its very existence proves the importance of the route itself apart from the destination. Pilgrims' tales about their experiences traveling to Santiago de Compostela exist throughout the Middle Ages and Renaissance. Nineteenth-century travelers such as Kathryn Lee Bates, Edith Wharton, and Georgiana Goddard King visited Santiago de Compostela to see the *Pórtico de la Gloria* and to marvel at the swinging of the *Botafumeiro*, while writing about the awful conditions of the roads and lodging along the route. From its beginning, the pilgrimage site of Santiago de Compostela has been integrally tied to the process of getting there.

Remembering the Medieval Pilgrimage: 1957–1980

The pilgrimage to Compostela was moribund in the eighteenth to early twentieth centuries, but it never truly died out. The story of the modern Camino begins in the 1950s and 1960s as organizations such as the *Société Française des Amis de Saint Jacques de Compostelle©* (Paris, 1950), the *Amigos del Camino de Santiago* (Estella 1961), and the Spanish Ministry of Information and Tourism (established 1951) worked toward the revival of the medieval pilgrimage route, based on the description in the *Codex Calixtinus*. These groups promoted the pilgrimage as an historical artifact, a route to be re-created, and the Cathedral of Santiago de Compostela as the goal to be reached.

One of the earliest travel narratives of this period, *The Road to Santiago* (1957) by Irish Hispanist Walter Starkie inspired future pilgrims and set the tone for the next pilgrimage narratives. In Part One, "Early Pilgrims," provides the origin of the cult of Saint James, medieval literary references to the pilgrimage, and background on early pilgrims to Compostela. Part Two, "A Modern Pilgrim," offers a compilation of Starkie's thirty years of experiences along the *Camino francés*. His story is tightly interwoven with local history (political and literary) and his discussions with priests, drivers, gypsies, farmers, and shopkeepers. Although he meets a few pilgrims, the majority of his conversations are with locals. He relates to the route as a modern re-creation of a medieval phenomenon, always attuned to the past as he describes the cities' monuments and churches, and the countryside's beauty: "For me as a humble pilgrim of today the vision of the Sangüesa portal was a profoundly moving experience, for it enabled me to understand the universal significance possessed by the pilgrimage to Santiago de Compostela in those early centuries" (157). Just as the medieval pilgrims did, Starkie clearly sees Compostela as the goal for his journey: "Less than a mile after Lavacolla I came to the '*Monte Gaudi.*' ... Like the French pilgrims of the Middle Ages, when in the joyousness of their hearts they saw the *portus quietis* and the end of their long toiling, I, too, cried out, '*Mon Joie! Mon Joie!*'" (306).

At least one of Starkie's pilgrimages was undertaken for religious, not scholastic reasons: "My 1954 pilgrimage bore for me a deep significance, for it marked the time of my retirement from official life, and I wished to perform religiously all the rituals, in order to prepare myself for making my examination of conscience" (83). He ends by affirming the similarity of life to pilgrimage: "Looking back, my various journeys along the Jacobean road became a huge rambling peregrination through life with many deviations into side roads and bypaths in quest of other shrines, but always with the firm intention of picking up again the trail to the tomb of the Apostle" (306–307).

American author James Michener did not write a book solely about the pilgrimage to Compostela, but the last chapter of his personal travelogue, *Iberia* (1968), introduced the Way of St. James to a general audience. In the brief but well-researched opening, he recounts the facts, tradition, legends, and history of St. James and his pilgrims. He imagines the route from the perspective of the Middle Ages, classifying six types of pilgrims one might have encountered. Michener traveled the route by car, stopping in key cities, and meeting with local scholars and priests. His detailed descriptions of Romanesque architecture and inclusion of stories from the *Codex Calixtinus* give a sense of reading a "history-light" of the Camino. Differing from virtually all other travel accounts, however, is Michener's fascination with the history of both the Carlist and Napoleonic wars, and the retreat of the British Sir John Moore through Galicia. Like Starkie, Michener is not introspective about his reasons for travel to Compostela, except, tellingly, in closing the chapter. After suffering a heart attack in 1965 he was unsure whether he would ever recover sufficiently to travel: "As I lay in that fitful slumber which is not sleep I thought of the good days I had known in northern Spain ... and I thought then that if I ever were to leave that restricted room.... I should like to see Compostela again" (938). In 1966, Michener, a Quaker, fulfilled his medieval vow, closing this chapter (of his life and his book), saying, "I hid in the darkness as if an interloper with no proper role in the ceremonial except that I had completed my vow of pilgrimage and stood at last with my arms about the stone-cold shoulder of Santiago, my patron saint and Spain's" (938).

A third Camino travel narrative written before the large-scale recognition of the pilgrimage route in the 1980s is Edwin Mullins' *The Pilgrimage to Santiago* (1974). Mullins begins his journey by car in France and, like Starkie, provides detailed descriptions about the medieval history of the pilgrimage, the four routes in France, and the monuments, churches, and relics along the way. He is less contemplative, less reverent, and less awed about Spain's medieval past than either Starkie or Michener. He admits his ambivalence toward the "relics and rubble … that depressed life of rural Spain scratched on to the surface of the Middle Ages" (141). His description of the Baroque church portal of Santiago el Real in Logroño brings a bit of levity into what has largely been a serious account:

> high on the north side … poised a monument to St. James such as I had never hoped to see. It was a colossal equestrian statue in stone of Santiago Matamoros, with our hero thundering into the attack like Don Quixote in drag, sword flailing, his billowing robes destining him for certain to the fate of Isadora Duncan: he was mounted, what was more, on a stallion equipped with the most heroic genitals in all Spain, a sight to make any surviving Moor feel inadequate and run for cover [142].

Mullins' reaction at the Monte de Gozo separates him from the sacredness of the medieval pilgrimage while still acknowledging its importance:

> [I] tried to imagine something of the sense of elation a pilgrim would have felt at this moment in the Middle Ages. Impossible. Sadly so. A non-believer who was catching no more than a whiff—scented perhaps with a little sentimentality— of that joy. Yet happy, radiantly happy in a way that maybe no mediaeval pilgrim could have known, because I had not only the city of St. James lying before me but the whole perspective of history, of *its* history, of the follies and lies and achievements, amazing bravery and persistence which were woven together into the intricate pattern of this story to which I had devoted a slice of my life. Why had I done so? I did not in all honesty know, except that I was glad I had [197].

Mullins, like many future pilgrims, undertook traveling the Camino for vague, unknown, or unexpressed reasons, but his goal was to arrive at the Cathedral of Santiago and to experience the pilgrimage in its context as a great cultural-historical event.

Creating a New Medieval Pilgrimage: 1980–1989

Multiple factors led to a marked increase in the number of walking pilgrims in the 1980s. The official signaling of the *Camino francés* with the now famous yellow arrows, a task originated by Cebreiro's priest Elías Valiña Sampedro, made it more accessible to a general walking population who no longer needed trail maps or to speak Spanish to find their way. In 1985 UNESCO designated the old town area of Santiago de Compostela as a World Heritage Site, and the Archicofradía of the Cathedral of Santiago held its *Primer Encuentro Mundial de Cofradías de Santiago* (First Global Meeting of Santiago Confraternities). But it was the 1987 designation of the *Camino francés* as the first European Cultural Itinerary by the Council of Europe that began promotion of the *process* of pilgrimage rather than its destination. The number of walking pilgrims along the route was still minuscule but growing: 690 in 1985, 2,905 in 1987, and 5,769 in 1989, compared to the average of only183 per year in the 1970s.[1]

Pilgrimage accounts of this period still regard the experience as an adventurous, physical re-creation of a medieval ritual. Their narratives tell of extraordinary events and sights that they experience on their journey, recounted for the reader's enjoyment and edification. These authors were pioneers on the *Camino francés*, often traveling for days without seeing other pilgrims. Their focus, therefore, is on the terrain, the weather, their meals and lodging, the sights and history of the towns through which they pass. Stories of camaraderie with other pilgrims are limited, and they offer only an occasional glimpse into their own emotions or motivations. These accounts focus on the external. The goal is the Cathedral of Santiago de Compostela, regardless whether the pilgrim is religious. The authors struggle to understand what it means to be a "real" pilgrim for they have only the medieval model on which to base their identification.

Canadian Laurie Dennett's *A Hug for the Apostle* (1987) tells not only of her experiences walking alone from Chartres, but of the logistics required to publicize her pilgrimage as part of a "Pilgrimage for MS" campaign: "Many people have asked how the idea of re-enacting the historic journey made by medieval pilgrims to Santiago de Compostela came to be linked to fund-raising in the fight against multiple sclerosis. Strangely … how the original idea came to me is a mystery" (xxi). Her daily journal entries describe the weather, sights, terrain, and her occasional interactions with locals who live along the Way. Although her religious background is Catholic, and she mentions lighting candles in many of the churches she visited, her narrative for the most part is neither spiritual nor introspective:

> I have a vague mental image of the walk marked out in stages that correspond, in a way my medieval fellow-pilgrims would have recognized, to the major shrines along the way.... I have resisted thinking about the journey in its full immensity.... Walking doesn't so much allow me to live in the moment as force me to [14].

Her initial arrival in Compostela is somewhat chaotic because of her "Pilgrimage for MS" campaign. It is only after the news and radio reports, awards, and interviews are over that she is able to consider a more private end to her journey. She closes her narrative explaining, "Tomorrow I will walk back out to Monte del Gozo.... I will walk back slowly, right to the cathedral steps.... I shall give St. James another hug, and, in some quiet chapel, light my last candle" (224).

Although Ellen Feinberg's (now Elyn Aviva) book, *Following the Milky Way* (1989), was published two years after Dennett's book, Feinberg had actually walked four years prior, during the 1982 Holy Year. Like Dennett, Feinberg writes her tale in chronological and geographical order beginning with her (and partner Bill's) arrival in St Jean-Pied-de-Port. Her intention in walking the Camino de Santiago is academic, not spiritual, "It wasn't faith that had impelled me—a non-religious, non-athletic graduate student in anthropology. I was doing fieldwork for my dissertation on the modern-day pilgrimage to Santiago de Compostela. I focused on those who upheld tradition by walking the Camino" (*Princeton* 18). In her narrative, she incorporates debates with Bill over the nature of a "real" pilgrim, adding detailed portrayals of early pilgrims and their lives. She also reports conversations with some of the few pilgrims they meet, including an elderly French gentleman who is walking in order to fulfill a vow made during World War II:

> I thought: now there goes a real pilgrim, a pilgrim motivated by faith.... I was puzzled;
> he was fulfilling a religious vow made during World War II, yet he found nothing wrong with taking a bus occasionally, while we, having little or no faith, had scruples about not walking every foot of the way! Was it because we were substituting external ritual for interior belief? Was I a pilgrim? I surely was suffering enough, but did suffering make a pilgrim? [*Following* 46]

In asking these questions, Feinberg frames the debate that continues to be raised today in relation to the bestowal of the "Compostela" by the Pilgrim's Office of the Cathedral of Santiago. Her arrival in Compostela is both upsetting, and eye-opening:

> I had thought that only pilgrims could pass through the Holy Doorway, and we and our companions from the road were the only pilgrims I knew of. We were "real" pilgrims. We had walked the Camino for over a month to reach Santiago, the cathedral, the Holy Door.... They had come by car or bus.... They hadn't walked.... But according to the Church, they were pilgrims too.... The realization shocked me. They were pilgrims, just like us [258–59].

Bert Slader's more modest book, *Pilgrim's Footsteps* (1989) tells of his solitary 1985 walk. Like Feinberg, he questions whether he is a real pilgrim:

"To follow the cult of St. James to Santiago requires a sense of religious purpose based on a sincere belief in its truth, a belief which I did not have. I was on the Camino for the journey, to follow the footsteps of those who had gone before" (38). He meets other pilgrims along the route, most notably two young Belgians who chose making the pilgrimage from Vézeley over incarceration for offenses committed in their home country. More frequently, Slader includes conversations with Spaniards—shepherds, farmers, barkeeps, bank tellers, grocers—who are curious about his journey and his reasons for making the trip. He muses about times during the trip when he felt lonely, but is grateful for those times allowed him to think, uninterrupted. He does not share those thoughts with the reader. His inspiration had come from reading Starkie, and so he views the pilgrimage from a past viewpoint, "At times it felt as if I was tramping through scenes in a medieval play, the drama of the people and places unfolding around me as I moved across the stage" (173). In the end he enters the Cathedral and realizes, "The reason for my pilgrimage had been the journey, but now I was here, the power of St. James was in the very air of this place. The arrival in Santiago is a new beginning—not an end" (168).

Not all pilgrimages were on foot. *Spanish Pilgrimage: A Canter to Saint James* (1990), describes an unusual pilgrimage undertaken in 1989—a journey on horseback, symbolically beginning at the Tower of London where Robin and Louella Hanbury-Tenison paid their traditional medieval twelve pence fee required of all pilgrims traveling from the Thames to Compostela. Because of their mode of travel, they moved in much longer stages than walking pilgrims, and had less direct contact with persons living and working along the Route or other pilgrims. A large portion of their book describes the environment through which they rode and the care of the horses. Hanbury-Tenison clearly used Mullins' book as his main source of historical knowledge, and quotes the passage describing St. James' equestrian statue in Logroño (see above). The "Aftermath" chapter leads the reader beyond Compostela, to Finisterre and Padrón; the author guides the reader away from the medieval notion of pilgrimage and suggests a new purpose of the Camino: "The myth is what matters, inspiring unnumbered [medieval] men and women to lead—if only for a time—lives of hardship and self-sacrifice, buoyed up by the spiritual ecstasy their journey created. St. James was very real for all those people.... We need to search urgently for new and relevant myths to cling to..." (154–156).

By the end of the decade pilgrim narratives had begun to shift away from the sense of re-creating the medieval pilgrimage with the Cathedral as the goal. The Camino, the journey itself, is becoming the transformative experience to a new spiritual center.

Creating a Modern Pilgrimage: 1990–2000

Thanks in part to the political support of the Galician government in forming the *Consejo Xacobeo* in 1991 to promote pilgrim tourism, Holy Year 1993 marked the greatest upsurge in pilgrim numbers in the 20th century with 99,436 pilgrims being granted the "Compostela," a ten-fold increase over the numbers in 1992 (9,764). The availability of multiple guidebooks, easily booked accommodation, and a strong infrastructure, encouraged more diversity among pilgrims walking the Camino. As pilgrims' experiences change so does the focus of their narratives. While their travelogues still (briefly) describe key medieval stories and monuments, they are more likely to regale the reader with tales of new places and people who are soon to become modern legends of the Camino. The purpose of their pilgrimage becomes more personal in nature, and their writings provide insight about their motivation to follow the Camino—a personal loss, an illness, the need for space or time away from the mundane. A successful pilgrimage was often less about the physical goal (Santiago de Compostela) and more about the metaphysical one.

Edward Stanton (*Road of Stars to Santiago*) and Jack Hitt (*Off the Road*) were both pilgrims in 1992, and both published their Camino chronicles in 1994. Like Hanbury-Tenison, Stanton foresees a new future for the pilgrimage. His work also sets a tone about the ultimate purpose of being a pilgrim that breaks away from the medieval model: "To make the pilgrimage has been a way of proving that we could free ourselves from our daily existence, from all those small routines and obligations that mean nothing by themselves but together can prevent us from doing the things that really matter to us, can prevent us in fact from being ourselves." (187)

Hitt also begins by suggesting that the pilgrimage to Compostela is at the point of great changes, but based not on our belief in the efficacy of pilgrimage itself, but on how we speak about religion in general.

> The problem with pilgrimage is that, like so much of the vocabulary of religion, it is part of an exhausted and mummified idiom…. Religion has become a kind of nonstop PBS seminar on ethics, conducted in a shout…. The result is that other unarticulated notions and yearnings once associated with religion have become intensely private. And that is why I wanted to walk to Santiago [14–15].

Both authors write archetypal first-person travel narratives, telling their stories in geographic-chronological order, but not as day-by-day journal entries. Both include stories about modern legends such as the *hospitalero* "El Ramón" of Casa Santa Bárbara in Torres del Río, and both impart historical tidbits through conversations with fellow travelers. Of the two, Hitt is the more nimble storyteller, irreverently interjecting humor and exuberantly absurd flights of fancy into his narrative. Yet in the end, his pilgrimage closes solemnly as he stands ready to place his hand in the column in the *Pórtico de la Gloria*: "The old stone is worn smooth in one place, about an inch deep, in the perfect shape of a human hand. With my new pants and shirt and fresh-washed face, I have no privileges now. No one notices me. So I take a place in line. One cannot make literature here. When my time comes, I put my hand into the stone and pray" (255). Stanton is more somber and reflective throughout, discussing rather than joking about the miracle of the reborn hen in Santo Domingo, for example. In the end, after attending mass and praying for all those who requested his attention, he agrees with a fellow pilgrim, "Santiago's not in here, is he?" (191), and sets out alone to finish his pilgrimage at Finisterre.

A third Camino narrative of 1994, *Pilgrim's Road*, by Bettina Selby is literally a change of pace as she writes about biking from Vézeley to Compostela. Selby had already written about several other long-distance biking adventures. Like Hanbury-Tenison, her mode of travel allows her to traverse greater stretches of the road each day, and minimizes her interactions with other pilgrims. She does add to Camino lore of the period in describing her encounter with Madame Debril, the Camino gatekeeper in St.-Jean-Pied-de-Port. (Stories of this legendary figure are also included in Dennett's, Hitt's and Egan's books.) Selby's assessment of her pilgrimage is a bit less personal than those of Hitt and Stanton, but she too determines that the spirit of St. James is more ephemeral and less rooted in Compostela:

> The St. James I had gradually become aware of on the pilgrimage, was what had come from the hearts and minds of the thousands and thousands of people who had walked the *Camino de Santiago* for all these hundreds of years, struggling with meanings, with conscience, with faith and with the lack of it. It was because of them that there was a *Camino*, and all I could hope to do was to add my prayers to theirs [207].

As a pilgrim during Holy Year 1993, Lee Hoinacki, professor of political science and former Dominican priest, approached the pilgrimage from a decidedly different angle. His account, *El Camino* (1996), is the first volume of the Penn State Series in Lived Religious Experiences. Like many pilgrim narratives, Hoinacki bases each chapter on a reworking of his daily journal entries. His recounting of his pilgrimage frequently touches upon the intersections between Catholic ritual, the lives of biblical characters, medieval pilgrims, and his own lived experiences on the Camino. He is thoughtful, and introspective in describing his daily routines and interactions with others he meets along the road—both Spaniards and pilgrims. Upon arriving in Compostela, Hoinacki ponders the faith of the medieval pilgrims, and their draw to places with relics, the physical remains of the saints. However, the pilgrimage for Hoinacki is no longer tied to a specific sacred space, but to a communal way of living, not just with others who are physically here, but with those who came before:

> I exist only to the extent that I participate in the innumerable practices that collectively establish the living tradition that is my heritage, which my parents and the pilgrims have given me. All the "inner" experiences of these four weeks only occurred insofar as they had real links with the experiences of the dead who accompanied me…. The relics I touch are they, their real presence. I have met, embraced, and kissed them … and their lips were not cold [278–79].

The destination of the pilgrimage shifts slowly from Santiago de Compostela, to the Camino itself. Being a pilgrim becomes less about re-creating the medieval Camino as a fixed geography, and more about creating a meaningful interior journey. In examining pilgrims' narratives through this point in time anthropologist Nancy Louise Frey observes:

> The meanings that the journey comes to have usually appear to emerge over time and space—forward, backward, inward—through movement. Pilgrims' stories are not only about moving through the landscapes but also about odd encounters, refuges, and people and pilgrims they meet during the journey. The Camino, which begins as an abstract space, comes to be an accumulation of internalized places made up of stories, sensations, and changes in perception [*Pilgrim's Stories* 87].

Remembering the Pilgrimage: 2000–2010

In the 21st century, the numbers of pilgrims again increased dramatically. The upsurge in pilgrims requesting a "Compostela" during the 1993 Holy Year led to the establishment of a 100 kilometer minimum required distance for the 1999 Holy Year, and with good reason—even with a 100km minimum 154,613 pilgrims arrived, up from 30,126 in 1998.[2] Depending on the year, the 100km pilgrims, often referred to as *turigrinos* (tourist-pilgrims) make up between 27–40 percent of the total number requesting "Compostelas"; they, however, do not generally publish travel narratives. From reading earlier travel narratives, many pilgrims begin with expectations about what they will experience along the route. They begin their accounts by expressing their intentions about why he or she is walking the pilgrimage route. Rather than chronicling their adventures and the Camino environment as they move through it, this generation of pilgrims writes more personal reflective journals about their individual experiences, feelings, and beliefs, often creating a personal memoir rather than a travelogue.

Shirley MacLaine, an American actor and writer noted for her nontraditional spiritual beliefs, ushers in this new era of Camino memoir with the publication of *The Camino: A Journey of the Spirit* (2000) in which she recounts her 1994 experiences along the French Route. Spanish-language books about the *Camino esotérico* or *mágico* had been popular since the early 1990s, but MacLaine's book is the first to bring this viewpoint to a general English-speaking audience: "I have never been religious, opting instead to seek spirituality, so what interested me about the Camino was the energy of the ley lines themselves, as well as the challenge of walking alone for 800 kilometers" (5). MacLaine follows a geographic trajectory in her story, but not necessarily a chronological one, as she travels backward in time to describe her dream-visions, often seeing life from the perspective of a Moorish girl in the court of Charlemagne. Her dream-guide, John the Scot, reminds her: "The trail enables you to recall who you are. You are the repository of many experiences along the road of time. In truth, you are seeking to travel forward to the beginning. *Ultreya*" (90). She describes few interactions with other pilgrims or Spaniards except for the paparazzi, and her attempts to avoid or flee from them.

In her memoir, *Sue Kenney's My Camino* (2004), Kenney is clear about her motivation to walk the Camino: "As my goal for this journey was the discovery of my higher purpose, I would have to learn the secrets to mastering what I wanted to accomplish through ritual" (22). She insists on her need to be alone: "I tried to avoid any dialogue about the religious aspects of this pilgrimage, making it perfectly clear to myself and others, this was my own personal spiritual journey. Determined not to have a dogmatic religious experience, I resisted being expected to go to this Catholic pilgrim's mass [in Roncesvalles]" (47). The geographical stages of her journey are punctuated by the lessons each one teaches her: "With each lesson I had experienced throughout this journey, I had gained a respect for the mystical nature of the Camino" (133). Her initial arrival to Compostela is anti-climactic, "I had been through a life-altering ordeal which filled my world with absolute love, yet somehow at this place, I felt almost no emotion. Definitely, I felt no joy" (175). After attending the Pilgrims' Mass and reflecting on her journey, she recognizes:

> Through enlightenment, I learned the Camino is God. Through God, I am guided to my higher purpose…. Through my higher purpose, I inspire by sharing my light. By sharing my light, I instill absolute love. Through absolute love, I find peace. Through peace, I find joy…. Through joy, there is happiness. All I really wanted from the beginning of this journey, was universal happiness. On the Camino, I had finally found my way [179–180].

Today she continues to "share her light" through coaching others on how to "reflect, transcend, and transform" on her guided Camino tours, complete with yoga instruction, wine and cheese receptions, cooking lessons, all while staying in lovely accommodations on the last 100 kilometers.

Another tale of spiritual renewal, *Fumbling* (2004), by Kerry Egan is as personal as Kenney's work, but upon starting out Egan has no goals, only questions about why she feels compelled to walk the Camino at all. When she walked (in 1998) she was a student in the Divinity program at Harvard and her father had recently died. Her personal reflections and questions about life, God, the nature of suffering, and joy are couched in theological history and belief. She includes a few typical Camino stories, but *Fumbling* consists primarily of her conversations with Alex, her boyfriend and co-pilgrim. When they arrive in Compostela, she has no answers to her questions: "I was glad there were rituals at the end of the pilgrimage, otherwise I don't know what I would have done. I probably would have fallen apart. Instead, I got there and had something to do…. Ritual can transform space and time, can help us tap into the holy" (220–221).

Personal spiritual and religious lessons are also promoted from a more traditional religious perspective in several books from this period. Sister Joyce Rupp, *Walk in a Relaxed Manner* (2005), shares her experiences while walking with Father Tom Pfeffer in 2003. Her story is only loosely tied to their itinerary, the chapters are not their nightly destinations, but rather the lessons she learned—dealing with disappointments, savoring solitude, trust, humility, to embrace beauty, among others. She bases many of these lessons on interpersonal exchanges with other pilgrims and *hospitaleros*. Her work does not culminate in the arrival at Compostela, but in a gentle reflection of how it prepared her for the end, in Finisterre, as well as in life, for Father Tom died suddenly only six months after completing the pilgrimage.

Mennonite pastor and pastoral theology professor Arthur Boers' *The Way Is Made by Walking* (2007) follows a format similar to Rupp's book with chapter divisions by subject rather than by strict geographic order. His observations are often punctuated by scripture, formal prayers, and comments about the role of worship, service, and spirituality on the Camino and in the world. He writes:

> I heard intriguing theological insinuations in discussions of "the Camino." People personalized, even divinized this route. They spoke of it mystically, as if a wise, caring mentor…. People were correct that something spiritually unique was afoot. But we err by elevating the Camino too much. A pilgrimage route may help someone get in touch with God, but is not itself divine [105–106].

Like Rupp, Boers also ends his narrative, not in Compostela, but in reflections and support for future pilgrims.

Father Kevin Codd, an American Catholic priest and head of a seminary in Belgium, follows a more traditional travel journal format for his narrative, *To the Field of Stars* (2008). His aspiration for his pilgrimage refers to the miraculous discovery of St. James's tomb, "when all is said and done, what I really wanted was to see those stars of Compostela dance for myself" (xvi). The lessons he offers are not overt, but are implied in his descriptions of sacred places and sacred people of the Way. He tells of his own rituals—of prayer, meditation, gratitude, the rosary—and describes the spirit of camaraderie that permeates relationships along the Route. In those relationships he reaches his destination of the field of stars, "So do I see the stars dance at seven thirty this evening in the *Plaza del Obradoiro*? I see José laugh. I see Toni laugh. I see Marisa laugh. I see Elena laugh. I see Nicoletta laugh. I see Alessandra laugh. And I laugh. Yes, I see the stars dance. I surely do" (260).

For some, however, following the Camino is still just a great travel adventure. Two popular books deserve a brief mention. Tim Moore's *Travels with My Donkey* (2005) and Jane Christmas' *What the Psychic Told the Pilgrim* (2007) are entertaining travel narratives in the vein of Jack Hitt, bringing to life new characters, hostels, and rituals that may develop into new Camino legends as did Madame Debril or "El Ramón." These day-by-day adventures are enjoyable tales that just happen to occur on the Way of St James, and are far removed from the majority of the more serious introspective spiritual pilgrimage journals of this decade.

The Pilgrimage Goes Viral: 2010 and Beyond

The expanding awareness of the Camino, thanks in part to the success of Emilio Estevez and Martin Sheen's 2010 movie *The Way*, the ever-multiplying numbers of pilgrims (272,135 in the 2010 Holy Year, 327,318 in 2018) and the ease in self- and on-demand publishing means that the numbers of Camino books is increasing exponentially. The commercialization of the now multiple Caminos to Santiago is reflected in the commodification of the pilgrimage narratives.

Technological advancements have changed both life on the Camino and Camino narratives dramatically. Tablets and smart phones, easy internet access via free Wi-Fi, and the introduction of blogging platforms, have opened the doors for more pilgrims to share their first-hand reports to a wider audience. No longer do pilgrims have to handwrite journals each evening, to be carried home, rewritten and polished into a Word document, and shopped to an editor. E-publishing had been on the rise, but with the launch of Kindle Direct Publishing (KDP) in 2007 it became even easier for individuals and author-wannabes to offer their books to a wider (electronic) market. When Amazon acquired CreateSpace, a print-on-demand service in 2005, then fully merged it with KDP in 2018, the publishing loop had come full circle.

Internet Camino forums, blogs, and Facebook groups now affirm there is no one "right way" to walk the Camino. Suddenly, everyone can share his or her journey of discovery—no need to be a Spanish scholar, historian, or professional author. The quality, polish, and creativity of these publications vary enormously. While some pilgrims simply want to share their experiences with a minimum of effort and expect a minimum (monetary) return, others use e-publishing as a platform to launch (or continue) a writing or speaking career. Keith Foskett wrote his first book in 2015 (*The Journey in Between*) about his 1000-mile trek from Conques, France to Compostela, launching his career as a long-distance hiker and travel-adventure writer. Steve Watkins (*Pilgrim Strong*, 2017) gained a large following as he blogged about his 2015 journey and parlayed that into a book and a career as author and speaker. Kurt Koontz (*A Million Steps*, 2014) continues to promote himself as an inspirational speaker. For Patrick Gray and Justin Skeesuck (*I'll Push You*, book and video, 2017), the book was secondary to the video documentary; their company, Push, Inc., provides courses and curriculum, not about the Camino per se, but about overcoming obstacles and building relationships. Beth Jusino (*Walking to the End of the World*, 2018) published her book through Mountaineers Books, but also has used it to recreate her own business, helping other authors to "tell a better story" and to market it successfully. All of these books are better described as travel journals or memoirs, rather than travel narratives. Their goal is to tell each author's personal stories—of blisters, weather, landscapes, food, and people they encountered day-by-day. Some may have had only a vague notion of the religious importance of the medieval pilgrimage to Santiago de Compostela or the historical basis of many of the rituals in which they participate when they set out. Foskett, for example, learns the French pilgrimage hymn "*Ultreya*" during the communal supper in Conques:

> I realized it centered on both faith and the Camino…. I saw the words scrawled in visitors' books, sung it around meal tables, and stumbled across it written in dust on the trail…. If there was one word signifying El Camino, it was *Ultreya*. It was not until five years later that I learnt it was derived from Latin and meant "Onward!" It was used by pilgrims past to greet and encourage others [71].

For some becoming a pilgrim and writing about it is a cathartic act for coping with grief at the loss of a loved one, just as Tom (Martin Sheen) in the movie *The Way* walked the Camino to make sense of his son's death. Father Brendan McManus (*Redemption Road*, 2011) uses Loyola's *Spiritual Exercises* to guide him on his solitary journey on the Camino del Norte as he mourns his brother's suicide. *The Man with the Camino Tattoo* (2018) is the second volume of a trilogy of pilgrimage memoirs by Dermot Breen who also walked the Camino del Norte, guided by, and along with the spirit of his wife Jacqui who died from cancer.

There is, however, little to set the majority of these blogs-cum-adventure books, travel journals-cum-spiritual life lessons apart from each other. Most stress the importance of the building of relationships with other pilgrims, the creation of a "Camino family," over the individual experience, a logical development given the increasing numbers of pilgrims at all times of the year. They are, for the most part, repetitive in form and intent. The majority replicate a simple daily journal or blog entry format easily reproduced as an e-book, soon after arriving home from the Camino. This is not to say they are not enjoyable reading, or are not well written. Only a few, such as Mary O'Hara Wyman's epistolary account *Grandma's on the Camino* (2012), are self-published with a distinctive format.

* * *

This decade is not yet over. The year 2021 is a Holy Year. How will the pilgrimage change in the next ten years? How will pilgrimage narratives reflect those changes? The path is unclear. The pilgrimage to Santiago de Compostela is no longer a single route, a straight path to the tomb of St. James. Meanwhile, the stories told by pilgrims about their experiences on the Caminos twist and turn like a labyrinth, crossing, mimicking, repeating, and copying each other. The stories are all alike, yet different. Only the pilgrim's movement—forward, backward, inward, onward—is constant, in a never-ending exhortation: *¡Ultreya!*

Notes

1. Statistics are based on the number of Compostelas granted by the Pilgrim's Office of the Cathedral of Santiago de Compostela. Searchable statistics from 2004 to the present are available at www.oficinadelperegrino.com.

2. The choice of 100 kilometers seems to have developed from the Galician Xacobeo 1993 theme "Todo el Camino" ("All the Route")—more appropriately "Toda Galicia" as all the 100km starting points are within Galicia.

Works Cited

Alighieri, Dante. *Vita Nova*. Trans. by Andrew Frisardi. Northwestern UP, 2012, Ch. 29.

Boers, Arthur Paul. *The Way Is Made by Walking: A Pilgrimage Along the Camino de Santiago*. InterVarsity Press, 2007.

Codd, Kevin. *To the Field of Stars: A Pilgrim's Journey*. William B. Eerdmans, 2008.

Dennett, Laurie. *A Hug for the Apostle*. Macmillan of Canada, 1987.

Egan, Kerry. *Fumbling: A Pilgrimage Tale of Love, Grief, and Spiritual Renewal on the Camino de Santiago*. Doubleday, 2004.

Estevez, Emilio, Martin Sheen, and Deborah K. Unger. *The Way*. Icon Entertainment International & Elixir Films, 2010.

Feinberg, Ellen. *Following the Milky Way: A Pilgrimage on the Camino de Santiago*. Iowa State UP, 1989. 2nd ed., Elyn Aviva, Pilgrim's Process, 2001.

_____. "Pilgrimage to Santiago." *Princeton Alumni Weekly*, vol. 86 (Sept. 11, 1985): 18.

Foskett, Keith. *The Journey in Between: A 1000-Mile Hiking Adventure on the Camino de Santiago*. CreateSpace, 2016.

Frey, Nancy. *Pilgrim Stories: On and Off the Road to Santiago*. U of California P, 1998.

Hanbury-Tennison, Robin. *Spanish Pilgrimage: A Canter to St. James*. Hutchinson, 1990.

Hitt, Jack. *Off the Road*. Simon & Schuster, 1994.

Hoinacki, Lee. *El Camino: Walking to Santiago de Compostela*. Pennsylvania State UP, 1996.

Kenney, Sue. *Sue Kenney's My Camino*. White Knight Publications, 2004.

MacLaine, Shirley. *The Camino: A Journey of the Spirit*. Simon & Schuster, 2000.

Michener, James. *Iberia*. Penguin Random House, 1968.

Mullins, Edwin. *The Pilgrimage to Santiago*. Secker and Warburg. 1974.

Slader, Burt. *Pilgrims' Footsteps: A Journey to Santiago de Compostela*. Little, Brown & Co. 1994.

Stanton, Edward. *Road of Stars to Santiago*. U of Kentucky P, 1994.

Starkie, Walter. *The Road to Santiago*. J. Murray, 1947.

Looking for the Simplest Question

A Pilgrimage to Compostela in Anne
Carson's "The Anthropology of Water"

ANNE MCCONNELL

In Book 4 of *The Odyssey*, Meneláos tells Telemakhos of his voyage home after the Trojan War, specifically detailing his encounter with Proteus on the island of Pharos. Not knowing how to get home and suffering alongside his men, all of them "thin-bellied from the long fast," Meneláos learns from Proteus's daughter how he might obtain the answers to his questions: "If you could take [Proteus] by surprise and hold him/he'd give you course and distance for your sailing/homeward across the cold fish-breeding sea" (64). Of course, as Meneláos suspects, getting a hold of Proteus could prove tricky, and he begs the nymph for more information that might help. She counsels: "He'll make you fight—for he can take the forms/of all the beasts, and water, and blinding fire;/but you must hold on, even so, and crush him/ until he breaks the silence" (65). Proteus's defining characteristic, his ability to change form, allows him to elude challengers—not by running faster than everyone else, or taking flight, but by transforming into matter that his challenger cannot grasp. After all, how can one hold onto water? Anne Carson's "The Anthropology of Water" unfolds as a meditation on that question. She begins, "Water is something you cannot hold. Like men. I have tried. Father, brother, lover, true friends, hungry ghosts and God, one by one all took themselves out of my hands" (117). Yet, despite the definitive statement that initiates the text—the keen awareness that water escapes— each of the poem-essays that make up "The Anthropology of Water" traces the narrator's continual efforts to get some sort of a hold on men, the world, language, herself.[1] From that perspective, in each of the texts in "The Anthropology of Water," the narrator lives out the punishment of Danaos's forty-nine daughters, who "were sent to hell and condemned to spend eternity gathering water in a sieve" (118). I would like to focus, in particular,

24

on the essay, "The Kinds of Water: An Essay on the Road to Compostela," where the narrator takes up the pilgrimage to Compostela in order "to look for the simplest question, the most obvious facts, the doors that no one may close" (123). In that search, the narrator-pilgrim finds herself wandering, tracing the steps of the thousands who came before her, yet simultaneously erring, unable to establish a foothold along the way. She meditates upon the way the world slips through her fingers—much like water through a sieve or Proteus through the grasp of his challengers—and defines her act of pilgrimage, her wandering, in terms of that slippage.

In "Thirst: Introduction to Kinds of Water," we read an anecdote about Kafka. According to the anecdote, Kafka's poor health prevented him from swimming, and those circumstances prompted him to write a parable about swimming. The parable focuses on a man who receives a prestigious swimming award, despite the fact that he doesn't know how to swim. The literal water of the sea no longer accessible to the writer, Kafka turns to the watery environment of writing—an environment where meaning always seems to scatter, to exist "over there," rather than "right here." Theodor Adorno describes the elusiveness of Kafka's parables in "Notes on Kafka": "It is a parabolic system the key to which has been stolen [...] Each sentence says 'interpret me,' and none will permit it" (96). For Carson's narrator, the interest in the story lies in the fact that the man "begins to mount the steps" to receive his award, accepting the new reality he has been assigned, without question (119). She notes, "I like the people in Kafka's parables. They do not know how to ask the simplest question. Whereas to you and me it may look (as my father used to say) as obvious as a door in water" (119). The man's silence, his inability to figure out how to ask what he needs to know, keeps him trapped within the confines of the narrative imposed upon him. Carson's narrator admits she likes that silence, perhaps because not asking the right question—one which, we presume, would elicit an answer—sustains the story. And it creates a situation that defies both the man's and the reader's attempt to interpret a situation, a text, in a meaningful way. For that reason, Kafka's protagonists commonly emerge as pilgrim-figures, wandering through strange environments that they never come to know and understand, largely because they can't figure out the right question to ask. Carson's narrator-pilgrim moves through her environment in a way that resembles Kafka's wandering protagonists—despite her commitment "To look for the simplest question," and her initial confidence: "Look I will change everything, all the meanings!" (123).

One of the complexities of "The Anthropology of Water" is trying to determine the value of finding the simplest question, of capturing the water in a way that keeps it from slipping through one's fingers. The narrator-pilgrim clearly seeks the simplest question, at the same time that her journey relies upon the persistence of the question, beyond the ability to discover it, and to pose it. After all, the journey will seemingly end once she arrives at her destination. Carson's discussion of another Kafka parable in the Preface to *Eros, the Bittersweet* provides insight into the play between question and answer, framing it as the movement of desire. Carson reflects upon desire's requirement of an ever-elusive love object, since attainment and accomplishment mark the end of desire—a movement toward that which we don't have. In the Preface, Carson discusses the parable, "The Philosopher," where the main character chases after a spinning top and grabs it, in the hope of capturing movement; and the top, of course, stops spinning. Carson gives Kafka's philosopher the benefit of the doubt, suggesting that he doesn't really seek understanding, but, instead, wants to "furnish himself with pretexts for running after tops" (xii). She explains, "To catch beauty would be to understand how that impertinent stability in vertigo is possible. But, no, delight need not reach so far. To be running breathlessly, but not yet arrived, is itself delightful, a suspended moment of living hope" (xi). Carson describes the delight in desire, in the movement toward something beyond our reach. In this case, then, Carson seems to argue in favor of endless pilgrimage, of the persistence of the question. After all, who wants a "silly piece of wood" (xi)?

In *The Infinite Conversation*, Maurice Blanchot also reflects upon the relation between the question and desire, arguing that a question poses a sort of radical openness, one that in its incompleteness allows for a sense of possibility and unfolding: "Through the question we give ourselves the thing and we give ourselves the void that permits us not to have it yet, or to have it as desire. The question is the desire of thought" (12). Questions provoke thought, affirming their own incompleteness and pointing us toward that which we don't have. And, though they perhaps demand an answer, that answer conflicts with the movement and openness of the question that prompts it:

> But the question is not pursued in the answer. On the contrary, it is terminated, closed again by the answer. The question inaugurates a type of relation characterized by openness and free movement; and what it must be satisfied with closes and arrests it. The question awaits an answer, but the answer does not appease the question, and even if it puts an end to the question, it does not put an end to the waiting that is the question of the question [14].

Blanchot argues here that what the answer has to offer cannot address or negate the movement of questioning, which persists, in excess of any attempt to answer, to produce closure, to make the world comprehensible. In a sense, the question invites us into that failure, asking us to chase down an answer, like a spinning top. Perhaps that's one way of viewing the narrator's search for the simplest question in "The Anthropology of Water." Like

Kafka and Blanchot, she values the persistence of a question over the discovery of an answer, recognizing movement, openness, and desire as fundamental to the act of pilgrimage.

The narrator does not begin her pilgrimage with that recognition, though. Her proclamation that she will "change everything, all the meanings!" shows that she seeks a destination in earnest, implicitly defining herself against the swimmer and other Kafkan protagonists who fail to ask the right questions (123). In "Thirst: Introduction to Kinds of Water," the narrator sets out the circumstances that provoke her to take the pilgrimage, describing herself as a "locked person" looking for clarity in an increasingly murky environment, where objects, words, and people refuse to stay in place (122). The narrator's father suffers from dementia, and his worsening condition causes the narrator to confront the silence and tension underlying their relationship. One of the father's most pronounced changes involves his use of language: "He was all his life a silent man. But dementia has released some spring inside him, he babbles constantly in a language neurologists call 'word salad'" (120). In the beginning of the disease, that particular symptom leaves room for playfulness and even delight: "Dementia can be gleeful at first" (121). Yet, Carson suggests, even a poet can only take so much joy from nonsensical juxtapositions of words, tossed together in ways that feel like they continually re-invent the world. When words behave like water, leaking and slipping, perhaps especially when we most want them to stay in place, the gleefulness quickly transforms into a sense of loss and despair. The narrator admits her avoidance of her father, preferring distance to intimacy: "There are a number of simple questions I could ask. Like, Father what do you mean?" (120). Despite her desire to define herself against Kafka's characters, the narrator recognizes the resemblance, as she doesn't know how, or is unwilling, to ask a simple question that would presumably help her to understand her father's thinking.

At the same time, the narrator sees her father as impenetrable, rendering any question-asking pointless. She describes him as a private man whose disease simply exaggerates his resistance to intimacy: "Now his mind was a sacred area where no one could enter or ask why" (121). Tanis MacDonald, in her article on "The Anthropology of Water" emphasizes the unreachability of the father, and the sense that the narrator has lost him, despite the fact that he is still there: "The father remains beyond the reach of the narrator's love, even as she strives to read him as an untranslated (and ultimately untranslatable) text that will not yield to traditional consolation" (MacDonald 67). The narrator's father is unreadable—a trait that seemingly characterized him in the past and now puts him definitively out of reach, given his dementia. The father's mind, perhaps like the worlds Kafka creates in his writing, remains impervious to questioning, especially since it resists logic and mastery, changing form and eluding one's grasp at every turn. Is there really a simple question in such circumstances, in a language composed of words tossed together like a salad? Interestingly, the narrator does have brief moments of insight into her father's world: "To live with a mad person requires many small acts of genius—reverse of the moment when Helen Keller shouts 'Water!'—when you glance into the mad world and suddenly see how it works" (122). But she also notes a certain resistance: "My mother got good at this. I did not" (122). What does it even mean to glance into madness, to dive into the water, where any satisfying answer eludes one's attempts to chase it down? Ultimately, the narrator turns away from her father's madness, and her life, looking for the simplest question somewhere else. She goes on the pilgrimage to Compostela, presumably hoping she will become the type of person who discovers and asks simple questions, and probably assuming that the world "out there" will feel more stable and comprehensible than the one that makes her feel like a "locked person," unable to get her bearings (122).

There is something solid about the road to Compostela, a well-worn path, traveled by pilgrims since the 9th century. The narrator explains, "Since ancient times pilgrimages have been conducted from place to place, in belief that a question can travel into an answer as water into thirst" (122). History, tradition, and ritual have carved a path in the earth, allowing contemporary pilgrims to connect with past walkers by repeating their steps and committing themselves to the same road. In her essay, "How Is a Pilgrim Like a Soldier?," Christine Hume points out that a pilgrimage, "by [its] very nature eschew[s] more exploratory walking strategies" in favor of a regimented, pre-determined path (51). In other words, the road to Compostela contrasts the labyrinthine space of, for example, Kafka's castle, protecting the pilgrim from the anxieties of wandering without a clear destination. Carson's narrator seems to seek the sort of structure and clarity provided by the pilgrimage, given the sense that she is drowning in the waters of her father's illness, where nothing has a definitive shape or logic. Instead of feeling like a locked person, the narrator pronounces with confidence: "I was a young, strong, stingy person of no particular gender—all traits advantageous to a pilgrim. So I set off, into the late spring wind blasting with its green states" (123). The narrator sets off with clear goals and a well-trod path ahead of her; she feels up to the task, propelled by the desire to find "the simplest question, the most obvious facts, the doors that no one may close" (123). As a "person of no particular gender," the narrator identifies herself as pilgrim—evoking a sort of universal voice of pilgrimage that arises consistently throughout "Kinds of Water."[2] Rather than an isolated individual, trapped in her circumstances, the narrator emerges here on solid ground, joining with pilgrims of the past and present to reach Compostela.

The narrator's approach to her journey, and her choice of companion, also reveal an interest in crafting an environment that feels manageable, accessible, and stable. Her traveling partner, to whom the narrator refers as "My Cid" for the rest of the piece "[is] a pious man who [knows] how to ask questions"; he travels with a map, seeking mastery of the path and its history, and trusting that he will arrive at its end point (122). The narrator explains that she calls him "My Cid" because "It speeds up the storytelling" (126). Identifying her partner by way of a well-known historical and literary figure, the narrator encourages the reader to infer certain things about the man without having to slog through explanations or analyses of his character traits. The narrator points us in that direction: "You will see this as the journey proceeds, see him sailing through danger and smiling at wounds" (126). As a Cid-like figure, the man seems to represent the hero of the journey, triumphant and masterful in the face of adversity. As far as traveling partners are concerned, the Cid represents the type of guy who provides a sense of security and confidence, largely through the performance of his own mastery.

In addition to choosing a competent, self-assured companion, the narrator takes an academic approach to the journey, emphasizing documentation in her search for "the simplest question, the most obvious facts, the doors that no one may close" (123). She refers to that approach as anthropology, suggesting that her pilgrimage, and the information she collects on that pilgrimage, represent a study of humans and humanness. Keeping a journal of her experiences and snapping photographs along the way, the narrator creates a record of her travels, including descriptions and images of the places through which she passes. Hume discusses the narrator's documentation, and the photographs in particular, in terms of the way the narrator becomes observer, recording her experiences as if from an outside perspective: "Photographs set the narrator where she wants to be, a witness to her own story, allowing her to embed a third-person perspective in a first-person voice" (53). Carson's anthropologist resembles the description of the historian she provides in her book, *Nox*: "One who asks about things—about their dimensions, weight, location, moods, names, holiness, smell" (1.1). Both in *Nox* and in "Kinds of Water," we see an interest in getting the facts down, through careful study and observation—perhaps especially when the object of study feels elusive and complex, more like water than a thousand-year-old stone road. But, as the journey begins, she trusts in anthropology, in history, so that she may begin to understand: "What is it others know?" (125).

It does not take long for the narrator's sense of certainty at the initiation of the journey to begin eroding. If the pilgrimage at first promised the solid ground of a pre-determined path, it soon reveals itself as more complex than a linear voyage from point A to point B. Along the road, the narrator describes one particular stretch: "We circle, circle, circle again. Around each bend of the road, another, bending back" (167). Even the most linear of paths reveal their circularity, and give one the sense of backtracking even when moving forward. Jennifer K. Dick, in her essay, "The Pilgrim and the Anthropologist," notes, "['The Anthropology of Water'] advances in a kind of mutation-progression where the repetitions of words such as gold, water, loneliness, love, light, wolves, penance, God, the road, fire, blood, fish, bread, stone, heart, red, moon, and drown vary because their meanings and contexts mutate" (66). In this way, the repeated images and language provide a sense of circling back at the same time that each repetition also draws attention to difference, or the newness we might associate with a particular repetition of the same experience. From that perspective, the road that the narrator-pilgrim travels, though worn by the steps of thousands of pilgrims, has never before been traveled.

In addition to the journey's circularity, it also lacks closure. While the road to Compostela leads to Compostela, the road also continues to Finisterre—the promise of the destination transforming into more road. The narrator explains, "Just as no mountain ends at the top, so no pilgrim stops in Santiago" (183). Of course, eventually the pilgrims will reach Finisterre, and thus the coast, but the narrator's description of the end of the pilgrimage suggests that it feels anti-climactic, especially given the fact that the last leg of the journey is not on foot: "Tomorrow, the ultimate absurdity. We will hire a car and drive to Finisterre" (182). In addition, the comparison to a mountain that doesn't end points to the way that a pilgrimage continues to unfold, and perhaps *is* the unfolding, even after the road stops. The narrator brings the issue of non-closure, of elusive end-points, back to the theme of questions and answers, since, of course, she set out to find the simplest question:

> it is an endeavor as old as civilization to set out on a road that is supposed to take you to the very end of things, if you keep going. What do you find there? That is a good question. Who would you be if you knew the answer? There is one way to find out. So a pilgrim sets off. One thing is certain, one item is constant in the set of beliefs with which he travels. It is simply this, that when you reach the place called the end of the world, you fall off into the water. Some pilgrims drown, some do not. *Claro* [184].

Pilgrimages generally have a destination, yet, in reaching the "very end of things," the pilgrim sacrifices the ground on which he or she stands, the road of pilgrimage. The pilgrim becomes a swimmer, even if he or she, like the man in Kafka's parable, doesn't know how to swim. According to the narrator's logic, pilgrims know this—that they will confront the water one way or another, and that they will learn whether they will drown or will manage to stay afloat. Whether or not an answer exists in that moment remains unclear; but, if it does, it would seemingly resemble the narrator's flash of insight into the mind of her father, where one, even when swimming, can't help but drown.

At the end of the narrator's pilgrimage, as all pilgrims do, she confronts the water, "knocking back and forth slightly in the force of the waves" (187). As she teeters at the water's edge, she listens closely, briefly hoping for a moment of revelation, or insight: "What is it they are saying? Perhaps—no. Words never went on in me" (187). It would seem that the narrator's pilgrimage ends in failure—that she never discovers the simplest question or the most obvious facts. The moment of completion brings silence, or, at least, reveals an inability to decipher words, to make meaning out of the journey. The narrator thus enters the water, suggesting her own fate by evoking the drowned dog she sees floating in the river at the beginning of her journey: "You take hold of my paws and cross them on my breast" (187). While MacDonald argues that "the narrator's attempt to go beyond pilgrimage brings her not to transcendence but to a failure of the mind that echoes the father's madness," I would argue that there is also a sense that the narrator comes to understand pilgrimage precisely in terms of the pilgrim's failure to "get there"—to an end point that would bring closure, meaning, accomplishment. After all, with "paws" crossed, the narrator is sent into the water as "one who has been to the holy city and tasted its waters, its kinds" (187). And she ends "Kinds of Water" in the traditional expression of pilgrims who have completed the road to Compostela—"¡E ultreja e sus eja Deus adiuva nos!" ["Let's keep going further; let's keep going higher.... God help us!"]—an expression that suggests that the pilgrimage never ends, and that all pilgrims must go beyond the end of the road (187). Tasting the waters of the holy city does not furnish answers, or even simple questions; nor does it allow the narrator to transcend the complexities and absurdities of the world. But that failure defines the work of the pilgrim, trying to capture water in a sieve.

Not only does the pilgrimage reveal itself as much more complicated than the narrator initially conceives of it, but so do the pilgrims—herself and her traveling companion, in particular. At the beginning of the pilgrimage, the narrator perceives that a singularity of purpose and action brings focus and clarity to the pilgrim: "You step forward. You shiver in the light. Nothing is left in you but desire for that perfect economy of action, using up the whole heart, no residue, no mistake: *camino*" (154). Yet the narrator soon admits that simplicity, when it comes to humans, is a ruse, theoretically possible and definitely seductive, but, in reality, unattainable: "It would be as simple as water, wouldn't it? If there were any such thing as simple action for animals like us" (154). The complexity of the pilgrimage comes from the pilgrim, not the road. Even the most seemingly transparent of pilgrims, the Cid, ends up feeling opaque and unknowable early on in the pilgrimage: "Who is this man? I have no idea. The more I watch him, the less I know. What are we doing here, and why are our hearts invisible?" (139). Something about the Cid remains totally bewildering and inaccessible to the narrator, perhaps especially because he hides nothing and tends to accept the world as it is, with little reflection. When the narrator notices the drowned dog floating in the river at the beginning of the journey and points it out to the Cid, she notes his response: "The man I am traveling with peers vaguely toward it: 'Ah!' and returns to eating bread. His concern is with the more historical aspects of pilgrimage" (126). The narrator, who has spent a significant portion of the first two entries of her travel journal reflecting upon the dog's corpse, realizes that the Cid does not swim around in the complexities of an object, an image, a moment in the same way that she does. She later describes him twice as someone who "rarely gets thirsty"; and, when noting, "I am making this journey to find out what appetite is," she adds "And I see him free of it" (138, 143). The narrator, driven by desire, by her search for the simplest question, cannot relate to the Cid, who remains totally unreadable and foreign—precisely because he seems to have little interest in catching a spinning top, or seeking to hold onto something that will necessarily slip through his fingers.

The Cid seems to find the narrator as confounding as she finds him, again, as a result of their completely different modes of navigating and experiencing the world:

> Sometimes when I speak to him, My Cid looks very hard and straight into my face as if in search of something (a city on a map?) like someone who has tumbled off a star. But he is not the one who feels alien—ever, I think. He lives in a small country of hope, which is his heart. Like Sokrates he fails to understand why travel should be such a challenge to the muscles of the heart, for other people. Around every bend of the road is a city of gold, isn't it?
>
> I am the kind of person who thinks no, probably not. And we walk, side by side, in different countries [131].

The Cid wants to read the narrator's face in the same way he reads a map, looking for the markers that will allow him to navigate the space with mastery. Just as the narrator can't make sense of his transparency, the Cid seemingly searches in vain for some clue that would provide insight into the narrator's ways of processing her experiences—not necessarily because she withholds anything, but because he simply can't relate. The narrator's comment that the two pilgrims "walk, side by side, in different countries" demonstrates the way that the singular path of the pilgrim disperses or multiplies when considering the diverging perspectives of the pilgrims who walk it. For that reason, the pilgrimage, which at first seems to offer the possibility of intimacy and shared spiritual journey, draws attention to an unbridgeable otherness that leaves the narrator feeling painfully distant from the Cid.

Part of the issue concerns the narrator's own disappearance into the morphing, watery landscape of the pilgrimage—a waning sense of self that contrasts her initial self-identification as a "strong soul"—a "young, strong, and stingy person" (123). Referring to a line from Carson's book, *Glass, Irony, and God*, Adam Phillips notes the way that Carson's exploration of humanness seems to blur the lines between the self and something outside of the self:

> It is as if the continual risk (and temptation) of self-exposure is made bewildering by the possibility that there may be "another human essence than self." This is the mystery that the heroes and heroines and narrators of her poems are always being initiated into. They are always discovering something in themselves that doesn't seem quite human, that leaves them on the edge, teetering at the limits of the available stories [1].

In "Kinds of Water," we see that fluid sense of self—one that seems to converse with and integrate experiences and objects from outside the self, undermining the singularity and clear definition of a distinct self— early in her journey. After seeing the body of the drowned dog, the narrator describes herself as she and the Cid leave a bar to continue walking: "I wipe the table with my hat: paws still dripping" (127). The narrator's identification with the drowned dog persists for the entire text, until the very end when she enters the water "paws" crossed on her chest (187). Hume sees this final transformation from human into dead dog as "an act that reinforces the radical instability of her identity and our sense of her as an object" (55). The narrator becomes the dog floating in the river, an object of contemplation, a signifier of that which exceeds the end—of the pilgrimage, or life—and resists comprehension. The pilgrimage, rather than disrupting the narrator's identification with the drowned dog when she first spots it in the river, affirms it.

The narrator also emphasizes animality in her relation to the Cid. She describes the two of them as "Two small ensnared animals howling toward Finisterre" and continually comes back to the imagery of trapped animals who get tangled up in one another (157). That imagery, the narrator explains, consistently pops up in the sculptures and other artwork along the road to Compostela: "Animals ride on top of one another. Animals ensnare themselves in plants and tendrils" (144). For that reason, the narrator reads herself and the Cid through the framework of the imagery, wondering how it might shed light on the dynamics of their relation. It seems that she's interested in seeing the pilgrimage, and her relation to the Cid, from the position of a non-human animal, as if one's humanness has the tendency to get in the way of seeing. The narrator, at one point, remarks on a particularly intimate moment with the Cid, where he rubs her back and tells her of his sick mother: "A voice coming from behind your back can be different. Animals who ride on top of one another do not have to see one another's face. Sometimes that is better" (150). In this case, animality does not lead to entrapment or ensnaring, but to a shift in perspective and relation made possible by the absence of the face, the self, the gaze of the other.

Coming from that perspective, it seems that Carson's "anthropology," though interested in humans, is perhaps even more interested in how one might shapeshift a bit, getting out of that humanness—at least at points when the human gaze distorts and limits, rather than offering insight. After all, Carson's use of the term "anthropology" necessarily evokes humanness, at the same time that it shifts the object of study to something non-human: water. One can understand that shift in multiple ways, including the notion that the human *is* water—not just in terms of bodily constitution, but also in terms of the fluidity of a human self, which continually changes, inhabits different positions or roles, and integrates and reflects experiences of the environment. Jennifer K. Dick notes the difficulty of such a study:

> For how might one study water as if it were of man (from *anthrop* and *ology*), or observe water, that which is "something you cannot hold" (117) but which also does not lend itself to consistent observation—altered so radically by wind, light, or reflection? In the end, this is the study of something running away, mourned, sought, ungraspable slipping off through the fingers, touched, perhaps seen or seen through or which has only a projected reflection on its surface [63].

The object of study doesn't stay in place for us to train our gaze for more than a minute or two; and thus, the anthropologist approaches the water with a sieve. She can make observations, document her experience even, but the "most obvious facts" of any particular moment always threaten to take their leave as soon as she has gotten them down (123). And, as we have seen, even the most seemingly transparent of humans take on different shapes, depending on the angle of the observer. Of course, the very notion of angling implicates the observer—the way her position determines the shapes she perceives, and, also, the way her presence can affect the humans she observes (the perennial problem of cultural anthropology, as Dick notes as well).

For the narrator of Carson's anthropology, the facts also often feel out of reach due to obscured vision or the inability to capture a particular moment in the way she wants—as becomes evident in almost all of the descriptions of the photographs she takes. For example: "In the photograph the two of us are bending over the map, looking for Castrogeriz which has been obscured by water drops. Here is an enlargement. You can see, within each drop, a horizon stretching, hard, in full wind" (146–7). Interestingly, though water drops obscure this picture, they also magnify the image, simultaneously distorting and making visible. As the journey continues, though, the narrator seems to have increasingly negative feelings about the photographs she takes, as if the imminence of the end of the road makes her more aware of the inability to document what she observes:

> I have to confess the photographs of the *emparedadas* are something of an embarrassment. I tried to angle my lens so as to shoot through the bars but the grillwork was too high. None of them printed properly.... The picture has been taken looking directly into the light, a fundamental error [165].

In the case of this photograph, both darkness and excess of light produce barriers to capturing the object, as does the narrator's own decision-making about how to position herself and her camera. The photographs generally fail to do what the narrator wants them to do: document her experience of the journey. In the end, she notes, "the light is not something you see, exactly" (156); it makes seeing possible, and also sometimes prevents seeing through over-exposure, but it cannot itself be seen. Light, the narrator suggests, exceeds visualization. Lastly, it seems important to note that the photographs often feature both the narrator and the Cid: "From outside it all, looking down: two tiny figures moving on the Meseta. Two animals enraged with each other" (156). While one can imagine a scenario where such a photograph would be possible, it doesn't really make sense— who took the picture?—unless we consider the notion that a photograph, at least in this case, might take linguistic shape. After all, Carson's text does not include any images, but, rather, describes them. The photographs, like other objects in the text, require that we read them as fluid, merging visual and linguistic forms of representation.

In "Diving: Introduction to the Anthropology of Water," the narrator relates the teachings of an anthropologist, who "emphasized the importance of using *encounter* rather than (say) *discovery* when talking about [alien cultures]" (117). "Encounter," it would seem, expresses the confrontation of two or more positions, whereas "discovery" implies a sort of subjugation, or a subject uncovering the truth of an object of study. The narrator tells the anthropologist, "I am not interested in true and false," parenthetically admitting that claim to be "one last lie" (117). The narrator's pilgrimage, at least as it begins, reflects an attempt at discovery, at coming to know the world, others, and herself—a turning away from the waters of the unknown, represented by her father and his illness. At the same time, like Kafka's philosopher, she feels deflated, even angry, at the moment of acquiring some sort of knowledge, of knowing the answer to a question instead of reveling in its persistence. At one point on the pilgrimage, she poses a question to the Cid, and, as soon as he begins speaking, she knows what he will say and lashes out at him. She reflects:

> I know. I know what you say. I know who you are. I know all that you mean. Why does it enrage an animal to be given what it already knows? Speaking as someone who is as much in love with knowledge as My Cid is in love with the light on the plain of León, I would say that knowing is a road [165].

While earlier in the journey the narrator seems to lament the fact that the Cid represents an unknowable "alien culture" of sorts, she becomes infuriated by his transparency and predictability here. It seems he is too easy to know, especially since it's the striving toward knowing that drives the narrator. Another way of putting it: she prefers encounter to discovery, as advised by the anthropologist, even if she sets out to discover.

Part of what changes in the way the narrator positions herself on the pilgrimage and in the text has something to do with the recognition of her own hand in the work of anthropology. The word "encounter," implies that, since it suggests the meeting or confrontation of multiple positions. When we "encounter," we are not passive observers/discoverers of objective truths; rather, we come from a specific position and perspective, coming into contact with other positions and perspectives. In doing so, we try to make sense of what we observe, and that sense-making always reflects what we already know. In the middle of the journey, the narrator and the Cid find themselves trying to find their way through thick fog:

> Shapes of life loom and vanish at us, grow grotesque. Fog invents the imagination. We do not like to be surrounded by meaningless grotesquerie, we are animals who take it upon ourselves to find form in the misshapen…
> Shapes of life change as we look at them, change us for the looking [173].

The narrator suggests here that obscured vision, blindness to the "shapes of life" around us, provoke us to form the world in a way that makes sense to us and feels meaningful, to take water and turn it into something more concrete. Those acts of imagination change the world into what we want to see; and they also reflect back to us, changing the way we navigate and experience the world. Of course, the self-aware anthropologist recognizes all of this and plods forward on the road, knowing she will necessarily reach the water, and that the documentation of her observations represent her propensity to find and create forms as much as they reflect stable, objective truths.

Interestingly, Carson's narrator never identifies herself as a writer, choosing instead to see herself as pilgrim, and, implicitly, as anthropologist. At the same time, the work of writing remains present throughout the entire text—not just because we literally read the narrator's journal-like account of the pilgrimage, but also because the questions the narrator addresses both as pilgrim and as anthropologist also pertain to writing. The narrator employs writing as a form of documentation, alongside the (absent) photographs, since "On the road you can think forward, you can think back, you can make a list to remember to tell those at home" (129). Since the entries have dates, they trace the way the narrator's sense of things shifts and changes along the way, makes the work of writing feel like it unfolds with the road. At the same time, the work of writing, like anthropology, reflects the work of forming the world into shapes we recognize. The narrator points to the limitations of writing:

> I am a pilgrim (not a novelist) and the only story I have to tell is the road itself. Besides, no one can write a novel about a road, any more than you can write a novel about God, simply because you cannot get around the back of it. [...] Now I think it is true to say of the road, and also of God, that it does not move. At the same time, it is everywhere. It has a language, but not one I know. It has a story, but I am in it. So are you [152].

The narrator clarifies that she is not writing *about* the road, but that the writing *is* the road, the unfolding toward an unknown, unreachable destination. And that destination, it would seem, is the road too—a destination, we might imagine, with questions and answers, composed in a language that belongs only to the road and thus escapes our reading. The narrator, as pilgrim, walks the road to Compostela, and she writes the road—a road necessarily made of water, slipping through her grasp—inspired by the question on the horizon (187).

Notes

1. "The Anthropology of Water" is the final section of Carson's book, *Plainwater*. "The Anthropology of Water" contains seven sub-sections, the first three of which I will discuss in this essay: "Diving: Introduction to the Anthropology of Water"; "Thirst: Introduction to Kinds of Water"; and "Kinds of Water: An Essay on the Road to Compostela."

Carson's *Plainwater* bears the sub-title, "Poems and Essays." Whether any given text represents a poem or an essay, or both, remains unclear. I will refer to "The Anthropology of Water" as a text, an essay, or a poem-essay, and to the "I" of the text as the narrator (though "speaker" and even "Carson" might also work). In addition, the various sections in "The Anthropology of Water" do not all necessarily belong to the same genre, nor do they necessarily feature the same first-person subject—especially since some of the sections, at least nominally, are "introductions," which in some sense positions them "outside" or "before" the narrative texts they introduce. In any case, all identifications of genre and the first-person subject simply intend to facilitate discussion of the work, not to define the work in any way.

2. The narrator's self-identification as someone "of no particular gender" complicates pronoun use, although I generally see it as an extension of the difficulty in trying to pin down the "I" of the text. The narrator implicitly identifies herself as a daughter to her ailing father, like the daughters of Danaos, which leads me to use the feminine pronoun throughout the chapter. That said, the feminine pronoun misses the ambiguity or ambivalence of the narrator's description of gender in "Thirst: Introduction to Kinds of Water."

Works Cited

Adorno, Theodor. "Notes on Kafka." *Franz Kafka*, edited by Harold Bloom. Chelsea House Publishers, 1986, pp. 95–105.

Blanchot, Maurice. *The Infinite Conversation*. Translated by Susan Hanson, U of Minnesota P, 2003.

Carson, Anne. "The Anthropology of Water." *Plainwater: Essays and Poetry*. Vintage, 2000.

_____. *Eros the Bittersweet*. Dalkey Archive Press, 2003.

_____. *Nox*. New Directions, 2010.

Dick, Jennifer K. "The Pilgrim and the Anthropologist." *Ecstatic Lyre*, edited by Joshua M. Wilkinson, U of Michigan P, 2015, pp. 62–68.

Homer. *The Odyssey*. Translated by Robert Fitzgerald, Doubleday, 1963.

Hume, Christine. "How Is a Pilgrim Like a Soldier? Anne Carson's 'Kinds of Water: An Essay on the Road to Compostela.'" *Ecstatic Lyre*, edited by Joshua M. Wilkinson, U of Michigan P, 2015, pp. 50–55.

Macdonald, Tanis. "The Pilgrim and the Riddle: Father-Daughter Kinship in Anne Carson's 'The Anthropology of Water.'" *Canadian Literature*, vol. 176, Spring 2003, pp. 67–81.

Phillips, Adam. "Fickle Contracts." *Raritan*, vol. 16, no.2, Fall 1996, pp. 112–19.

The *Río Salado* Incident

The Intertextuality of the Liber Peregrinationis *in Contemporary First-Person Camino Narratives and the Creation of an Etiological Myth*

Annie Hesp

Nothing is its own author, nothing exists of itself.
—Lee Hoinacki

Since the early 1980s, over a million pilgrims from around the world have walked or ridden their bicycles or horses along the revitalized Camino de Santiago. At the end of each day on the trail, pilgrims jot down their daily experiences, noting who they met, what they witnessed and how many new blisters developed. Many pilgrims talk about publishing their diaries; however, each year only a few do so. Collectively, their number is becoming significant as a shared body of work.[1] Within these published first-person narratives, one of the most striking features that emerges is the use of embedded medieval texts to retell the contemporary experience. The most commonly embedded text is an episode in the *Codex Calixtinus* (ca. 1170).[2] (This is a copy of the *Liber Sancti Jacobi* [*Book of Saint James*] and the oldest surviving illuminated manuscript describing the XII century Camino de Santiago and its dangers.) Authors draw specifically from its fifth book, the *Liber Peregrinationis* (*The Pilgrims' Guide*), something of a guidebook that, along with typical travel advice, describes a disastrous river crossing at the *Río Salado* where a pilgrim's horse dies from drinking the water and then is immediately skinned by locals. This essay examines how three authors fold this incident into their own first-person Camino narratives in three distinct stories, Elyn Aviva's *Following the Milky Way: A Pilgrimage on the Camino de Santiago* (1989, 2001), Lee Hoinacki's *El Camino: Walking to Santiago de Compostela* (1996) and Edward Stanton's *Road of Stars to Santiago* (1994). In doing so, I seek to draw attention to the contribution the

39

Liber Peregrinationis episode has in the telling of each individual's story and how this and other medieval texts connect the protagonists to the medieval pilgrimage, to fellow past pilgrims and, ultimately, to show how they create an etiological myth. What becomes evident is that Camino authors are highly invested in the narrative experience—this pilgrimage is as textual as it is spatial or spiritual: while authors/protagonists move along the space of the trail, they move through texts. Medieval texts, especially, play an important role in these post–1980s Camino narratives. The inclusion of the past functions as more than a pastiche of Camino folklore, it serves as a constitutive part of their articulated, lived experience.

It can be argued that the inclusion of medieval texts serves simply as part of the travelogue genre, in which authors use bits of history or stories to contextualize their journeys and to help readers understand the cultural and historical context in which the authors find themselves.[3] More than paying homage to the historical legacy of the trail, or providing authorial knowledge, in the Camino context, the use of the embedded medieval texts creates a sense of timelessness and community that stretches back through and across time with other pilgrim authors. However, I want to argue that the repeated use of the *Liber Peregrinationis (LP)* episode also places the authenticity of these stories at stake. While these stories are not "inauthentic," it becomes apparent that the repeated use of the same texts at the same geographical sites can make Camino narratives sound formulaic and predictable. This is especially the case as Camino narratives continue being published and this scene is replicated. In the context of the Camino, authors want a unique story to tell, but rely on others as markers of authenticity. An examination of the embedding of the *Río Salado* episode reveals tensions between the individual and the communal, the authentic and the formulaic in many first-person Camino narratives, particularly those published in the 1980s and 90s.

In their introduction to *Pilgrim Voices: Authoring Christian Pilgrimage*, a book of critical essays about pilgrim narratives, Simon Coleman and John Elsner note, "To date, relatively little work has been explicitly devoted to the issue of pilgrimage as writing and specifically as a form of travel writing," emphasizing, "the relation of pilgrimage to the various narratives which it generates and upon which it depends" (4). This relationship that Coleman and Elsner refer to is one of *intertextuality*. This is a slippery word for literary scholars because of its multiple and imprecise usage. Here we employ literary theorist Gérard Genette's concept of intertextuality, which he defines "as the actual presence of one text within another" (2). This includes "quoting," "plagiarism" and "allusion" (2). This concept of intertextuality especially applies to the collection of recent Camino narratives.[4] In terms of intertextual relationships, these Camino narratives have a high correlative value. Nowhere does this seem to be more evident than in the shared use of the *Liber Peregrinationis* episode. Many authors in the 80s and 90s at least refer to it, and many quote it directly. These intertextual instantiations of the *Liber Peregrinationis* are embedded texts. That is, there is a distinct and sustained shift in time, characters, and sometimes place between the main narrative and the embedded text when this episode is mentioned.

In contemporary Camino narratives, the main narrative is the story of the protagonist (author/narrator) walking the contemporary trail. Interspersed within this narrative, Camino authors typically include brief interludes of other stories or excerpts of fiction and non-fiction (often historical information). In Camino narratives, the embedded texts are sometimes pieced together from two or three different sources, sometimes cited, sometimes not. This intertextual work then connects the author to the past. Collectively, we can also see another kind of intertextuality across the body of contemporary Camino literature in that many narratives share similar experiences at this same point on the trail. This is the "allusion" that Genette mentions. To at least scratch at the surface of these relationships in these recent Camino narratives, this essay focuses on one particular passage in three first-person Camino narratives where, when unpacked, these intertextual relationships to the past and across the contemporary corpus are most striking. While mention of this site and its history is frequent, in these three texts they are exemplary.

In terms of Genette's definition of intertextuality, the *Codex Calixtinus (CC)*, and more specifically, its fifth book, the *Liber Peregrinationis (LP)*, is the most influential book in contemporary Camino literature.[5] Almost every Camino author from 1980 to 2000 at least mentions the *CC* or *LP*, even if they do not heavily cite it. In the case of the narratives presented here, authors paraphrase and allude to the *LP* regularly. Some factors that account for the *LP*'s popularity are that it is one of the most important surviving Camino manuscripts,[6] as well as one of the most accessible because of its translation from Latin into Spanish and English by A. Moralejo, C. Torres, and J. Feo and Walter Muir Whitehill (1932); William Melzcer (1993); as well as Annie Shaver-Crandell, Paula L. Gerson, and Alison Stones (1995) respectively.[7] Two scenes in particular are most cited: the death of a horse from drinking bad water—the *Río Salado* incident, which is the one discussed here—and another that describes the sexual deviancy of the Basques.

For pilgrims who walked in the early 1980s and 90s, before the Camino gained its current popularity, much of the path as well as the actual *Río Salado* offered pilgrim authors very little to write about, presenting a representational problem for them: how do you write about a pilgrimage when it lacks many of the typical symbols or signs that differentiate a pilgrimage from a mere hike or trip across Spain? Authors resolve this dilemma by including the *Liber Peregrinationis* at this site to engage readers' interest precisely at a moment when the lived trail provides little. Many post–1980 Camino narratives mention the same location on the trail, a bridge between Chiraqui and Estella where protagonists cross the *Río Salado*, now a small, murky stream. Many pilgrim-authors stop and taste the water, others simply note its stench caused by heavy contamination. More interestingly, a notable number of authors follow the same pattern of embedding the actual story from the *LP*. This embedded text, like so many other medieval texts used in contemporary Camino narratives, is geographically bound, meaning that often pilgrim-authors tell or embed the same story at the same geographical place. Other examples of geographically bound stories that frequently appear in contemporary Camino narratives appear when protagonists reach Roncesvalles and retell the story of Roldan crossing the Pyrenees (sometimes using the story from the *Pseudo-Turpin* from the *LP*, but not always) and the miracle of the chickens in Santo Domingo de la Calzada sometimes referencing Gonzalo de Berceo's Miracle 6, Alfonso X's *Cantiga* 175 and also the *Codex Calixtinus*. In both of these cases, unlike the *Río Salado* episode, there are several different versions to choose from. In all instances, though, these embedded stories constitute and construct their journey *as* a pilgrimage: this rhetorical format gives meaning to their pilgrimage. These embedded texts have become literary *topoi* within contemporary Camino literature and thinking about them as geographically bound makes this concept of *topos* from its Greek roots, commonplace, even more compelling: these medieval texts are commonly retold when writing about these shared places.

Elyn Aviva includes the *Río Salado* incident in her book *Following the Milky Way: A Pilgrimage on the Camino de Santiago*, first published in 1989. For Aviva, the use of other medieval texts and stories provides her with a sense of pilgrimage that was not always present when she walked in 1982, before the Camino was remembered and restored. Other pilgrims were rare on the trail and the *albergues,* inexpensive lodging for pilgrims, were not consistent, nor reliable as they are nowadays. She is a self-proclaimed "old timer" on the trail (personal correspondence). Her pilgrimage served several purposes. Aviva walked the Camino as part of her fieldwork for her dissertation, "Strangers and Pilgrims on the Camino de Santiago in Spain: the Perpetuation and Recreation of Meaningful Performance" (1985), in cultural anthropology at Princeton University. Her pilgrimage also allowed her to test herself as well as her relationship with her then boyfriend. Her narrative, which was initially published by Iowa State University Press (1989) and later by her own independent press (2001), grew out of the first chapter of her dissertation.

Since Aviva walked in a time when Spanish locals had lost historical consciousness of the medieval trail, many of the embedded historical
moments provide Aviva's readers a sense of pilgrimage that they would
expect on a journey such as this. In her description of the *Río Salado*, the
protagonist walks down the *calzada romana* to the bridge. Upon crossing
it, she notes:

> We crossed a medieval stone bridge over the Río Salado. Aymery Picaud, in
> the "Pilgrim's Guide" in the *Codex*, advised twelfth-century travelers neither
> to drink the water of the Río Salado nor let their horses drink it, for the river
> is poisonous. He also warned that the Navarrese waited with sharpened knives
> to skin the dead beasts of the pilgrims. I tasted the water; it was salty, but not
> deadly [59].

At the narrative level, Aviva does not let her encounter of absence, her
encounter of few visual indications that would suggest she is on a pilgrimage, lessen her pilgrimage, she simply constructs one through the inclusion of the passage. The negative *topoi* of the Navarrese people at the bridge
crossing from the *Liber Peregrinationis* makes the walk through Spain feel
more like a pilgrimage. While Aviva draws from the past, it does not seem
like she is trying to remember how things were. She does not suffer from
a case of nostalgia so much as the present and past coming together, connected by the "medieval stone bridge." Without the help of the historians
and pilgrims who wrote about these places previously, Aviva would find
herself with very little pilgrimage to write about convincingly since the
time she walked and wrote about the revived pilgrimage was still relatively
unmarked and incomplete (1980s); the *LP* infuses a sense of pilgrimage and
adventure where otherwise none existed in a way that readers would understand her journey as pilgrimage. Without the help of medieval texts, her
journey would feel more like two Americans lost on a Spanish back road
than the pilgrimage it is meant to be. The rhetorical strategy of embedding the *LP* and other medieval texts creates an organic feeling of a lived
pilgrimage steeped in the past and present. As Aviva herself mentions in
the preface of her narrative, "It [the trail] is both quintessentially contemporary and incredibly ancient" (xxvii).[8] This observation is not limited to
Aviva or only the lived experience. Paul Genoni, in his article "The Pilgrim's
Progress Across Time: Medievalism and Modernity on the Road to Santiago," notes that the medieval pilgrimage appears as a reoccurring theme in
many Camino narratives (157). I would add that one of the most prominent
ways this theme is conveyed is through the use of embedded medieval texts
like those that appear in Aviva and many other Camino authors' stories.

Like any practical guidebook, the *Liber Peregrinationis* relates where
to find good food, lodging, what to see and what to avoid. The section
that Aviva, and many contemporary Camino authors, include tells of the

protagonist's dreadful encounter with Navarrese. Arguably, hyperbole and politics seem to be more at play than a truthful account of the situation (Melczer 143). The episode reads:

> In a place called Lorca, towards the east, runs a river called Río Salado. Beware from drinking its waters or from watering your horse in its stream, for this river is deadly. While we were proceeding towards Santiago, we found two Navarrese seated on its banks and sharpening their knives: they make a habit of skinning the mounts of the pilgrims that drink from that water and die. To our questions they answered with a lie saying that the water was indeed healthy and drinkable. Accordingly, we watered our horses in the stream, and had no sooner done so, then two of them died: these the men skinned on the spot [Melczer 88–89].

In contemporary Camino narratives, embedded medieval texts usually mirror (either in correlation or opposition) the main protagonists' feelings or experiences. The added appeal of this passage is its ability to provide both opposition and correlation. The scene is framed in opposition because today nobody ever dies from tasting the water and few go by horse. Yet, it provides a correlative experience of adventure and limit pushing shared by all pilgrims who endure this pilgrimage across Spain. This interplay of time seems to happen seamlessly, allowing readers to occupy both past and present at once.

As mentioned, Aviva walked in a time when the Camino didn't exist as such, the use of medieval pilgrim narratives seems practically necessary to transmit the sense of her own pilgrimage. However, once the Camino did regain its popularity, its infrastructure rebuilt, its historical consciousness restored and the creation of a network of consistent *albergues* (sometime during the late 90s, I would argue), subsequent authors have continued this trend of embedding medieval texts into their narratives.

Lee Hoinacki's book, *El Camino: Walking to Santiago de Compostela* (1996) tells the story of his Camino. Hoinacki, an ex-priest who completed a PhD and later quit a tenure-track position in order to pursue a simpler life as a subsistence farmer, walked in 1993. Hoinacki writes about his arrival at the bridge:

> After some time, I cross the Río Salado, near the place where Aymeric Picaud claims his two horses died from drinking the water. The river's name, Salado, means "salty"—the same name Picaud gives—a condition that has not changed since the twelfth century. Other authors have disputed Picaud's claim; they think the water could not have killed the horses. It's salty, and does not taste good; but it's not poisonous [47].

In Aviva's text the *LP* episode stands in for the lack of visual signs that she is on a pilgrimage because the Camino had barely begun its revival. In Hoinacki's case, the *LP* episode, and the many other medieval texts he includes, populate his story with medieval pilgrims with whom he can share his experience. Hoinacki is primarily concerned with the complicated proposition of walking with past pilgrims. Throughout his story, he openly declares that he doesn't want to share his pilgrimage with other present pilgrims, and thus often walks alone; however, he is quite open in sharing his journey with pilgrims from the past. Unsurprisingly then, he regularly employs this strategy of embedding past texts as a way to develop his "friendship" with these past pilgrims.

In her book *Pilgrim Stories: On and Off the Road to Santiago* (1998), Nancy Frey writes about how the pilgrims experience friendship on the Camino: "The formation of friendships and groups of walking and cycling companions that cut across normal divisions such as gender, age, class, nationality and marital status is an important aspect of becoming a pilgrim and feeling part of a larger community" (91). In post–1980 Camino narratives this community is articulated in several ways. The most frequent strategy includes descriptive scenes of pilgrims walking and eating together as well as curing each other's injuries. While this creates a large community of pilgrims to accompany the protagonists, it fails to include the pilgrims of the past, another group whose presence contemporary pilgrims feel. Frey notes, "Pilgrims commonly experience themselves with pilgrims of the past as they walk, rest, take shelter, drink at a fountain, cross a bridge, pray in church. Many pilgrims in previous centuries died on the way to Santiago, and some modern pilgrims feel their presence strongly" (81–82). Embedded medieval texts convey that sensation well. In the written medium that is the first-person narrative, embedded texts from the Middle Ages are ideal for articulating the feeling of walking in the footsteps of past pilgrims as well as *with* the pilgrims of the past.

Hoinacki, like many of the earlier contemporary Camino authors (those from approx. 1980–2000), is also well-versed in its history. The embedded text situates Hoinacki's experience squarely within the medieval legacy. The *LP* episode adds to the overall depth of the work; however, as a subordinate story, it could be removed completely without losing the essence of Hoinacki's adventure, who is walking in a time in which the sense of pilgrimage *has* been fully reestablished on the trail. Unlike many older pilgrim narratives, like Chaucer's *Canterbury Tales*, where the embedded texts serve as the primary story, or even arguably Walker Starkie's Camino narrative *The Road to Santiago* from 1957, where his walk seems to serve more as a framework than as the main story, here the embedded episode is a secondary marker of authenticity. This is not the case in most post-1980 Camino narratives. In these narratives, primacy is given to the protagonists' adventures while the pilgrimage's history is secondary.

Edward Stanton wrote *Road of Stars to Santiago* in 1994. Stanton is a professor of Spanish who, by his own admission in his Introduction, needed a break from academia and his personal life (1). In this narrative, it's clear that Spain is both a passion and profession for Stanton, affirming his mastery of the country and its culture through his narrative. Like Aviva and Hoinacki, Stanton's bridge crossing reads in a strikingly similar fashion even though his intentions for walking the Camino are markedly different. In this third example, the scene starts to feel uncanny. He writes:

> After getting lost in a field crossed by lines of rushes, I reach the second famous bridge on the Camino de Santiago, over the Río Salado. Not majestic like the Puente de la Reina, it looks quaint with its two uneven arches, dwarfed by a modern aqueduct. Even armchair pilgrims know that this river and bridge are the scene of the most notorious passage in the *Book of St. James*. The probable author of that manuscript, the French priest Aymery Picaud tells how he and his companions on the pilgrimage asked two Navarrese, who were seated on the shore sharpening their knives, if the water was fit to drink. When the two men said yes, the French watered their mounts in the Salty River whose name should have put them on guard; the horses died almost at once and were quickly skinned by the Navarrese, who must have sold the meat and hide for a profit.... Today the trickle in the Río Salado—it can be called a river only by an act of the imagination—doesn't carry enough volume to kill a horse, even if the water were poisoned. Walter Starkie and several modern pilgrims have tasted the supposedly brackish water without keeling over dead. A doubting Thomas, I decided to confirm their reports, walking to the middle of the almost dry-riverbed, sticking one finger in the warm, gentle flow: not even a salty taste to justify the name [51–52].

Stanton's use of the *LP* episode performs much of the same work that it does for Aviva and Hoinacki. It also adds another layer of complexity by serving as a reference to Walter Starkie, Stanton's former professor and the author of arguably one of the first modern Camino narratives, *The Road to Santiago* (1957). The intertwining of the three books (Stanton's, the *Liber Peregrinationis* and Starkie's) creates a multi-vocal description that reaffirms the authenticity of Stanton's observations as well as a conversation with an older historian who shares his intellectual interest. Analyzing similar instances of pilgrimage literature, Simon Coleman and John Elsner note that "[a]s such narratives shift and move into each other, authorship can be shown to be complex and multivocal" (3). The interweaving of the singular with plural histories adds richness and texture to the individual scene, and to the overall narrative, and although no direct dialogue occurs, the affect makes it appear as though it has. The sustained appearance of embedded texts, moreover, adds to the authors' authority. In other words, the multiple voices provide a doubling of the authors' authority: first, for having experienced the trail first-hand, and second, through the historical knowledge transmitted through the embedded texts. Sidonie Smith and Julia Watson, note a similar effect in multivocal autobiographies:

> In his collaborative narrative *Black Elk Speaks* (1932), the Lakota shaman incorporates the voices of multiple others as he tells his story through the dreams, visions, and voices of other spiritual leaders. Doing so, Black Elk secures the authority of his own visions by situating himself in a genealogy of visionaries [66–67].

In the case of the Camino authors, using the work (and words) of other respected pilgrims improves the authors' own position among other authorial voices and among readers.

Most striking is that the three authors here and others who include this episode from the *Liber Peregrinationis* are doing something akin to a literary reenactment by writing about the same location and embedding the same story. Curiously, no post–1980 author acknowledges that other post–1980 authors have also written about this place in a similar fashion. Both this form and content can be traced back to a 1957 Camino author, Walter Starkie, who includes a verse from his Latin source. Starkie is the first author I find who embeds this story at this geographical point:

> Soon I reached the River Salado and crossed by a picturesque bridge with two uneven arches. Here Aymery Picaud warns pilgrims not to drink the water or allow their horses near it (*quia flumen letiferum est*). He describes how when he reached the bridge he saw two Navarrenses sharpening their knives in readiness for skinning the pilgrim mules or horses who would drop dead when they had drunk the water. And when Aymery asked them whether the water was fit to drink they replied in the affirmative. "And so" he continues, "we watered our horses, and two of them straightway died, and the two men skinned them." I tasted the brackish water without any sinister results [180].

It's quite likely that Aviva and Hoinacki are aware of Starkie's quote; Aviva may or may not have used his text at least to refer back to the original or a translation of the *LP*. In Stanton's case, however, he explicitly refers to Walter Starkie, who seems to have unwittingly initiated this ritual of tasting the water.

Furthermore, it appears that Aviva, Hoinacki and Stanton and the other Camino authors are interested in more than re-enacting and re-telling; they all make reference to a specific person Aymery Picaud (others provide variations on the name Aymeric, Aimery), an individual whose exact relation to the medieval manuscript is uncertain. Even in the manuscript, multiple versions of Aimery are offered, Aymericus and Aymeri are likely two different people (Stones and Krochalis 19) and William Melczer reminds us that the "traces we have of Aimery's presence in the work are of indicative value only. All told, nothing firm may be said at this point of him or of anybody else as the author of the compilation" (32). In these narratives, Aymery's identity is no more settled in that the authors will at times talk about him as the protagonist, and at other times as the story-teller, but no one seems too concerned with his true relationship to the *LP*. Scholars continue asking the question, by whom and for whom is this text intended with little resolution. (Cf. "*El Codex Calixtinus: Volviendo sobre el tema*" by Manuel C. Díaz y Díaz, and the extensive section and footnote in Stones and Krochalis's critical edition of the *Pilgrim's Guide* [16]). For Camino authors, finding the actual identity doesn't seem like a constitutive element of their project and, indeed, perhaps too much searching for it would detract from their story, a laborious detour most readers and academics wouldn't be interested in making anyway. Stones and Krochalis's critical edition of the *Pilgrim's Guide* calls pursuing authorship simply a "red herring" (12). So while authors don't pursue the question of authorship, they do include a specific name adding to the episode's appeal and value. The authors appear to be as interested in connecting their story to the ancient text as with connecting themselves to this conflated medieval figure. The use of the embedded text here as a rhetorical ploy seems as much about making a personal connection with Aymery (and to a lesser degree Starkie), regardless of whether he even existed as a real person or not (a more literal sense of Anderson's *imagined community*, by means of a shared experience with an identified individual) as with giving meaning to the space through which our pilgrims are traversing.[9]

This is where the etiological myth comes to be. Tasting the water was never part of the medieval pilgrimage rite, but rather one that contemporary authors reenact as something of homage to their medieval predecessors. By thinking about the Camino authors who cite the same passage at this bridge crossing, we see another kind of reenactment occurring: all drink the water for themselves. For them, reenactment is not limited to walking the trail, but also citing the passage and drinking the water. Since they have no horses to water, they are enacting the pilgrim part as best they can by sampling it themselves. In addition to citing the passage from Aymery, the authors make an even deeper connection with the protagonist by drinking the water at the same spot where his horse drank. Conversely, one could argue that it is not medieval pilgrims who contemporary authors are emulating, but rather Starkie. Stanton, an accomplished academic who had Starkie as a university professor, honors and engages with his former professor by including his participation within this episode. At the same time, there is something deeply satisfying about the former student figuratively and literally following the same path as his former professor: he too became a professor and also followed Starkie on the Camino.

By tasting the water, each individual becomes a member of the group of Camino authors by means of a brackish baptism. Within the contemporary context this episode has practically become a rite of passage: when crossing the *Río Salado*, a Camino author is expected to include the story from the *LP*, then taste the water for him or herself. The relation to the images of holy water is obvious. Yet the experience has, much like the trail itself, become highly secular (the water has become tainted or brackish). On an individual level, each author might make a claim of authenticity because of the connection through the shared water (this is the authenticity of reenactment and ritual). Collectively, however, the repeated use of the *Liber Peregrinationis* and the authors' perfunctory tasting of the water can also serve to diminish these claims of authenticity in that once everybody begins to perform the same act, that uniqueness dissipates (this is the authenticity of unique quality or originality). The incompatibility of these two somewhat irreconcilable meanings of authenticity create, at least on paper, a representational dilemma: there's a deep desire to drink the water in order to replicate the medieval experience, yet doing so anymore seems to wash away one's uniqueness.

The post–1980 Camino narratives have started functioning like guidebooks themselves by providing interpretations of these unmarked sites for future pilgrims.[10] Eric J. Leed, a prominent travel historian, talks about how sites such as these create a set of rituals:

> The site continues, so long as it is sacred, to generate a literature, texts, guidebooks, testimonies, miracles, and travel accounts that perpetuate its now famed and contained power. This literature generates an audience to consume the site in and through travel to encounter the actuality implicit in its reproductions and representations [143–44].

The history of sites along the trail, like el Río Salado, has been perpetuated in part by the many Camino narratives that include its past. When they write about the historic places and events, Aviva and other Camino authors collectively participate in an etiological myth by embedding these texts and retelling these stories in their narratives. A certain reflexivity exists then: the past is reiterated, remembered and potentially altered by new Camino narratives. Drinking the water was never part of a religious act of this pilgrimage, but feels like it has through the repeated use of this scene in contemporary first-person Camino narratives. Because the history of the trail has not been as well controlled by the Catholic church, as, for example, the Mormons' highly-centralized writing of history (Mitchell 135), the authors of these Camino narratives have considerable influence when deciding what Camino history will be remembered, forgotten or changed through their words and choices of embedded texts.[11] At some point after 2006 a sign was erected at this site, telling pilgrims about the incident that purportedly took place there, something that likely would not have happened had this scene not been repeated throughout this body of literature. With the signage, even more individuals will be tempted to try the water for themselves.

Thinking about these passages in the light of re-enactment is fascinating because yet another kind of re-enactment taking place, a literary one, which also tangentially is like Genette's idea of intertextuality. In this case, it's his third kind, that deals with form. While all of these narratives share many common formal elements that one might find from travel literature, such as the day-to-day format and the diary-like voice, there is also another formal element of writing not unlike that of Egeria, considered one of the first pilgrims to write about her pilgrimage to the Holy Land. This intertextuality comes from the nuanced way of writing which, in addition to describing the place, also describes events from other books that have taken place at that site. For example, Egeria writes, "The place where was the inscription concerning Lot's wife was shown to us, which place is read of in the Scriptures. But believe me, revered ladies, the pillar itself cannot be seen, only the place is shown, the pillar is said to have been covered by the Dead Sea" (trans. McClure and Feltoe 23). While Egeria did not get as lucky as our narrators who got to touch the water, the biblical reference, like the *LP* reference, adds meaning to this site and broadens her lived experience. In other words, our contemporary authors are also reenacting the way, the form, medieval pilgrims, like Egeria, wrote about their lived experience.

Together, these shared scenes reveal how these post–1980 first-person Camino narratives are highly mediated through previous Camino texts, both contemporary and medieval ones. Had none of these authors read about this episode in the *Liber Peregrinationis*, where the graphic scene of poisoned horses first appeared, it is doubtful that they would have even noticed or written about the seemingly insignificant stream. The repeated use of this story has created an etiological myth for an unremarkable place—pilgrims are now invited to taste the water for themselves as well as a trope that has become a stand-in for an uneventful bridge crossing. Stopping, tasting and then writing about the water has become ritualized within Camino narratives. In an article titled "The Miracles of St. James," Klaus Herbers talks about medieval pilgrims to Santiago as agents of cults, using a term coined by Manuel C. Díaz y Díaz (11, 15). Along the same lines, these authors are doing something similar by perpetuating the stories of the *LP*; however, they do so in a way that surely the author of the *Codex Calixtinus*, whoever he was, never imagined.

This pattern of embedding the *LP* at this geographical place is not limited to Aviva, Stanton and Hoinacki. Other contemporary authors like Mary Victoria Wallis (2003), and Conrad Rudolph (2004) as well as Spanish authors Manuel Mandianes (1993), Víctor Luengo (2004), and Carlos López

(2000), also embed the same story when they arrive at this bridge thereby giving meaning to this otherwise uneventful place; however, none acknowledges that other first-person Camino authors have practically identical passages describing the same incident. It is not that an unimportant creek is mentioned, or that the same scene from the *LP* is reused, but rather that recycled moments—both in form and content from other Camino texts—permeate these Camino narratives. For more recent Camino authors, this example highlights a dilemma authors face when writing about their pilgrimage: drawing from previous pilgrim raconteurs risks being derivative, yet not including them might weaken contemporary authors' claims to a common literary and experiential heritage, and rupture the air of seamless continuity they work so hard to construct.

Individually and collectively, embedded texts in these contemporary first-person Camino narratives repeatedly create a trans-temporal sense of community and experience that pays little attention to the boundary between the lived and written experience. Examples such as Aviva, Hoinacki and Stanton's narratives make it clear that the use of medieval texts renders their unique stories as pilgrimage, and that the use of *Liber Peregrinationis* is not merely illustrative or supplementary, but, indeed, constitutive of their pilgrimage, as well as creating a sense of pilgrimage for those who read them and set out on their own Camino.[12]

Notes

1. I believe that there is nowhere in the world that has become as widely documented on the same space—there are easily over 100 published account of the Camino just in English. An interesting project would be to compare the many different ways people from different cultures have described the same Camino spaces and experiences, for example, a study of Asian narratives and how they differ from Western European ones, especially with the increase of Asian pilgrims in recent years.

2. Williams, John "Introduction." *The Codex Calixtinus and the Shrine of St. James*, p. xi.

3. Cf. Dunn, R.E. *The Adventures of Ibn Battuta, A Muslim Traveller of the Fourteenth Century*. University of California Press, 1986.; Morsey, M. *La relation de Thomas Pellow, une lecture du Maroc au 18 ième Siècle*. Edition Récherche sur les civilizations. Paris: 1983; Abderrahmane El Moudden, "The Ambivalence of *Rihla*: Community Integration and Self-Definition in Moroccan Travel." *Muslim Travel*, edited by James Piscatori and Dale F. Eickelman, 2nd ed., University of California Press, 1990, pp. 69–84.

4. Pilgrim narratives refer to narratives written about *any* pilgrimage; I use the term "Camino narratives" to refer specifically to narratives about the Camino de Santiago.

5. In their introduction to an English translation of the *Pilgrim's Guide*, Alison Stone and Jeanne Krochalis note that during the Middle Ages, it was the fourth book from the *Codex Calixtinus*, the *Pseudo-Turpin*, that was most popular. I would argue that it is now the fifth book, the *LP* that has gained in popularity, particularly for pilgrim authors.

6. On July 6, 2011, church officials reported the theft of the *Codex Calixtinus* in Santiago de Compostela, Spain. It was under less than desirable surveillance and the effects were the realization of its historical value and a concern that it would be desecrated and sold on the black market in pieces. It was later found in the thief's garage.

7. I use the William Melzcer translation of the *Pilgrim's Guide* for the purpose of this paper.

8. I use Aviva's second edition.

9. Curiously, most authors/protagonists connect with the pilgrim even if, as in this case, the individual's identity is unknown. It's at least worthy to mention that their treatment of this passage is much like authors/protagonists' dealing with those who they meet on the trail. In first person Camino narratives as a whole, priority goes to other pilgrims, while those who live and work on the trail received little attention.

10. On Amazon.com, there are numerous comments of readers of these Camino narratives mentioning how they have used these books in various ways as guidebooks.

11. This becomes particularly noticeable in electronic listservs, chatrooms, and Facebook sites, when people ask about avoiding problems they have read about in Camino narratives.

12. As a final note, the trend of using embedded texts is definitely subsiding in post-2010 publications. Without elaborating extensively, this can be explained by both literary and non-literary reasons. Many earlier Camino writers came out of academia or had extensive experience writing previously. In many ways, this embedded-text format is not unlike an academic style of writing. The earlier Camino authors also wrote at a time when gaps needed to be filled to describe the lived-pilgrimage experience when there were few markers of pilgrimage remaining from the Middle Ages. Medieval stories and history did just that. Nowadays, plenty of the post-2010 Camino authors have little to no writing experience and are able to self-publish. Furthermore, pilgrim rituals and markers are readily available along the trail. Worthy of further research is the absence of pilgrimage in first-person Camino narratives, simply Camino as a trip or experience. The trend, it seems to me both as pilgrim and as researcher, is that the Camino is entering into something of a post-modern pilgrimage where it means many different things to many people. In more and more cases, pilgrimage isn't one of them.

WORKS CITED

Anderson, Benedict. *Imagined Communities.* 1983 ed., Verso, 2002.

Aviva, Elyn. *Following the Milky Way: A Pilgrimage on the Camino de Santiago.* 1st ed., Iowa State UP, 1989.

_____. *Following the Milky Way: A Pilgrimage on the Camino de Santiago.* 2nd ed., Pilgrim's Process, 2001.

Coleman, Simon, and John Elsner. "Pilgrim Voices: Authoring Christian Pilgrimage." *Pilgrim Voices: Narrative and Authorship in Christian Pilgrimage.* Berghahn Books, 2003, pp. 1–16.

Díaz y Díaz, Manuel C. "El Codex Calixtinus: Volviendo sobre el tema." *The Pilgrim's Guide to Santiago de Compostela." The Codex Calixtinus and the Shrine of St. James,* edited by John Williams and Allison Stones, G. Narr, 1992.

Frey, Nancy Louise. *Pilgrim Stories: On and Off the Road to Santiago.* UP Press, 1998.

Genette, Gérard. *Palimpsests: Literature in the Second Degree.* 1982. Translated by Channa Newman and Claude Doubinsky, Nebraska UP, 1997.

Herbers, Klaus. "The Miracle of St. James." *The Codex Calixtinus and the Shrine of St. James,* edited by John Williams and Allison Stones, Narr, 1992.

Hoinacki, Lee. *El Camino: Walking to Santiago de Compostela.* Penn State UP, 1996.

Leed, Eric J. *The Mind of the Traveller: From Gilgamesh to Global Tourism.* Basic Books, 1991.

López, Carlos. *Paso a paso por el Camino de Santiago.* Ediciones Beta, 2000.

Luengo, Víctor. *El Camino de las Estrellas: Cuaderno de viaje de un peregrino a Santiago de Compostela.* Milenio, 2004.

Mandianes, Manuel. *Peregrino a Santiago: Viaje al fin del mundo.* Ronsel, 1993.

McClure, M.L., and L.C. Feltoe. *The Pilgrimage of Etheria.* The Macmillan Company, 1919.

Melczer, William. *The Pilgrim's Guide to Santiago de Compostela.* Italica, 1993.

Mitchell, Hildi J. "Postcards from the Edge of History: Narrative and the Sacralisation of Mormon Historical Sites." *Pilgrim Voices: Narrative and Authorship in Christian Pilgrimage,* edited by Simon Coleman and John Elsner, Berghahan Books, 2003, pp. 133–158.

Moralejo, Juan Jose, and C. Torres y J. Feo. *Liber Sancti Iacobi, "Codex Calixtinus,"* edited by Juan José Moralejo Álvarez, CSIC, 1951.

Rudolph, Conrad. *Pilgrimage to the End of the World: The Road to Santiago de Compostela.* Chicago UP, 2004.

Shaver-Crandell, Annie, Paula L. Gerson and Alison Stones. *The Pilgrim's Guide to Santiago de Compostela: A Gazetteer.* Harvey Miller Publishers, 1995.

Stanton, Edward F. *Road of Stars to Santiago.* UP of Kentucky, 1994.

Starkie, Walter. *The Road to Santiago: Pilgrims of St. James.* John Murray, 1957.

Stones, Alison, and John Krochalis. *The Pilgrim's Guide to Santiago de Compostela: A Critical Edition.* Harvey Miller Publishers, 1998.

Wallis, Mary Victoria. *Among the Pilgrims: Journeys to Santiago de Compostela.* Trafford, 2003

The Making of Emilio Estevez's *The Way*

Merging Family Ties, Literary Texts and Cultural Identities

Javier Torre Aguado

The film *The Way* (2010) by Emilio Estevez is an inspirational story about the friendship developed by a cohort of pilgrims on their way to Santiago de Compostela. Four peculiar characters—an irascible American doctor who has recently lost his son, an uninspired Irish writer, a tortured Canadian smoker with a secret, and a light-hearted Dutch food-lover trek together as they search for remedies to their innermost anxieties, hoping that the Camino will provide the solutions.

The film is loosely based on the book by Jack Hitt entitled *Off the Road: A Modern-Day Walk Down the Pilgrim's Route into Spain* (2005); to add to that, this free adaptation includes different themes linked to the familiar background of the film director. The personal, the artistic and the ideological are seamlessly weaved into this deeply intimate work of art, motivated by the artist's desire to reconnect to his ancestral land. A book that helps interpret the film and understand the artistic choices made by Emilio Estevez in the making of it is a memoir titled *Along the Way: The Journey of a Father and Son* (2012).

The film *The Way* was released in 2010 and both the father, Martin Sheen, and the son, Emilio Estevez, felt that it wasn't enough to satisfy their need to address their family saga and their ties to the land of their ancestors, so they published the book. The book has an original structure; it's a memoir that alternates in every chapter between the voices and perspectives of the father and the son. It was written with the help of professional writer Hope Edelman. The work recounts, with a tone of humility and honesty, different episodes of their respective professional and personal lives, including the reasons for making the film and the process of filming it.

In this essay, I explore three intersecting aspects of the genesis and the making of the film *The Way*:

1. Father and fatherland as core components of the film, in other words, familiar and cultural ties lie at the heart of the story. I interpret the film as a reflection of the director Emilio Estevez's reconnection with his ethnic and cultural roots, as the film is dedicated to his grandfather, a Galician peasant who emigrated to America decades ago. I also evaluate the complex role of actor Martin Sheen in the making of the film, as he plays the role of the father, and Emilio Estevez plays the role of the deceased son. These topics are particularly relevant because the making of the film itself was a way for the director and his father to reconnect with their own Galician-Spanish heritage and with each other. Furthermore, Martin Sheen's deep religious beliefs shaped certain aspects of the plot of the film, such as the treatment of the topics of abortion and Catholic devotion.

2. The adaptation of Jack Hitt's book *Off the Road. A Modern-Day Walk Down the Pilgrim's Route into Spain* (2005), and the relationship between the film and other travel accounts about the Camino, like the first travel account describing the pilgrimage, the *Codex Calixtinus*, written by Aymeric Picaud during the 12th century. Also, other intertextual and filmic references such as the films *The Wizard of Oz* and *Sideways* that enhance the metanarrative function of the film and provide deeper layers of interpretation of *The Way*.

3. The depiction in the film of national and ethnic identities such as the American, the Spanish and the Gypsy characters, within the general framework of a Spanish travelogue. These depictions are the result of difficult artistic and ideological choices that the director had to make, as he confessed to me during the long conversation that we had after the debut screening of his film in Denver (Winter 2011).

The Way is both a portrait of characters in search of meaning, and the director's quest for a fictional story that would tie him to the land of his ancestors and his descendants. The film also represents Estevez's attempt to understand Spain and portray the nuances of different identities found in the Iberian Peninsula.

Father and Son

Fatherhood and the dynamics between father and son are a powerful theme in *The Way* and something that extends well beyond the film. In this section of the essay I'll explain how the fictional father/son relationship relates to real father/son relationships in four different generations of the Estevez family and how impacts the plot and the character development of the protagonists.

The film tells the story of a doctor who has lost a son to the Camino de Santiago. Tom is a well-established eye doctor living in California who has had a difficult relationship with his son, Daniel. Daniel is a thirty-something graduate student of cultural anthropology at UC-Berkeley who has decided to quit his studies to instead learn about people by traveling abroad. In the film Tom describes his son as "smart, confident, stubborn, pissed me off a lot." When Daniel dies in an accident on the Camino, Tom decides to walk the Camino to reconnect to his son, to try to understand him (something he failed to do when his son was alive) and to literally put himself in his shoes. As the narrative progresses, the haunting image of his son appears on the side of the road on different occasions: quiet, relaxed, looking his father in the eyes. The father, committed, carries on with his pilgrimage, bringing with him the ashes of his deceased son, which he spreads at different places along the Camino.

As I mentioned above, the actor that interprets Tom, the father in the film, is Hollywood star Martin Sheen. The film director, Emilio Estevez, who is also a Hollywood star, plays the role of the son in the film. Their different last names might mislead you, but Martin Sheen and Emilio Estevez are father and son in real life. Although both Martin Sheen and Emilio Estevez are well-known actors with careers that span several decades, not everybody knows that Martin Sheen is an artistic name and that his real name (and the official one on his passport) is Ramón Estevez, the son of a Galician immigrant to the U.S. at the beginning of the 20th century. Ramón changed his name to Martin Sheen when he decided to try his hand as an actor in Hollywood; he was advised to do so because some thought his Hispanic name would become an obstacle for him to be cast in non–Hispanic roles. Decades later, when his son Emilio Estevez decided to also try his hand at acting his father Martin Sheen strongly advised him against changing his name, he confessed that he had regretted changing his own. Consequently, Emilio Estevez maintained his original Spanish name and used it professionally, while his brother, the infamous Charlie Sheen, adopted the artistic name that his father had created. While Charlie Sheen and Emilio Estevez are brothers, each decided for personal reasons to use a different name. As Estevez has explained numerous times, he always felt very connected to his Galician-Spanish ancestry.

How is all of this relevant to the film *The Way*? It is relevant because the film is dedicated to Emilio Estevez's grandfather, the Galician immigrant whose last name he still uses. The genesis of the story is even more pertinent and intricate. How this film came to be made has been explained by both Martin Sheen and Emilio Estevez on different occasions, particularly in a series of interviews they gave to a variety of media outlets in the U.S. and in Spain.[1] It was a combination of ideas of the father and the son that made the film possible. This is explained in the book they wrote together, *Along the Way: The Journey of a Father and Son* (2012), a book that provides critical information to interpreting the film.

Along the Way starts *in media res*, in Saint-Jean-Pied-de-Port, the French town on the border between France and Spain, where the mountain pass that leads to the Spanish section of the Camino is located. In September 2009, the father and son with the rest of the crew started to shoot the film. Estevez explains how the movie came to be:

> In 2003, my father, his close friend and fellow actor Matt Clark, and my son, Taylor, saw the Camino for the first time when the three of them took a trip to Spain. My father was on hiatus from *The West Wing* and didn't have enough time to walk the Camino's length, so they drove along it for a few weeks instead. At an inn for pilgrims outside the city of Burgos, Taylor met and fell in love with the Spanish woman who would become his wife. Later that year he moved to Spain with her, and they live there to this day [6].

During that period in his life, after having had problems with alcohol, Martin Sheen had returned to Catholicism and visited different spiritual places, the most memorable being the Camino de Santiago, which ends in Galicia, his father's place of birth.[2] After that trip, Sheen started bugging his son about making a film that would underline the value of the Camino not only for Catholics but also agnostics, and would serve also as an homage to the memory of his father and his Fatherland: "I have a great idea. Write something for me set in Spain. A documentary" (6). When his son replied that he had no experience with making documentaries, or interest in making one, Sheen replied, "How about a story where two old guys go to Spain with a young guy who speaks the language and shepherds them along the way?" (6). Emilio Estevez thought intensely about it, he really wanted to please his father, so he added his own personal apprehensions—that is, the major shift in his relationship after his son Taylor moved to Spain—into the kernel of the film:

> What did I know about being an old guy or a young guy walking in Spain? Nothing. But I knew what it felt like to lose a son to the Camino. That's what it had felt like after Taylor moved to Spain, and something in that theme felt right. This film needed to be about a father who loses his son [8].

In one of the many interviews Estevez offered while marketing the film, he stated: "I'd lost my own son on the Camino, not tragically, but I lost access to him."[3] Thus, the metaphorical loss of his son experienced by Emilio Estevez in real life became a literal death of a son in the film, and the heart of the story. The first chapter of the book explains how they decided on filming the disappearance of the son in the Pyrenees: it was simply because on the day the film crew arrived, there was an intense fog, and they needed to use every single shooting day available.

So, the film is a story about a father-son relationship, a relationship that was never harmonious when the son was alive, because they didn't share a common set of beliefs. The son is adventurous and wants to see the world while the father is satisfied with his successful career and luxurious lifestyle as a doctor who plays golf in his free time in California. Only after the son has died and the father has placed himself in his son's shoes, finishing the pilgrimage that the son was never able to complete, only then does the father gain enlightenment.

Although the plot of the film only involves two generations (the father and the son), we know by reading the memoir that the themes and personal links expand two more generations. The film director Emilio Estevez dedicates the film *The Way* to his grandfather, the Galician immigrant who left Spain in 1916. The story of Emilio Estevez's grandfather, Martin Sheen's father—whose name is Francisco Estevez Martínez—is retold in different chapters of *Along the Way*. In Chapter One, Martin Sheen remembers the life lessons taught to him by his father, and his father's trip from Galicia to the sugarcane fields in Cuba (where he worked for three years) and later on to his arrival in Dayton, Ohio, where he lived "with the rural sensibilities of northern Spain" (14). Martin explains how his father met his mother, a young immigrant from Ireland, and how the Catholic religion was the cornerstone of their intercultural marriage. His father's side of the family left a stronger impression on him. As Martin explains in the book, "Spain and Ireland were the twin enchantments of an Estevez childhood, distant lands that maintained an emotional pull on both my parents. My father had brothers in Cuba and Argentina by now and my siblings and I romanticized those countries, too—but Spain was our Golden Land" (20).

One important section addresses the topic of cultural identity, and how badly Martin Sheen felt after adopting an Anglo-American name when he was starting his acting career and, in a way, renounced the cultural legacy of his father for professional reasons. Parallel to Martin Sheen's family story, Emilio Estevez reconstructs his younger years raising his son Taylor. The difficulties that he faced as a very young actor having to support a family, just like his own father's struggle when he was a child.

The Way, besides being a film about four strangers who meet on the Camino as each one of them experiences their own revelation, is the product of a father and son settling old disagreements after death and also trying to get back to their cultural roots in Northern Spain. The family story expands, outside of the film, two more generations, including the first Estevez, the Galician immigrant in the U.S., and the last one, the young Taylor who ends up marrying a girl from Burgos, Spain, and returning to the land of his ancestors. Through the story of the four generations of the Estevez family and their circular trip away from Spain and back, various generational disagreements and confrontations are condensed and metaphorically synthesized into the story of Tom's pilgrimage carrying his son's ashes and settling matters with him on a metaphysical level.

The Adaptation and the Literary Tradition, Intertextual References and Meta-Narrativity

I have already explained that the original idea for the film came from Martin Sheen and his religious and personal experiences on the Camino, but some other key ingredients make up the core of the film. *The Way* owes much of its structure and theme development to two books and two films.

In adding elements to the story, Emilio Estevez thought of the similarities between the pilgrims on the Camino and other travel films that he was familiar with. One of those inspiring films, one that serves as a constant intertextual reference in *The Way*, is one of the greatest films of all time: *The Wizard of Oz*. *The Wizard of Oz* is a 1939 American musical film directed by Victor Fleming with a story that revolves around Dorothy, a girl from Kansas who is caught up in a tornado and ends up in the wonderful Land of Oz. In trying to find her way back home, she is joined by a peculiar group of characters: the Scarecrow, who needs a brain so that the crows don't tease him, the Tin Man, who wants to have a heart; and the Cowardly Lion, who needs courage in order to fulfill his natural duties. All four new friends continue in their search for transformation as the film progresses. They encounter numerous obstacles until they finally achieve enlightenment and find new meaning in their lives. It's the inner transformation that is revealing, and that makes the journey worth doing. The four members of this varied group travel together learning from each other and changing along the way. *The Wizard of Oz* is considered a children's film, but it offers many more readings. It's, above all, a metaphor for life, just like *The Way* is. It's also, for example, a cult film among the LGTB community because one of the characters, the cowardly lion, has been interpreted as a closeted gay person. Indeed, singing the film's main song "Over the Rainbow," has become a staple at LGTBQ events.[4]

In an interview with film critic Bob Verini (and also in other interviews), Emilio Estevez acknowledged that the *Wizard of Oz* served "as a template" that would model the story of *The Way*. In discussing it with his father, Martin Sheen, who was going to play the main role in the film, he told him, "I think this is a retelling of the *Wizard of Oz,* and you're Dorothy. The son's death is the catalyst to get you to Spain, but you're going to meet a cowardly lion, and tin man and scarecrow along the way. And it becomes a four-hander" (52).

This is how Estevez decided that there would be three more characters, each representing a character from the classic film. For the equivalent of the Cowardly Lion, he envisioned a large but gentle Dutch character. For this affable character he was also inspired by a real Dutch winemaker that he had met years earlier in California. Some of the most celebrated lines in the film come from Joost, the Dutch foodie/Cowardly Lion character—like "if it ain't Dutch, it ain't much," or "We Dutchmen are always looking for the fastest way to the nearest party"—are actual statements made by this real person.[5]

Another character from the *Wizard of Oz* that is reinterpreted in *The Way* is the Tin Man. The Tin Man is looking for a heart, so Estevez decided to incorporate a character with a broken heart, that character is Sarah, the Canadian smoker who keeps a secret that is revealed to Tom as the film progresses. That heart-breaking secret is that she had an abortion years ago that has laid heavily on her conscience ever since. Finally, Estevez wanted to create a fourth character to replicate the Scarecrow who needs a brain. Estevez struggled to come up with a character that would somehow relate to the Scarecrow, but he found the solution when he read the book *Off the Road: A Modern-Day Walk Down the Pilgrim's Route into Spain,* by American writer Jack Hitt.

As noted earlier, the film is an adaptation of Jack Hitt's *Off the Road,* the book in which he recounts his own misadventures doing the pilgrimage. That the film is an adaptation is acknowledged at the beginning of the work, in the credits: "Story by Emilio Estevez and selected stories from *Off the Road: A Modern-Day Walk Down the Pilgrim's Route into Spain* by Jack Hitt." Nevertheless, the film adaptation of the travel book is only partial, as there are substantial differences.

The main character in the film *The Way* is Tom, the father who decides to start walking where his son died (in a difficult pass in the Pyrenees, between France and Spain) and continue the pilgrimage. Tom tries to reconnect with the spirit of his deceased son, and to understand his philosophy of life, his desires and fears better than when Daniel was alive. As Tom embarks on this journey, he will get to meet and interact with a wide range of characters, pilgrims, *hosteleros,* and locals, and will change in the process, in ways he could have never imagined. None of this can be found in the book that inspired the film. There is no young adventurous American pilgrim who dies in the Pyrenees, no grieving father who continues on his journey. The main character in the travelogue is an American writer with writer's block who decides on doing the pilgrimage as a way to find inspiration for his future book. Much of the narrative centers around his hesitancies and his determination to become a true pilgrim, but also about his fears and self-doubts, because, after all, "what does it take to be a good pilgrim?"

How, then, do the novel and the film intersect? How does the latter adapt the former?

The main figure in the novel, the American writer Jack, becomes a secondary figure in the film, The Irish writer with the same name. Not only that: Jack, the neurotic writer is modeled after the Scarecrow in search of the brain that Emilio Estevez needed to complete his four characters reminiscent of the film that partially inspired him. Jack, the uninspired writer, suffers from brain emptiness, as he has difficulties coming up with an idea to write a book. Emilio Estevez saw this as equivalent to the Scarecrow's lack of a brain. In Estevez's own words, "What if Jack were an Irishman (you see a lot of Irish people on The Way, as well), and he was, in fact, struggling to write this very book during his own bout of writer's block? And isn't that really sort of the same thing as looking for his brain? I have my Scarecrow!" (Verini 54). Estevez even made the character of Jack appear in the film for the first time next to a pile of straw bales, to establish the parallel between his Irish character and the Scarecrow in *The Wizard of Oz*. This is not just my interpretation, Emilio Estevez himself acknowledged this in his memoir.

The change in nationality from the book (an American writer) to the film (an Irish writer) adds to the international flavor and composition of the film, but the character maintains his main traits: he lacks confidence, is neurotic and gets excited easily about the prospect of writing a masterpiece. He is, both in the book and in the film, a funny, likable character that brings emotion and intensity to both works. In his memoir, Emilio Estevez is more specific: "I modelled the character after the author Jack Hitt, whose deeply insightful and hilarious 1994 book about walking the Camino, *Off the Road: A Modern-Day Walk Down the Pilgrim's Route into Spain*, was my inspiration as I wrote *The Way*" (198).

The Irish writer is not the only character that comes out of Jack Hitt's book, one of the "selected stories" adapted by Emilio Estevez from the book into the film is that of Ramón. Ramón is a crazy *hospitalero* met by the pilgrims in the small town of Torres del Río (Logroño). He is described by Hitt in his book (70). Creepy Ramón lives alone but displays a clinical case of double personality disorder, as he impersonates his deceased mother, in what looks like still another intertextual reference, in this case, to the film *Psycho* by Alfred Hitchcock. Apparently, Ramón was a real character who owned an *albergue* called Casa Santa Barbara that no longer exists.[6]

One very relevant topic brought to the story by Jack, the self-conscious writer, is the meta-narrative traits that it introduces. This is the essence of Jack Hitt's travel account, and it permeates the film, where it continues to be a main component. Both the film and the book posit a medieval pilgrimage in the realm of post-modern metanarratives. This is a trend of contemporary travel writing, is present in the work of relevant contemporary figures such as Pico Iyer, Juan Goytisolo or Maximilian Sebald, who are all self-conscious travelers that constantly contrast their experience with those of their predecessors. Literary critic Jorge Carrión calls these writers counter-spatial travelers, because their writing is a re-writing of a very dense, sometimes overwhelmingly dense, inherited cartography, that is, the literary tradition around a given space. Carrión summarizes well the anxiety experienced by these contemporary travel writers: "in postmodernity, the shape of the travel account is not given. To find it is an agony, a conflict" (24).

In the book, the traveler-writer is constantly concerned about living up to the expectations of a true medieval pilgrimage, there is an excess of self-awareness that mortifies the travel writer. This figure, the archetypical medieval "true pilgrim," becomes a sort of ideal that the writer wants to incarnate, but constantly feels he is not up to the task. This is accompanied by the humorous, self-deprecatory tone used often by the travel writer, in the tradition of authors such as Mark Twain in *The Innocents Abroad* (1869) or Bill Bryson in *I'm a Stranger Here Myself* (1998).

In the film *The Way*, all of this is present, some of the most characteristic lines of the writer and dialogues in the film come directly from the book. What adds even more meta-narration is the combination of the writer's character with Tom's personal drama. When the writer learns about Tom's story (that he carries a little box with the ashes of his son and leaves little piles of ashes along the way) he experiences an illuminative moment, "That's brilliant!" he exclaims, and immediately has to hide his enthusiasm, showing more respect for the sad story of Tom: "I mean, tragic, of course." He quickly returns his original excitement to have found a story that could enhance his own travel account: "but brilliant!" He has been asking pilgrims about the reasons for their pilgrimage (a recurring topic throughout the film), now he believes that he has found the ultimate, *real*, pilgrim's story, and he wants to capitalize on it. Paradoxically, the story of Tom will be an important component of the travel book that the Irish writer Jack is composing. This writer-narrator within the narration, exposing the process of the making of a travel account about the Camino, is certainly a great component of the film that adds a new more complex layer of interpretation.

A travel book that is an inevitable reference in Hitt's book is the

Codex-Calixtinus. In *Off the Road*, Jack Hitt makes several references to the *Codex Calixtinus* through the narrative. In fact, in his first reference, at the beginning of his travelogue, he provides a brief synthesis of the medieval book: "I spot on her shelf a copy of an ancient book I have read in translation. The *Codex Calixtinus* is the first book ever written on the pilgrimage, in 1160. It has reports on the inns, the food, the quality of the rivers, the character of the people. Devotees of the road call it the first tourist guide" (32). By mentioning it on different occasions, Jack wants to prove—to other pilgrims, to the locals (like Madame Debril in the French town of Saint-Jean, in Chapter Two) and to his readership—that he is a well-read and a well-prepared modern pilgrim, perfectly aware of the literary tradition that precedes him and that he is attempting to engage with, as a true, contemporary pilgrim that carries on the torch.

The *Codex Calixtinus* (also known as the *Liber Sancti Jacobi*) is the 12th century anthology of texts aimed at providing advice to pilgrims on their way to Santiago [Saint James]. The book contains a compilation of texts (five books total) that include sermons and liturgical texts related to Santiago. It also includes a description of miracles attributed to Santiago. Probably the most interesting section (Book Five) is the "Liber Peregrinationis," which is the actual medieval travel guide because it contains descriptions of the sections of the route to Santiago (the so-called Camino francés), the towns it passes through, and the peoples who live in those areas. The *Codex* is mentioned in the book, and is also cited in the film *The Way*. Jack lectures his comrades about the *Codex Calixtinus* in one of the stops, while they all drink wine at a *posada*. The long explanation provided by Jack is focalized through the perspective of Tom in the film, who has been drinking heavily, and adopting a tone of confrontation, calls Jack an "arrogant bore" and a "true fraud." Not all pilgrims are interested in learning about the intricate story of the pilgrimage and its literary tradition, certainly not Tom, who is tired of listening to Jack's erudite fanfare. To put an end to the confrontation, after Tom is put in jail for being drunk and disturbing the peace of the small town, it's Jack who bails him out, teaching Tom a lesson in generosity.

Another explicit and implicit literary reference in *The Way* as well as *Off the Road* is the classic Spanish novel *Don Quixote* (1606–1616), by Miguel de Cervantes. The book is the obligatory book of travels and adventures in Spain, the tale of contrasting characters, the dreamy Don Quixote and the down to earth Sancho Panza, who learn from each other as they spend months traveling together. No, they're not pilgrims on the Camino, but they encounter an endless number of atypical characters, unexpected exploits and, at every step, learn a new lesson. Early on in the book *Off the Road*, the travel writer Jack is called "Jack Quixote" (4). Likewise, in *The*

Way, in the scene where Joost, the Dutch foodie, and Sarah, the Canadian chain-smoker, meet with Tom; Sarah calls them "Tom Quixote and Sancho Panza," and Joost replies that she, then, must be Dulcinea. Perhaps this is an easy and even predictable literary reference to a Spanish masterpiece inserted into Estevez's script, but nonetheless it increases the intertextuality of the resulting artifact, inviting more subtle layers of meaning in the dynamics among the characters. Visually, Estevez adds beautiful shots of modern windmills that are also perhaps too obvious references to the classic Spanish novel and one more reminder of the contrast between travels centuries ago and contemporary ones.

Finally, another film that is an important model for *The Way* is the film *Sideways*, a low-budget modest film directed by Alexander Payne that earned critical success in 2004. It tells the story of two middle-aged men, who were once college roommates, on a wine tasting road trip, as they say goodbye to their youth. One of them, Jack, is about to get married to a young woman from a wealthy family but still wants to get laid in this last adventure; his friend is a divorced, depressed, failed novelist called Miles, who is passionate about wine. The combination of complementary characters is very effective in the film, this is an odd couple on a road trip, something we've seen before, but that resonates in this film. Jack is enthusiastic about life; the road ahead is always full of possibilities. On the other hand, Miles considers life to be a succession of disasters. They meet other characters along the way, specifically two female counterparts that results in a double-date situation. The film provides reflections on friendship at a leisurely pace. There was so much to admire and reproduce from that film: the low budget, the road, the contrasting characters, and the success. Emilio Estevez acknowledged this model in many interviews and also in his book *Along the Way*.

In the film *The Way*, and in *Sideways* and *The Wizard of Oz*, the four main characters are also on a search, and they learn from each other. Emilio Estevez himself has summarized what walking the way in the company of each other provides to the pilgrims:

> This is a common story on the Camino: Many pilgrims encounter people they can't seem to get away from, but by the time they all reach Santiago de Compostela they've discovered the lessons they need to teach one another along the way. From Sarah, Tom learns compassion; from Jack he learns honesty; and from Joost, kindness and tolerance [203].

All of these narratives—the three films, and the books—naturally fall closely into the patterns and steps meticulously described in "the hero's journey," a universal motif of adventure and transformation, the backbone of all mythic (and non-mythic) narratives, particularly of travel narratives, as originally described by Joseph Campbell and later on adapted and reduced by Christopher Vogler. Although structuralist analysis has fallen out of fashion and has been displaced by poststructuralist cultural analysis, it's worth noticing that at the core of a travel account a fundamental structure continues to exist, and that Campbell's tools of analysis are as pertinent today as they were in 1949, when his book *The Hero with a Thousand Faces* was released to immediate success.

Tom returns to the world completely renewed after his descent into hell (which, in many ways, is his pilgrimage to Santiago). During his pilgrimage, he battles his foes (loses his son, falls into a river, gets robbed, gets drunk and is detained by the police), but also he encounters new friends and allies, and finds new meaning in his life. This is symbolically represented in the last, but very significant, scene of the film, as Tom walks confidently in the streets of Morocco a transformed person, more open, embracing diversity and otherness.

Depiction of the Other

The depiction of the other has always been a key issue in travel accounts, in fact theorists of travel writing consider it a central theme to analyze in travel books and travel films.[7] How is the local depicted? As a heinous enemy or as a fellow human to whom the traveler can relate? Are different ethnic or cultural groups differentiated? Are all local people considered to be the same? Are they depicted as individuals or as clichés, stereotyped by some national or ethnical traits?

Travel accounts about the pilgrimage to Santiago are not an exception to the general bias expressed by travel writers throughout history. In fact, if one opens the *Codex Calixtinus*—the first travel guide about the Camino— one is appalled at the outrageous bias shown by the travel writer and his disdainful depiction of Spaniards, particularly of people from the region of Navarre. In his book, Jack Hitt touches on this sensitive topic. He explains:

> The Codex is attributed to a French cleric named Aimery Picaud. The book is amusing because the author's pro–France/anti–Spain bias is the most comically exaggerated in history. His critical reviews of the towns and food along the way are filled with crazed invective. France is all elegance, and Spain is a country of poisoned rivers, granite bread, and lethal fish [52].

Hitt quotes directly from the *Codex Calixtinus* to show his readers the biased depictions of Spaniards in this text:

> This is a barbarous people unlike all other peoples in customs and in character, full of malice, swarthy in color, ill-favoured of face, misshapen, perverse, perfidious, empty of faith and corrupt, libidinous, drunken, experienced in all violence, ferocious and wild, dishonest and reprobate, impious and harsh, cruel

and contentious, unversed in anything good, well trained in all vices and iniquities […] in everything inimical to our French people [53].

It is of no surprise that modern day Spaniards are concerned about their image, as they have been for centuries. This is something noticed by many scholars today, particularly those who study the Black Legend.[8] Hitt broaches this topic in his book when he notes that "Spaniards still fear that they are inferior to the more brutal capitalists one finds in parts of Italy and all of Germany. The lazy Spaniard, drunk and stretched out in *siesta*, is an image they seek constantly to dispel" (62).

Perhaps because Hitt wants to dispel stereotypes, a Spanish pilgrim that appears a few pages later is characterized as anything but lazy. He is introduced in these terms: "Javier, my Spanish friend, is a banker with a wife and kids. He's in his forties, bald, with tufts of graying hair above the ears, and possesses a lanky body riven with restless tics. Javier is anxious to talk. He confesses that he has longed to walk the road all of his life" (66). They trek together, but when Hitt wants to "sit down to a plate of lamb chops and greasy Spanish fries, maybe half a carafe of red wine," his Spanish friend insists on "just throwing down a fistful of shelled pistachios, gulp a quart of water, and move on" (67).

Emilio Estevez, like Jack Hitt in his book, addresses head-on issues of representations of ethnic groups, particularly gypsies and Americans. One of the more typical topics in the travel literature about Spain is gypsies, to the point that, since the Romantic mythification of gypsy people, they have been associated with Spanish identity and culture.[9] No gypsies appear in the book by Jack Hitt, but Estevez wanted there to be an important scene with gypsies. Actually, it was his father who wanted a scene in which his backpack gets stolen, Estevez decided that it would fit that it was stolen by gypsies, only to give the episode an unexpected twist. A gypsy kid steals Tom's backpack in Burgos, and a frantic scene follows in which Jack, Joost and Tom follow him through the narrow streets of the old town, only to find themselves in a gypsy quarter. Joost immediately warns Tom of the dangers associated with gypsies, they all leave the neighborhood in fear. The twist in the resolution of this episode is that the kid's father returns the backpack to Tom and makes his son apologize. Not happy with that, he invites all of them to spend the evening with his neighbors and family as they play gypsy music. In this case Estevez wanted to dispel negative stereotypes about gypsies by portraying them as *hombres de respeto*, which is exactly what he experienced while filming the sequence, as he explains in his memoire:

The Spanish crew has warned us about hiring gypsies, "They're not going to show up," we heard. "If they do, they'll steal from you and they'll leave early," but this group of Gitanos is magnificent. They arrive on time and play their instruments and dance beautifully. [...] They do it all for free and the only thing they take with them is the leftover food, which they ask for in advance [288].

One more cultural identity that the film explores is that of Americans abroad. Tom, in many ways, is a stereotypical ugly American, as recognized by Estevez: "By giving Tom this arrest scene in *The Way* I wanted to show a scene where an American who behaves badly in Spain, the typical ugly American, gets his comeuppance" (203). This connects to the idea that Tom represents, at least during the first part of the film, before the Camino has transformed him, an overconfident nationalistic American (perhaps even a hardcore Republican), that sees himself as superior to those around him. In fact, in his diatribe against his international travel companions he lists the faults of each of them. When Tom is arrested by the Spanish policemen, he screams arrogantly "I am American, I speak American!" Estevez has addressed this attitude in one of the interviews referring to Tom's character: "a character who in many ways is emblematic of America itself. We've built a wall around ourselves for how many decades now? And we've isolated ourselves to a great extent, which is ironic for a nation of immigrants" (Verini 53). Tom definitely learns a lesson in humility when his companions—those that he has been furiously screaming at—have to bail him out of jail. He learns that he also needs others to complete his personal journey. It's not just Tom's character that evolves in the film, it's ultimately Estevez's desire to see a transformed America, more engaged and responsive to the perspectives of other nations and peoples. This is represented in the last scene in which Tom has moved to a new level of travel and global identity, engaging with a much more radical otherness, in a predominately Muslim country like Morocco, and having adopted, at least partially, Muslim attire in the form of the symbolically charged Palestinian Keffiyeh that he wears around his neck.

To conclude, this essay has shown how the film *The Way* came to be by tracing the creative process of the film director, Emilio Estevez, as he combined familial challenges, unique characters and intertextual references. Being familiar with these references helps the viewer understand the work better and allows for more nuanced layers of interpretation.

NOTES

1. See, for example, this interview with a Spanish media outlet in which they state: "Somos gallegos, y nunca nos hemos ido." www.enclavedecine.com/2010/11/martin-sheen-emilio-estevez-somos-gallegos-que-nunca-nos-hemos-ido-pero-que-volvemos-a-casa.html

2. In this interview, Martin Sheen opens up about his religious transformation.

3. See Johnson, Brian D. Maclean's ."Martin Sheen's Family Baggage." 11–14–2011, vol. 124, Issue 44.

4. www.epgn.com/news/local/11176-the-wizard-of-oz-in-the-lgbt-community.

5. See Verini p. 53, also Sheen's *Along the Way* 2012.

6. Consult this website, which identifies all the locations where the film was shot: caminofacil.net/en/the-way/

7. Consult Tim Youngs' *The Cambridge Introduction to Travel Writing*.

8. Of the vast bibliography on the topic, I'll simply note that a book recently published in Spain by Maria Elvira Roca Barea with the title *Imperiofobia y Leyenda Negra* has become an instant best-seller, reigniting (once again) the intellectual debate about the image of Spain and of Spaniards.

9. On the conflation of gypsy, Andalusian and Spanish identities as "mutually interchangeable signifiers" see José F. Colmeiro, "Exorcising Exoticism: *Carmen* and the Construction of Oriental Spain."

WORKS CITED

Campbell, Joseph. *The Hero with a Thousand Faces*. Bollingen Foundation, 1949.

Carrión, Jorge. *Viaje contra Espacio. Goytisolo y W.G. Sebald*. Iberoamericana/Vervuert, 2009.

Colmeiro, José F. "Exorcising Exoticism: Carmen and the Construction of Oriental Spain." *Comparative Literature*, vol. 54, no. 2, 2002, pp. 127–44.

Estevez, Emilio. "Why I Wrote My First Memoir, *Along the Way*, with a Guy Named Martin Sheen." July 04, 2012, HuffPost.

Estevez, Emilio, Martin Sheen, and Deborah K. Unger. *The Way*. Icon Entertainment International & Elixir Films, 2010.

Hitt, Jack. *Off the Road. A Modern-Day Walk Down the Pilgrim's Route Into Spain*. Simon & Schuster Paperbacks, 1994.

Roca Barea, Maria Elvira. *Imperiofobia y Leyenda Negra. Roma, Rusia, Estados Unidos y el Imperio Español*. Siruela, 2016.

Sheen, Martin, and Emilio Estevez with Hope Edelman. *Along the Way: The Journey of a Father and Son*. Free Press, 2012.

Verini, Bob. "Showing Us the Way," *Script Magazine*, Sept/Oct 2011, pp. 51–55.

Youngs, Tim. *The Cambridge Introduction to Travel Writing*. Cambridge University Press, 2013.

Screening the Camino de Santiago

Suffering and Communitas in The Way and I'll Push You

Tiffany Gagliardi Trotman

World religions have long held pilgrimage as an important journey of the faithful. From the exodus of the Jewish people out of Egypt toward a Promised Land, Muslims traveling to Mecca, the Hindu journey to the Ganges and Christian pilgrimages to holy places revealed through miracles or the lives of saints, there is clearly a long tradition of pilgrimage for religious believers. Today, there is, also an increasing number of non-religious pilgrims undertaking these types of journeys. The consequence of this phenomenon is an increase in cultural texts in a variety of forms including documentaries and travel literature reflecting upon the topic of pilgrimage. These texts serve as an interpretive lens through which one can grapple with the journey of secular pilgrims. In this essay, I will focus on one specific pilgrimage site, the Camino de Santiago, whose principal route, the *Camino francés*, commences in southern France and travels nearly 800 km across northern Spain ending in Santiago de Compostela. Using Victor and Edith Turner's theory of the liminal I will examine two films, *The Way* (2010) and *I'll Push You* (2016), to discuss the presence of key features of liminality as they appear in the films. I will identify liminal/liminoid experiences and associate these with the role pilgrimage may play for those undertaking such journeys for non-religious/secular or spiritual purposes.

The Camino de Santiago, or the Way of Saint James, traces its roots back to the 9th century when Theodomirus, Bishop of Iria Flavia, told of the discovery of the remains of the Apostle Saint James the Great close to the current location of Santiago de Compostela. There is a rich history of legends and myths related to this discovery. From the 10th century, the Way of St. James became the most important pilgrimage route in Europe, with the road to Rome considered too dangerous, and the road to Jerusalem too far.

Early religious pilgrims were moved by their devotion or penance to travel the Way. In the 12th century, monks from Cluny initiated the tradition of travel guides through the commissioning of the *Codex Calixtinus*. This work is considered the first travel guide ever written, and it is also credited with popularizing the route for the next several hundred years. The 16th century saw a decline in the pilgrimage along the Way due to the Protestant Reformation. However, the route was reclaimed in the 20th century by the Spanish dictator Francisco Franco who used the pilgrimage as a means to foster Catholic unity. Subsequent to Franco's death, the Council of Europe championed the Camino as a cultural itinerary to help foster European cohesion and identity. In 1998, UNESCO declared the Camino de Santiago a World Heritage Site and today, after 1,200 years of existence, the pilgrims' route to Santiago is flourishing in part due to popular films, documentaries and literary works. For example, the number of pilgrims that received the *Compostela*, a medieval document recognizing the completion of a minimum of 100 km by foot in 2017 and 2018 was over 300,000. In 2007, the number of *Compostelas* issued was approximately a third of that number.[1] The causes behind such a steep increase in pilgrim numbers in recent years are complex. One factor that has contributed, however, is an increased awareness of the Way due to cultural depictions of the pilgrimage. Norman explains that

> part of the reason for this increase is undoubtedly the recent profusion of literature on the pilgrimage in popular culture, mostly in the form of travelogues and memoirs from authors who have walked the pilgrimage. These books tend to be filled with images of deep psychological exploration and mystical encounters [6–7].

In addition to generating a multitude of books and travel guides, the pilgrimage has also drawn the interest of filmmakers who have depicted the journey in both documentaries and feature films. The more popular of these works have featured those on secular pilgrimages rather than religious pilgrimages.

Secular Pilgrimage

Significant research in the area of tourism studies has attempted to grapple with the definition of a pilgrim or a religious traveler. For the purpose of providing some clarity around the type of pilgrim that features in the films examined here, Alex Norman's definition of a "spiritual tourist" is helpful. In contrast to a religious traveler, Norman writes,

> a spiritual tourist is one who includes an activity, such as yoga, meditation, following a pilgrimage … for the purposes of "spiritual betterment," such as

creating personal meaning, in a secular way. It is important to recognize the unstructured, individualized way in which they approach these activities, "which they see as concerned with meaning, identity, morality and transcendence" [20].

So what is known about the motivations of those undertaking the Camino as secular or spiritual tourists? Why do individuals without religious devotion from modern societies in which organized religion is being eclipsed by agnosticism and atheism, travel to this religious site? In her seminal anthropological study on the Camino de Santiago entitled *Pilgrim Stories*, Nancy Luis Frey explains that most of the travelers along this route are motivated by "the pains of the suffering soul" (45). Her research concludes:

> The journey of the Camino can reveal wounds—loss, failure, fear, shame, addiction—left festering from daily life. Experiences along the way often act as the catalyst that allows them to be exposed. It has been and appears to continue to be, a road for hopes and miracles of fulfilment of a different order. Some pilgrims, acknowledging this themselves, refer to the Camino as *la ruta de la terapia*, the therapy route…. The pilgrims' inner orientations often relate to issues of transition, loss, rupture, or marginality. Many are making a life-cycle transition—from youth to adulthood, from mid-life reflection and crisis to retirement. More serious wounds—or "critical gaps," as one pilgrim put it—also draw pilgrims to the Camino…. Pilgrims often have a difficult time explaining why they are making the pilgrimage [45].

Frey concludes, these travelers "may know what they are fleeing from but not what they are seeking" (45). Her research into motivations for the pilgrimage dispels the myth that the goal of the Camino is to reach Santiago de Compostela. Drawing a distinction between the Camino and other Marian shrines, she explains that "the goal is often the road itself, not the city" because these "[pilgrims] are not motivated by pains of the suffering body but by pains of the suffering soul" (45). Camino pilgrims require the time implied by the walk to work through their existential suffering. Frey explains:

> It is not just devotion (an instrumental purpose) that drives pilgrims to walk and cycle to Santiago, but in choosing to go in a nonmodern way pilgrims make statements (expressive and communicative purposes) about their society and their values. Broadly speaking, these values include an appreciation of nature and physical effort, a rejection of materialism, an interest in or a nostalgia for the past, a search for inner meaning, an attraction to meaningful human relationships and solitude [27].

Alex Norman's research confirms Frey's work through the exploration of a simple question, *"Why do Western spiritual tourists go to the Camino de Santiago?"* His conclusion is quite simple. The Camino for these tourists is part of a project of self-discovery or self-investigation (8).

Further motivation for traveling the Camino can be linked to the idea of the *biophilia hypothesis,* developed by Kellert and Wilson, which states that humans developed an affinity for nature and felt comforted by it, as part of the process of human evolution. So in essence, the motivation for secular pilgrims is may be somewhat unclear or ill-defined. What they experience is a sense of calling or a need to walk. This motivation to move the body, to disconnect from society, to discover something not fully understood or perhaps an identity lost in the fury of daily life sits at the heart of secular pilgrimages. As Norman explains, "the Camino has come to hold a popular mythological status as a journey of 'authenticity' and transformation" (48).

Liminality and Pilgrimage

With this motivation in mind, I will now move to Turner's theory of liminality which will shed light on the process that these pilgrims engage in and ultimately complete. It is through the lens of this theory that I will interpret the films *The Way* and *I'll Push You* as texts that depict secular pilgrimage.

In approaching liminality, the works of three key figures, Victor and Edith Turner and Arnold van Gennep, are important to understand. The concept of liminality was first developed by Arnold van Gennep, an early 20th century anthropologist interested in folklore, in his 1906 work "Rites of Passage." In studying rites of passage, van Gennep distinguished three specific phases or rites including: separation rites, liminal rites and finally, reincorporation. Separation rites consist of symbolic actions that reflect the detachment of an individual from a previous social structure. In the second phase, the liminal stage, an individual "passes through a cultural realm that has few or none of the attributes of the past or coming state" (Turner "Liminality" 327). Finally, reincorporation concludes a rite of passage as the ritual subject returns to their initial cultural conditions. The individual is no longer the same, however, having experienced a transformation through the rite of passage.

Victor and Edith Turner's works build upon the theory established by van Gennep. The Turners are credited with approaching the anthropological study of religion, not from a pure social science lens, but rather through the lens of humanistic studies. They were concerned with bringing to life the religious practices that they observed by concentrating on the transformative function of rituals within individual lives and within communities.

For the purpose of this analysis, the liminal phase is key to understanding elements that are specific to the Camino experience. Liminality is the middle phase of a rite of passage and is constituted by a state of being "in-between," after the individual has undergone a separation from a previous group, yet before their return to their original space. Within the liminal phase, an individual reflects upon many aspects of life through a process of change. The liminal subject is no longer who they were before, but rather "on the threshold" of a new way of being. Edith Turner, in her autobiography *Heart of Lightness*, describes liminality as possessing a strange "out of this ordinary world character." It is a place "where the normal does not apply. It is a kind of crack between the worlds like the looking glass world of Alice, where animals and chessman speak—and reprimand the visitor … it is hard to put into logical terms" (Ross xxx). Liminality ends when the rites of passage ritual moves toward the reincorporation of the individual into their former community as a changed person.

In order to understand liminality, the Turners outlined a dichotomy between two major models of human inter-relatedness that are "juxtaposed and alternating." Victor Turner referred to these models as the Liminal and Status models. The Status Model consists of "structured, differentiated and often hierarchical systems of politico-legal-economic positions with many types of evaluation separating men in terms of 'more' or 'less.'" In contrast, the Liminal Model of human relations is a society of mostly unstructured and undifferentiated *communitas* or community, an "even communion of equal individuals" (Turner "Liminality" 328). In practice, the human experience consists of a continuous fluctuation between these two models that operate in a dialectic. Specific binary oppositions exist based upon the nature of these two states of being or models.

Status

Heterogeneity, structure, inequality, property, status, distinctions of dress, selfishness, speech, secularity, avoidance of pain and suffering, pride of position

Liminal

Homogeneity, communitas, equality, anonymity, absence of property and status, uniform clothing, unselfishness, silence, sacredness/mystical, acceptance of pain and suffering, humility

Binary Oppositions: The Liminal and Status Models of Victor Turner. See "Liminality and Communitas" in *A Reader in Anthropology of Religion*. Ed. Michael Lambeck. Blackwell Publishing, 2008, p. 333.

Turner elucidates an interconnectedness between these two models in which those released from structure into liminality, return to structure revitalized by their experience of *communitas*. He concludes, "what is certain is that no society can function adequately without this dialectic." The oscillations between these two models effectively "constitute the 'human condition' in regards to man's relations with his fellow man" ("Liminality" 338–9).

In his book *Dramas, Fields and Metaphors* (1974), Victor Turner links pilgrimage specifically to the liminal stage. Through significant research into rites of passage within the context of African tribal culture, the Turners identified pilgrimage as Christianity's own form of liminality. He elucidates several features of this stage, including *communitas*, suffering and egalitarianism as important aspects of the pilgrim's journey. Bowie explains, "According to Turner, pilgrimage takes people out of normal society and throws individuals together, united by a common purpose. It is at odds with the normal social hierarchies and institutional norms and ideas. It is anti-structural, creative and transformative" (240).

Deborah Ross interprets present day pilgrimage as liminoid rather than liminal due to a clear distinction between present and past religious practices in Europe. She explains that previously such practices originated out of a "culture of obligation or duty." These practices have been shaped today by a "culture of consumption" which has created space for making choices among religious practices. She notes the Turners' distinction between obligatory religious practices within indigenous communities versus the optional religious practices of Western cultures. Ross writes, "the liminal-liminoid distinction anticipated the present religious moods in parts of Europe and it parallels the culture of obligation-culture of consumption difference … secular pilgrimage—with its emphasis on choice and the search for personal self-definition and its lack of defined traditional structure—is more liminoid than liminal" (xlii–xliii). In essence, because modern-day pilgrimage is voluntary, rather than obligatory, it is a liminoid experience.

Norman has previously linked the Camino de Santiago with the concept of liminality, particularly for secular pilgrims. He writes, "for the spiritual tourist the Camino de Santiago essentially offers one type of experience: a walking pilgrimage. However, far from begin a one-dimensional religious activity, the contemporary Camino bears witness to a suite of liminal, meditative, Romantic-inspired and life-changing processes and practices" (181).

The films *The Way* and *I'll Push You* serve as cinematic cultural texts based on pilgrimages to Santiago de Compostela the evidence various stages of the liminal process. In the next section, I will demonstrate two key features of liminality as they are depicted in these films. These features are *communitas* and suffering.

Communitas. *Communitas* is a common experience along the Camino, yet it is a slippery, difficult-to-wrangle, kind of term. In essence, it is a sense of a community in which individuals relate to each other as equals. *Communitas* flourishes in the absence of a structured society as it depends on the absence of social rank. Victor Turner, in *The Ritual Process*, explained it as an "experience of oneness or unity felt by those sharing a rite-of-passage experience"; a "sacred experience of mutuality with another" (Ross xxx). *Communitas* occurs throughout the Way but may be most evident at the end of each day when pilgrims converge to create meaning of their walk. Frey explains,

> The social element is vital for those on the Camino, not only for those people who live along the way but especially for those who are cycling and walking to Santiago. It is commonly said that many people start alone but always end accompanied by others. The formation of friendships and groups of walking and cycling companions that cut across normal divisions such as gender, age, class, nationality and marital status is an important aspect of becoming a pilgrim and feeling part of a larger community [91].

Pilgrims tend to feel geographically and emotionally removed from their homes and generally use only first names as they engage in an existence that has been described as "out of time" (Frey 86). The *communitas* experience is enriching as it allows individuals to return to their ordinary lives feeling rejuvenated and renewed.

The experience of the Camino itself is the driver for *communitas*. As pilgrims embark on each day of their journey they are faced with shared human experiences and sentiments as well as a plethora of physical and emotional obstacles. *Communitas* is built upon an equalizing force that permeates the pilgrim's journey. Pilgrims, as liminoid subjects, or those experiencing a liminal experience in a modern-day context, are not defined by their ordinary identities, and consequently there is a leveling of social hierarchies. Turner explains, "Liminal entities are neither here nor there; they are betwixt and between the positions assigned and arrayed by law, custom, convention, and ceremony." Pilgrims are united by a greater sense of community because:

> they have no status, property, insignia, secular clothing indicating rank or role, position in a kinship system—in short, nothing that may distinguish them from their fellow neophytes or initiands…. It is as though they are being reduced or ground down to a uniform condition to be fashioned anew and endowed with additional powers to enable them to cope with their new station in life ["Liminality and Communitas" 327–8].

This results in the development of "an intense comradeship and egalitarianism." Perhaps it is the awareness of the "out of time" nature of the experience that frees communication as many travelers will meet, walk, and share deeply personal feelings in the comfort of knowing that their fellow travelers will not be returning to ordinary life with them. Norman summarizes this writing, "[pilgrims] engage in deep thought and conversation with their fellow pilgrims about their daily lives at home" (5).

There is no doubt that *communitas* is difficult to describe. Indeed, esteemed scholars like the Turners wrestled with assigning words to the phenomena. Victor Turner writes, "it is neither by chance nor by lack of scientific precision that, along with others who have considered the conception of *communitas*, I find myself forced to have recourse to metaphor and analogy" ("Liminality and Communitas" 338). One could argue that the use of creative outlets, such as film, is an effective means of defining or evidencing an indefinable phenomena. Film in particular provides a means of showing, rather than telling.

Suffering. The second key aspect of liminality featured in these films is suffering. This theme is also multi-faceted. As previously mentioned, suffering is often a motivation for traveling the Camino. In his book, *Healing Places*, Wilbert Gesler writes:

> We know that many, if not most, societies around the world believe that nature has healing powers.... Many people feel that they can attain physical, mental and spiritual healing simply by spending time out-of-doors or seeking out remote or isolated places where they can "get away from it all," surrounded by undisturbed nature [8].

But, further to this, the Camino itself owns its own form of suffering in the shape of sore muscles, mental fatigue, hunger, swollen joints and blisters. All of these are a common experience of the pilgrim and they play a "crucial role in the formation of solidarity among pilgrims" (Frey 111).

For those choosing to walk the whole of the *Camino francés*, the typical time spent is four to six weeks, walking whilst carrying a pack with a maximum weight of 6.8 kilograms, or 15 pounds, over steep mountain passes. Norman describes suffering along the journey:

> Most pilgrims take at least three days to feel comfortable with the Camino experience, including the confronting physicality of it. In the first days, knees suffer under the weight of the pack and the many kilometers walked, and the blisters pilgrims often develop can be crippling and shocking to behold.... After four or five days the body adjusts. Around the same time the everyday social boundaries carried by pilgrims are shed and new types of bonds are developed, reflecting the intimacy of shared experience. The pains of the body continue, but they begin to become seen as part of the project the pilgrim is engaged in. The walking becomes a metaphor for the inner journey the pilgrim is on; one is walking through one's problems in life, just as one is walking through landscape. Participating in the walking thus designates one to all those around as participating in a greater journey of the heart and mind [51].

As mentioned previously, Frey has identified sufferings of the soul as a distinctive aspect of the Camino pilgrimage, in comparison to other Marian pilgrimages that focus primarily on seeking healing for physical ailments. She writes, "the experience of pain plays a crucial role in the formation of solidarity among pilgrims and among pilgrims and *hospitaleros.*[2] The pains that pilgrims suffer are an important topic of discussion as pilgrims give each other advice, help with cures, and lend each other band-aids, cotton swabs, and betadine" (111).

Turner underscores a process of chastening or humiliation that the initiand must go through in the liminal phase. Examples of this include a ritualized belittling that occurs as part of the installation of a new senior chief Kanongesha of the Ndembu people in Zambia or the medieval knight's vigil. Both are required to accept their own personal weaknesses prior to completing their liminal passage. He writes, "the ordeals and humiliations, often of a grossly physiological character, to which neophytes are submitted represent partly a destruction of the previous status and partly a tempering of their essence in order to prepare them to cope with their new responsibilities and to restrain them in advance from abusing their new privileges" ("Liminality and Communitas" 332). This may be linked to the humbling processes, both psychological and physical, that the pilgrim experience on the Camino. With these two aspects of liminality, *communitas* and suffering defined, it is now time to turn to the films.

The Way

The Way, a film partly subsidized by the *Galician Film Commission* as well as the *Santiago de Compostela Film Commission*, has been recognized as a significant contributor to the increase in North American pilgrims on the Camino since the film's release in 2010. López et al. have analyzed data from the Pilgrims' Office and concluded that "the American film, *The Way* can be considered the first promoter of the film-induced tourism" with little evidence of such a factor existing prior to 2011. In addition to a sizeable increase in pilgrims from the United States, the distribution of the film globally led to a significant internationalization of pilgrims, both non–Catholic and secular, from emergent markets that prior to the film had been the home country of very few pilgrims (26).

López notes that the marketing of the Camino through *The Way* extended well-beyond providing knowledge of the Camino's existence by portraying different purposes for the pilgrimage. These motivations include: "(1) living a unique experience (different from everyday life); (2) enjoying the landscape and environment; (3) enjoying heritage; (4)

experiencing ancestors' way of life; (5) discovering new places; (6) meeting new people, having time to interact with them, and rediscovering the art of conversation." The film is credited with "moving away from the traditional, historical background or symbolism, in order to reproduce the values of the human being, ideals and hopes" (30). Estevez's work provides a window into the Way that transcends the domain of a traditional pilgrimage and instead offers to a modern-day audience an experience beyond the ordinary day-to-day life in a world that increasingly seeks such escapes.

The film is a dramatic-comedy written, directed and produced by Emilio Estevez starring his father, Martin Sheen. It tells the story of an American ophthalmologist, Dr. Thomas Avery, who travels to Spain to recover the body of his son, Daniel, who has tragically died while walking in a winter storm in the Pyrenees. While Daniel is unable to experience the full potential of the Camino, his father's journey, albeit later in life, demonstrates the capacity of the pilgrimage as a rite of passage.

The father-son relationship between these two characters is one of emotional distance in which Tom proudly sticks to his tempered realism while his son Daniel, an anthropologist, sets off, determined to experience the world. Prior to leaving, Daniel invites his father to join him, "to pack a bag, grab his passport and forget his golf clubs," to embark on a trip with no fixed plan. Tom dismisses his son's suggestion. As an ophthalmologist who reserves his free time for the golf course, where he uses the golf cart for transport rather than walking because he is "old and tired," he fails to understand his son's free spirit and instead believes that he is "ruining his life." When he chastises Daniel saying, "most people don't have the luxury of picking up and leaving it all behind," his son responds, "I am not most people." The difference between these characters is starkly depicted in Tom's "choosing a life" versus Daniel's "living one." Daniel leaves phones messages for his father as he travels however, they rarely seem to connect.

It is with shock that Tom receives the news from France that Daniel's body has been discovered in the French Pyrenees, and he immediately travels to San-Jean-Pied-de-Port to recover his body. After meeting the gendarme, and cremating Daniel's remains, Tom decides to walk the Camino for his son, and to carry his ashes, stored in a small metal box, to Santiago de Compostela. He describes the journey to the gendarme captain, as a father-son trip, noting, "we are leaving in the morning … both of us." The following day, as Tom prepares to leave, the captain asks him, "Do you know why are you walking The Way?" When he replies that he is walking for Daniel, the gendarme explains, that one can only walk the Camino for themselves. Thus the journey is defined as Tom's journey. He begins his separation from society, his rite of passage, by removing his sportscoat, and donning Daniel's jacket and backpack. As he carries his son toward Santiago de Compostela he enters the homogeneity of the pilgrim community.

Communitas, as a unifying, self-sacrificing, all-together force, separate from class or social rank, is anathema to Tom's existence in Southern California. This force confronts him along his journey as he grapples with his own discomfort with community. His old life, in which respect and acceptance has been given due to his profession, vanishes on the Camino. He finds it difficult to accept the help of others, or to offer his own help to them. Initially he is guarded, hesitates to share personal information, the reason behind his Camino, the significance of the metal box. Ultimately, however, *communitas* triumphs and Tom renders himself a member of the pilgrim community.

On the first day of his journey, Tom ascends into the Pyrenees. Near Roncevaux, amidst a mountain fog, he notices a makeshift wooden cross along the side of the path. Glancing up the mountainside, he captures a glimpse of his son Daniel, who appears in a mystical fashion as if to encourage his father along. This is his first appearance, which is followed by several more as the journey progresses. In this manner, Daniel serves as a sort of spirit guide for Tom throughout the rite of passage.

Communal housing, in the form of *albergues* and *refugios*,[3] as well as shared meals provide an environment to instill the spirit of *communitas* in Tom. Just short of Pamplona, he arrives at an *albergue* unable to walk any further. As this is early days in his pilgrimage, Tom remains quiet, insular and removed from the community. This scene, however, depicts the impact of the community table, the sharing among equals. The host's welcome, *"Llegas tarde peregrino"* [You've arrived late, pilgrim], "We were expecting you," despite no knowledge of Tom's arrival, points to the open invitation and generosity of the Way. He comforts him, "we have plenty of beds and the food is still warm," and announces to the table already full of fellow pilgrims, "the Americans are here." The group salutes him as they hum the "Star-Spangled Banner." As the pilgrims engage in a dinner debate about who killed Charlemagne's commander Roland in the Battle of Roncevalles, Tom glances around the table to once again see, the appearance of his son sitting alongside others. Daniel smiles warmly as if enjoying the meal with him, and raises his glass. The jovial, warm and welcoming environment of the communal table reflects an atmosphere of instant friendship, the spirit of *communitas*. This is just one of several scenes in the film that incorporate the communal table.

Initially determined to avoid all social interactions and to keep his personal affairs to himself, Tom reluctantly forms relationships with three other pilgrims, Sarah, a Canadian seeking to escape an abusive past and give up smoking, Joost, a Dutchman wanting to lose weight and Jack, an

Irish poet who is desperately seeking inspiration for a new book. Through-out the film, a sense of camaraderie develops among these unlikely companions through their shared journey. Tom, Sarah and Joost meet Jack whom they find having an outburst of anger in the middle of a hayfield. He apologies for his behavior (tossing his pilgrim staff into the air and nearly hitting the others) saying, "Oh my God! I thought I was out here all alone." This is an interesting, existential comment. Tom's response brings Jack into the *communitas* fold, "You thought wrong." While Jack proves to be the commander of metaphors, particularly the significance of the "the road," he is himself lost on the road. Jack's verbosity irritates Tom who rebukes the writer's survey question about his motivations for walking. Despite this, ever-friendly Joost acquiesces to Jack's plea to walk with the group, to share the road.

Pilgrimage creates a space in which deeply personal stories, often of suffering and loss, can be discussed with a sense of anonymity and security. Members of the community learn to hold space and listen to others as they walk through their pain. Suffering brought to and gained on the Camino is accepted as a common, human experience. For many, suffering is lightened and wounds are healed through sharing stories with other pilgrims. There is, however, an unspoken code among pilgrims that one is not to judge or profit from others' suffering.

The spirit of protection among suffering pilgrims is clear in the film. Walking together, Jack questions Joost about the reasons behind Sarah and Tom's pilgrimages. When Joost reveals the accidental nature of Tom's pilgrimage, his loss and his practice of leaving small piles of ashes along the Way, the writer quickly grabs his pocket notebook and exclaims, "That's brilliant! ... Do you think that he'd want to talk to me about it?" Joost replies, "I think he sooner shove that walking stick down your throat." This scene captures the diversity of motivations of the travelers but also conveys the deeply personal nature of Tom's walk. Joost's quick attempt to shut down Jack's intention to profit from Tom's journey depicts the supportive and protective stance that he takes with respect to his traveling companion. This again is evidence of *communitas*.

Sharing and a sense of communal property, both aspects of *communitas*, also permeate the film. Joost enjoys offering his sleep aids, Ambien, ear plugs and marijuana, to fellow pilgrims. Sarah shares her "friends," cigarettes with others. When Tom meets Frank, a priest walking in the hope of a miracle to cure his brain cancer, he accepts a rosary. Assuming that it is Frank's personal rosary, he refuses the gift, however Frank reveals a pocketful that he carries for lapsed Catholics on the Camino. Despite the generosity around him, Tom hesitates to share with "strangers," the act is unfamiliar to him. This however changes when he agrees to share the thing most valuable to him, the story and memory of his son, with Jack, who intends to include it in his book. In Leon, Tom treats the others to a night of luxury at the *parador*,[4] a truly generous gift for his fellow, weary pilgrims. While the intention is to each have a restful night away from the communal sleeping arrangements of the *albergues*, one by one they arrive at Tom's suite to toast and to enjoy each other's company. The spirit of *communitas* has bound them together such that an evening in solitude no longer feels familiar or comfortable.

Shortly after arriving in Santiago, a further scene illustrates the sacred/mystical nature of liminality as the four travelers arrive at the Cathedral. It is here that the suffering of each character is most evident. Sarah approaches the statue of Saint James and lays down the cigarettes that she promised to quite at the end of the Camino. Joost approaches the statue crawling on his knees, expressing his gratitude as so many others have done before him. Tom carefully places the silver box containing Daniel's ashes before the relics of the Saint. Jack, who has yet to enter a church (which he has referred to as "temples of tears") during the pilgrimage, sits weeping in a pew within the Cathedral.

The weight of suffering that each has carried is offered up when they experience the Pilgrim's Mass. The pilgrims' faces reflect a sublime humility as they experience this end-stage ritual performed for hundreds of years in the presence of countless pilgrims. As the large *botafumeiro* swings back and forth over the pilgrims, bathing them in incense, Tom catches a final ghostly glimpse of his son, this time cloaked in monastic robes, swinging the large vessel. His gesture is an acknowledgment of his father's journey and transformation.

The film ends with a moving sequence in which, despite previous plans to go their separate ways, the group supports Tom on the final leg to Muxia to release the last of Daniel's ashes. While liminality is the focus of this essay, it is important to note that the final scene is one in which Tom is seen traveling through the bazaars of Morocco carrying Daniel's backpack. The rite of passage has entered the reincorporation phase. Tom has abandoned his quiet, restrained life and instead travels the world with a new curiosity and spirit.

I'll Push You

In contrast to *The Way*, *I'll Push You* (2017) is a documentary film that relates the story of lifelong friends Justin Skeesuck and Patrick Gray as they endeavor to complete the Camino, despite staggering odds. In 2012, Justin, who is confined to a wheelchair due to the rare neurodegenerative disease

Multifocal Acquired Motor Axonopathy (MAMA), learned about the route while watching a travel show. Patrick explains that when his friend mentioned the possibility of undertaking the pilgrimage together, his response was simple, "I'll push you," hence the film's title. The documentary is a moving testimony to the devotion of friends while also providing a window into the travails of the pilgrimage and how *communitas* carries many suffering travelers to the end. Ultimately the film provides a clear message to others through the lessons conveyed by the pilgrims as they reflect on their journey

As is the case with *The Way,* throughout the pilgrimage captured in *I'll Push You* the viewer bears witness to poignant scenes of suffering, both physical and emotional, as Justin and Patrick attempt to complete the *Camino francés* with a specially-designed wheelchair. Physical suffering comes in a variety of forms. While the infrastructure of the Camino has improved drastically over the last decade with increased accommodation as well as restaurants and cafés, this improvement has not considered the needs of travelers with disabilities. The pair struggle to negotiate the planes, trains, metro, taxis and hotels, which are not designed to accommodate Justin. Doors are too narrow for the wheelchair, hotels are without elevators or only have rooms with baths available. Between towns, the walking itself, particularly during the first few days as the Way traverses the Pyrenees, poses significant challenges and physical suffering. Fortunately Ted, a paramedic friend, joins them for the first two weeks and assists in the push-pull operation required to conquer this most difficult section of the route. Day One, leaving San-Jean-Pied-de-Port, involves a steep climb to Roncesvalles proves incredibly difficult for the trio as they push, pull and carry Justin over the rock and mud-laden path. Their pilgrimage is further complicated when the front wheel of the chair sheers off resulting in the need to harness another pilgrim to pull the front end of the chair and a desperate search for a professional aluminum welder in Pamplona.

While Patrick and Ted struggle to adapt to the physical demands of the route, Justin struggles with emotions related to his dependency on others. Despite his deep-seeded optimism, the loss of the wheel and the need to be carried by his friends to the nearest town, causes him to express a deep sense of humility. He explains, "It's hard not to feel like a burden when this happens … seeing your friends do what they need to do can be a difficult pill to swallow." As the search for a welder continues, Justin has time to reflect back at the hotel. He expresses the distress that he feels when his disability burdens others. In an emotional scene, he explains that he has had to learn to trust and to let go and allow others "to find their joy" in helping him. Through tears he acknowledges a lesson that he has had to learn: that his family and friends love helping him, and that he has learned to love them for it. Weeping he provides insight into his emotional pain:

To have my best friend with me across the world, breaking his back for me, doing what he can to move me forward in life is freaking amazing. It's really hard to let somebody do that for you … it's so hard. But I love him deeply because he is just there, he's there … on a freaking mountain, pushing me up a trail that is impossible with a broken wheel and not knowing where we are going to or if we are going to be safe … it's so hard to let it go.…

This process of learning to let go has come out of necessity for Justin, but it is a lesson that his friend Patrick has not yet had to learn for himself. With the wheelchair repaired, Ted returns to the United States as planned, and Patrick and Justin continue on the remainder of their journey. Patrick's sense of responsibility and determination drive them forward as he assumes the role of "pusher." The Camino teaches lessons, however, and no one is exempt. Patrick, despite his drive, will have to rely on the kindness of strangers, in the form of *communitas*, to carry them to the end.

As the documentary progresses, they meet individual pilgrims that walk with them for portions of each day or are joined by family friends for segments of the route. One new friend, Christie, has previous experiences helping others with adventure travel. She relates, "The whole nature of the Camino is looking out for each other. Supporting each other, encouraging each other, and making connections while you are here.… It's never just about you."

While walking the Camino was a goal set by Justin, Patrick is profoundly affected by his journey along the Way. As they walk through one of

I'll Push You (2016), Emota. Left to right: Ted Hardy, Justin Skeesuck and Patrick Gray push through deep mud as they ascend the Pyrenees section of the *Camino francés.*

the more challenging sections, the Spanish *meseta*, he reflects on a career change that he made four years ago which resulted in higher levels of stress that impacted his family. He remembers specific moments in which he was "an ass," "unkind," "not proud" of who he had been to his wife or one of his children. He realizes that it was not a matter of just a few bad days but rather day after day of interactions that left him not liking how he had treated his family. He explains, "that was not who I was called to be" and "it was not who I promised my wife that I would be." These are the thoughts and reflections that he carries to the Iron Cross as the team arrives at the *Cruz de Fierro*, the highest point along the *Camino francés*.

Since the 11th century, pilgrims have traditionally carried a stone (or several) with them from the start of the journey which they leave at the foot of this cross. The rock symbolizes something individual to each pilgrim. As Patrick contemplates the space, he reflects on what he needs and what he no longer needs in his life. He symbolically assigns his need for safety to the rock and climbs the mound to carefully place his at the foot of the cross, among many others. This scene reflects several liminal elements including sacredness, humility and the acknowledgment of pain. The distance walked and the time away from his normal life have provided Patrick with space to reflect. It has been a transformative experience that will allow him to re-enter society rejuvenated, and renewed as a different version of himself. Justin reflects on the mass of stones laden at the foot of the cross, noting that all of these people have carried burdens to this place. He realizes that because of his circumstances, he let go of his rock a long time ago

I'll Push You (2016), Emota. Patrick (left) and Justin share a moment of intimate friendship at the *Cruz de Fierro*.

After the Pyrenees, the largest single ascent in one day is the summit near O'Cebreiro. It is here that the spirit of *communitas* is best evidenced in the film. Despite wanting to experience the vistas from this place, Patrick and Justin consider bypassing the summit due to the raw trail conditions, which are both steep and rocky. *Communitas*, however, provides them with the support that they need to reach O'Cebreiro. Justin explains:

> Then when we stopped for lunch and at the café or bar there, there was a group of people and they were all welcoming us ... and I was going, is this normal for other people to wait for others? As we got up to leave, they all joined us and decided that they were going to be there to help us ... and they had planned that ahead of time ... and so what gets billed as a journey alone, became a journey of community.

I'll Push You (2016), Emota. Fellow pilgrims support Patrick and Justin as they begin the climb to O'Cebreiro.

The support of others, as Justin notes, "was a monumental shift in the way that Patrick perceived how he could help in the spectrum of our journey ... because he came into it with the role of 'I'm here, I'm the pusher, I'm going to make this happen' ... but I don't think he fully comprehended how much help we would need." This moving experience, allows Patrick to "let go of the reins," as others carry Justin in his wheelchair over the rough track. For Patrick, "this is the ultimate expression of community."

Justin notes that this release of control allows his friend to experience his own perspective, the experience of having to rely on others for help, and to feel the joy and love that this surrendering allows. He explains this simple lesson, "When you deny someone the opportunity to help you, you deny them joy in life. The joy that I saw in the faces, and the demeanor of

I'll Push You (2016), Emota. Justin (left) relinquishes the reins and allows others to step into the role of "pusher."

the people that helped that day, I'll never forget." The support of the community that develops around each pilgrim as they walk the Camino is clear in this scene.

Patrick admits that it is very difficult for him to relinquish the reins of his support to Justin but, due to the physical toll that the journey takes on his own body, he has to accept that assistance. When the pair have just over 100 miles remaining, Patrick's calves begin to cause him severe pain and cramping. The anguish he feels is evident not only by his inability to move further but also the anguish on his face.

I'll Push You (2016), Emota. Patrick stops to breathe through the pain of severe leg cramps in the final days of the pilgrimage.

Twenty-two kilometers outside of Santiago de Compostela, Patrick shares some of his final thoughts about the Camino which he describes as a "gift" that has "humbled" him. In the final days, the pair are joined by Michael Turner, a family friend, and his sons. Michael explains that he wanted to witness the pilgrimage, enjoy some time with Justin and Patrick and that he wanted to take his teenage son Matthew. It was an opportunity to demonstrate love for others and particularly wanted his teenage son to experience the journey. When Michael Turner is asked how he would explain the Way he replies, "how do you learn to live every day, in community and supporting those around you to achieve their goals and letting them help you achieve your goals? ... Ask people what their stories is ... and ask how you can help others on the way ... and get on their journey with them." *Communitas* is at the heart of the lesson he has learned on the Camino.

On the final day, as they approach the Cathedral, Patrick expresses a heartfelt desire for his "wife and kids to recognize that [he] is different" and ultimately that he does not want to "be who [he] was" before he began the Camino. He wants them to know that he "wants to spend every breath that he has with them." Here we see the subject of the rite of passage, Patrick, prepared and equipped to begin his reincorporation to society. It is interesting to note that Patrick has indeed became a different person. Upon returning from the Camino, he quit his job and he and Justin founded Push Inc. Today they travel worldwide speaking to businesses and organizations about the power of relationships and community. In addition, they have helped to lead several veterans-accessible Caminos.

Conclusion

Travelers in the 21st century are increasingly seeking time and space apart from their normal, everyday lives. It can be hard to truly escape the 24-hours news cycle and the constant interconnectedness generated by cell phones and the internet. Pilgrimage offers an opportunity to separate oneself from the everyday rhythm of life and to look beyond the ordinary to probe for spiritual and/or existential meaning. The Camino, as a physical journey, tests the human body and spirit, while also providing an opportunity to connect, in a transformative way, with others.

The Way and *I'll Push You* are just two films that sit among a growing body of cultural texts—film, documentaries, travel literature and novel— that reflect on the inner and outer journey of contemporary pilgrimage. As a medium, film uniquely captures the ineffable nature of pilgrimage through vistas of sweeping landscapes, the visual depiction of humility and suffering, and the joyous expression of human beings in communion with each other. These two films provide insight into the power of spiritual journeys and testify to the importance of stepping away from life, engaging with transformative endeavors and allowing oneself to be return to the world, renewed by the experience.

NOTES

1. Official statistics related to the Camino de Santiago are archived by the Pilgrim's Office in Santiago de Compostela.

2. *Hospitaleros* are volunteers who work in pilgrim shelters, catering to, caring for and receiving pilgrims. They are often seasoned pilgrims trained and organized by Confraternities of the Camino organizations.

3. *Albergues* and *refugios* are hostel-type accommodations available at an affordable price to pilgrims who identify themselves through their Pilgrim's Passport. These lodgings tend to consist of bunkbeds in large, communal areas with shared bathroom facilities. They also often provide a simple pilgrim's meal.

4. *Paradores* are luxury hotels found throughout Spain. They are usually located within a converted monastery or palace in a city or town of historical or cultural significance.

WORKS CITED

Bowie, Fiona. *The Anthropology of Religion*. Blackwell, 2006.
Frey, Nancy Louise. *Pilgrim Stories: On and Off the Road to Santiago*. University of California Press, 1998.
Gesler, Wilbert M. *Healing Places*. Rowman & Littlefield, 2003.
I'll Push You. Directed by Chris Karcher and Terry Parish. Emota, 2016.
Kellert, Stephen R., and Edward O. Wilson. *The Biophilia Hypothesis*. Island Press, 1993.
Norman, Alex. *Spiritual Tourism: Travel and Religious Practice in Western Society*. Continuum Books, 2011.
Ross, Deborah. "Introduction." Victor Turner and Edith Turner. *Image and Pilgrimage in Christian Culture*. Columbia University Press, 1978, pp. xxix–lvii.
Turner, Edith. *Heart of Lightness: The Life Story of an Anthropologist*. Berghahn, 2006.
Turner, Victor. "Liminality and Communitas." *A Reader in the Anthropology of Religion*. Ed. Michael Lambek. 2nd Edition. Blackwell, 2008, pp. 326–339.
Turner, Victor, and Edith Turner. *Image and Pilgrimage in Christian Culture*. Columbia University Press, 1978.
van Gennep, Arnold. *The Rites of Passage*. Routledge & Kegan Paul, 1960.
The Way. Directed by Emilio Estevez. Icon Entertainment International & Elixir Films, 2010.

Comic Camino

Two Graphic Memoirs Show the Way

Danielle Terceiro

Many pilgrims walk the Camino with the intention of documenting their journey along the way. For some, an important objective of the journey is the crafting of a memoir—a narrative of the pilgrimage that suffuses it with meaning that can be carried back into "real life." This essay will look at the work of two artists who have distilled their experience on the Camino into graphic memoirs. The chosen medium has allowed the authors to put both verbal and visual semiotic resources into play. The verbal text in each memoir will be considered in its interaction with "visual grammar" (Kress and van Leeuwen). Each author has shaped meaning by using the multimodal affordances of a graphic text, blending together ideas (the "conceptual blending" described by Turner and Fauconnier) to create an emergent understanding of the pilgrim experience. The authors show ways in which graphic memoirs can engage an audience and draw them into an experience: through a visual text that conveys emotion, through playful comic storytelling that interacts with popular culture, and by foregrounding the conceptual blending that occurs when the walking has finished and the "post-production" of the pilgrim narrative begins.

This essay compares and contrasts two graphic memoirs that depict a journey along the Camino: *Pelgrim of niet? Een voetocht naar Santiago* [*Pilgrim or Not? A Walk to Santiago*] (Vanistendael 2015) and *On the Camino* (Jason 2017). Both texts are graphic memoirs, but each uses different formats to create a narrative of each author's pilgrim experience. While Jason uses a comic strip format, with anthropomorphic animal characters standing in for humans, Vanistendael uses pen and watercolor images alongside her own handwriting. Her images are part of a "one drawing each day" enterprise she undertook on the Camino. Vanistendael prefaces her book with a typed introduction across eight pages, while the narrative in Jason's work is captured entirely within a comic strip.

While Vanistendael looks to the past to understand her artistic impulse, Jason looks to contemporary culture to interpret his inspiration, including "that movie" by Martin Sheen. Jason depicts his experience as crucially located within, and shaped by, the pilgrim community and the broader intertextual possibilities of contemporary culture. He first feels "part of the Camino experience" when other pilgrims are able to look up his comic books on Google and on their iPhones (44). By contrast, Vanistendael shows herself making friends along the way but remaining somewhat of an observer who uses the strenuous journey on the Camino as a medium for individual artistic expression, and a way to meet (what she considers to be) her deepest human needs (author's introduction).

Despite both of these northern European authors positions as self-consciously irreligious pilgrims, each text grapples with their identification as a "pilgrim" and with their different motivations for the journey. Vanistendael's typed introduction locates her motivation in the human being's evolved capacity and desire to walk and to make meaning through art. Jason reflects on his motivations toward the conclusion of his narrative, when he notes rather tentatively that his goal was "to become a bit more open as a person, maybe" (177). The implicit idea of pilgrimage here is that of an in-between space with the power to effect positive change upon return to "real life." Jason's pilgrim memoir aligns with the idea of *communitas* proposed by Victor and Edith Turner. *Communitas* is the in-between experience that pilgrimage offers; temporarily liberating a person from mundane realities and social hierarchies; fostering spontaneous comradeship; stirring rich emotion; evoking a "magical" feel and a sense of endless power (Turner and Turner, 250–251). Vanistendael, with her search for artistic privacy along the Camino, struggles with a tension within the concept of *communitas*: on the one hand, pilgrimage can be understood as a journey to uncover the "essential self," unencumbered by the social relations embedded in everyday interactions; at the same time the idea of transformation and liberation through *communitas* requires interaction with a community and the sense that pilgrimage is a universal human experience.

Genre: Comic or Picture Book?

Both texts are understood to be "graphic memoirs" that retell the author's experience of pilgrimage on the Camino, using a combination of visual and verbal text. *On the Camino* is produced using the conventions of representation of a comic book. It divides narrative into discrete panels, with "gutters" in between. Speech and thought bubbles and the text within them represent events that occur in the time and space pictured within a frame. *On the Camino* has a heightened sense of caricature, typical of comic books, through its use of anthropomorphic animals to portray characters that correspond to humans in "real life." However, while *On the Camino* is instantly recognizable as a "comic book," *Pelgrim of niet?* resists a neat categorization. It is clearly not a "picture book" intended for children, despite its use of full-page images, with text arranged around those images. The ink and watercolor drawings are not naturalistic representations, but they do not use the comic conventions described above. The verbal text is idiosyncratic handwriting rather than a regular sans serif or capitalized font, and it appears to be reproduced from the author's journal along the Camino.

The categories of "picture book" and "comic book" are somewhat contested, because a picture book may incorporate comic book "trademarks," and vice versa. Comic books tend to use multiple panels per page, with closure between them, in contrast to picture books, which tend to use full-page or double-page images, with closure coming at the gutter or during the page turn (Sutliff Sanders 78–79). However, any attempt to draw a line as to what is within the comic book medium, and what is not, is likely to be vexed by a medium that has a tendency to wriggle across boundaries (Wolk 16). This essay proceeds on the basis that, even though "comic book" and "picture book" are slippery categories, a "graphic memoir" can include a text from either category. Both texts are memoirs in that the verbal and visual text is clearly linked to authorial experience.

On the Camino is an extended comic narrative, in which the "I-narrator" is drawn as a dog. An endnote contains a cartoon caricature drawing of Jason in human profile, and notes that "Jason is not actually a cat or dog. He was born in Norway in 1965, but currently lives in the south of France. He walked the Camino de Santiago in 2015. One day he will walk it again." The back page notes explicitly frame the book as a "the first autobiographic work" of the "famed Norwegian cartoonist Jason" and describe it as a "graphic memoir of his 32-day trek." Even though the protagonist of the comic narrative is drawn as a dog and introduces himself in dialogue as "John from Norway" (rather than "Jason," which presumably is a shortened, "comic" version of the author's full name), the reader is left in no doubt that the author, narrator and protagonist of the text are the same character, and that the narrated experience is grounded in a reality exterior to the text. For ease of reference, the author and the protagonist will both be referred to as "Jason."

Lejeune notes that information in an autobiographical text need not be on the order of strict resemblance, where there is a clear identification of author/narrator/protagonist as the same person. He notes that, even where there is evidence that the author is "mistaken, lies, forgets or distorts, these utterances will be part of a narratorial enunciation that remains authentic" (25). Jason's comic text, with its depiction of animal characters, is a "distorted" reality but remains an authentic narratorial enunciation.

Jason presents his comic drawing as one of many possibilities for chronicling a pilgrimage journey, particularly in the digital age. There is a tension between the possibilities of the digital age and Jason's desire for an authentic pilgrim experience. While he smiles for a photo for someone's Facebook page, he then grumbles to himself that "[t]he original pilgrims didn't have Instagram, you know!" (24). When Jason rejects an attempt by a fellow pilgrim to record him for a YouTube video, he notes ironically that he would have given permission for this traveler to draw him as a dog (134). Jason's humor shows that he is not "precious" about his own form of artistic expression, even if he feels awkward at being the subject of another's narrative and their post on social media. His comic drawing perhaps allows him to draw near to himself as narrator/protagonist without feeling that awkwardness.

Pelgrim of niet? notes in its introduction that the book is a report of the author's hike from Santiago de Compostela to Saint-Jean-Pied-de-Port in the spring of 2010. The introduction asserts that the book is not an overview of "*de prachtige kerkjes die op de tocht vindt, van de boeiende stede of landschappen*" [the beautiful churches that you will find on the journey, or of the fascinating cities or landscapes].[1] Rather, "*het is een hoogst subjectieve waarnaming van een tocht die door honderdduizenden mensen is ondernomen. Een klein dagboekje van zes weken die een mens tekenen*" [it is a highly subjective perception of a journey undertaken by hundreds of thousands of people. A small diary of six weeks drawn by one person]. The extended introduction then ruminates on the universal human need to undergo pilgrimage, the link between walking and the evolution of the human brain, and the human need for meaning that is satisfied through the production of art. The introduction concludes with the author's note as to her chosen artistic medium: watercolor, a "deceptive" medium that she chooses to wrangle with each day, so that she can have a "few hours" out of the 10,000 that she may need to master the craft of drawing. It is this artistic endeavor that "delivers" the book to the reader. Vanistendael notes that her publishers wanted her to write an introduction to the text, perhaps this was to assist the reader in making sense of the author's pilgrimage, and to avoid any quick assumption that the text is a "coffee table" travelogue with pretty watercolors of "touristy" destinations.

Vanistendael's drawings are reproduced alongside handwritten diary entries that catalogue art according to a numbered day and provide commentary on the location and/or the experiences of that day. The sense that the text is intended to function as an artifact is enhanced by the photographic images of stamps and certificates in the inner and outer leaves of the book. The handwritten text provides an autobiographical link: it is messy and sometimes hard to decipher, suggesting that it may be a copy of the actual diary entries written by the author on her journey. The use of handwriting in multimodal texts often signifies individuality (Kress and van Leeuwen 22), helping to underline the author's (typed) assertion in the introduction that the book is a highly subjective representation of a pilgrim trek. Handwriting is an authentic "in the moment" record of an experience, whereas the typed introduction is implied to be somewhat of a reluctant, late insertion at the request of the publisher.

The author's photo at the end of *Pelgrim of niet?* highlights Vanistendael's identity as an autobiographical artist. The photo shows the author hiding most of her face behind a watercolor rendering of her features. Vanistendael's hand is shown in naturalistic detail at the bottom of the page, holding up the watercolor image. This highlights the individuality of the artistic hand at work in this text, and links the artistic hand and its work to a "real" person who prefers to reveal herself through her art.

Multimodal Meaning-Making

This section will consider how the visual and verbal text of each memoir is woven together to represent the pilgrimage experience. The "visual grammar" of each text will be given particular consideration, that is, the way in which depicted visual elements—people, places and things—combine into a meaningful, coherent whole (Kress and van Leeuwen 1). Each text uses a different form of material production, which can be an important aspect of the visual grammar of an image (215). *Pelgrim of niet?* contains reproductions of images produced with watercolor and ink while *On the Camino* contains black and white line-drawn cartoons. Both texts probably have used digital manipulation in the production of image and text. *Pelgrim of niet?* has arranged handwriting around framed images in a way that would not have occurred within the pages of a visual diary. *On the Camino* has the most overt use of digital manipulation: the cover of the book is colored digitally, and the black and white cartoons use the regular "digital dots" to effect shading.

Many of Vanistendael's drawings position her as an observer and chronicler of the local culture that surrounds the pilgrims and that can be observed as existing alongside them. She draws many local "characters" interacting in cafes, and pictures of landscapes and cityscapes along the Way. Some of the images have a "still life" quality, and depict typical pilgrim experiences, for example a picture of a chair and table to the side of a courtyard, and a picture of pilgrim socks hanging to dry. The fact that Vanistendael has chosen to reproduce pictures alongside her (apparently) synchronous handwritten notes, is in line with wider concerns to preserve the material in a world in which increasingly "the concrete becomes abstract, the material immaterial, the substantial insubstantial and reality 'virtual'" (Kress and van Leeuwen 223).

Vanistendael's subjective experience is sometimes highlighted in the handwritten text alongside a depiction of the social interaction around her. For example, on Day 30 she draws and writes about her encounter with *turigrinos* ("tourist pilgrims") as she enters Galicia.

The term *turigrinos* refers to Spaniards who take advantage of the affordances of pilgrim locations during their holidays. Tunistendael draws most of them from the back, emphasizing their group identity, and they are shown circulating around stalls that have postcards and pilgrim memorabilia for sale. The intensity of Vanistendael's experience of that encounter is concentrated in the words rather than the picture:

> *Het is ook de eerste keer dat ik me pilgrim voel. De blikken van de mensen maken een pelgrim van me. We observeren elkaar. Iemand wil een foto van me maken. Ik voel me een dier in een kooi. Ik voel me ineens vuil en vreemd.* [It is also the first time that I feel like a pilgrim. The looks of people turn me into a pilgrim. We

Pelgrim of niet?, Day 30.

observe each other. Someone wants to take a picture of me. I feel like an animal in a cage. I feel suddenly dirty and strange].

There is an interesting set of contradictions on this page. Firstly, Vanistendael feels like she has become a pilgrim under the eye of tourists, rather than through interaction with the pilgrim *communitas* (e.g., through "authentic" pilgrim experiences such as the communal washing of socks or cramped dormitory accommodation). Secondly, she writes that they observe each other, and yet the picture shows most *turigrinos* turned away from the viewer. The text suggests that the *turigrinos* are open about observing the pilgrims as an interesting specimen ("animal in a cage") there for the viewing, but the image suggests that Vanistendael's artistic purpose forces her into a more surreptitious mode of observing those around her, and a trickier method of recording her observations. Thirdly, it is the tourists, rather than the pilgrims, who are apparently interested in purchasing postcards and pilgrim memorabilia. This memorabilia is not presented as attractive or relevant to the pilgrims themselves. This is perhaps one reason why Vanistendael chose to reproduce her paintings in the context of a memoir, rather than to exhibit or reproduce them as standalone artworks: her artwork is ostensibly not destined for the front of a postcard, or to be subsumed into tourist culture on the pilgrim route.

Vanistendael uses different visual "modalities," that is, her images fall at different points along a continuum of abstraction to the standards of "contemporary naturalistic representation" (Kress and van Leeuwen 160). Modality addresses the question of how "realistic" an image is, while taking into account that each "realism" has its own naturalism and its own criteria for the most natural way of representing reality (Kress and van Leeuwen 158). Thus the conventions and affordances of Vanistendael's media—watercolor and ink—need to be taken into account when considering the effect of the different modalities she uses. For example, her drawing of the cathedral at Santiago de Compostela does not contain any watercolor, but the ink lines are intricate and draw attention to the "truth" of architectural detail. The use of watercolors would have perhaps distracted from this "truth."

There are other times where a limited color palette highlights that Vanistendael has moved away from the conventions of naturalistic representation, toward a more abstract representation of emotional states. In particular, there are a number of images that use bright red swathes of watercolor against black and sepia tones, and these images occur at times of pain and frustration. A pilgrim is painted with a bright red jacket during a period of rain that pauses the walking; a pilgrim suffering writer's block is also drawn with the same color jacket. The starkest use of red comes at times when the author herself is suffering physical pain. On Day

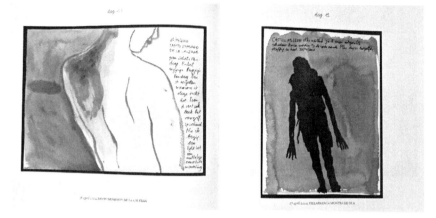

Pelgrim of niet?, Days 11 and 12.

11 Vanistendael uses simple red watercolor brushstrokes to outline her back and part of her facial profile, linking her back pain with her feeling that the walk has become a *"nutteloze, oververhitte"* [useless, overheated] enterprise (Figure 2). The use of bright red underlines the intensity of the pain and the "heat" of her emotional response. The simple brushstrokes are also the most overt invitation by the author for the reader to understand the marks on the page as the expression of her mental state. On Day 12 she uses black watercolor against a red background to show her shadow (Figure 2). The shadow, with its wobbly watercolor outline, detached from its "owner" and without any realistic background, is a disconcerting object. Vanistendael links the size of this is shadow figure to her mental state during the day. She notes on Day 16 that *"[m]orgen kan ik weer met een grote schaduw aan mijn dag beginnen"* [tomorrow I can start the day again with a big shadow]. Vanistendael's pilgrimage involves a daily reckoning with mental and physical pain. This is an unavoidable, "shadow" aspect of pilgrimage, continuous company along the way.

Vanistendael uses a low modality when she draws images of herself at the outset of the journey (Day 2 and Day 10), and this modality is the closest to cartoon caricature in the book. This lower modality is shown in particularly in the drawing of her face, which has a simple line drawing of nose and mouth (Day 2), and a dot for her eyes (Day 10). The Day 2 drawing is reproduced on the cover of the book and depicts the author's self-conscious and somewhat ironic representation of herself as a pilgrim at the outset of the journey. The lower modality reflects the author's own, objectified, view of herself, and it also enhances the self-deprecatory tone in the text to relieve the reader of any sense that the author will take herself "too seriously" as a pilgrim. The handwritten text notes in capital letters that *"ZO*

ZIE IK ER UIT" [THIS IS HOW I LOOK], and notes that because of the talismans *straal ik een zekere heiligheid uit*, [I radiate a certain holiness] which she explains is necessary to bring her journey to a successful conclusion. The labeling on the picture (three lines indicating a "talisman" and one line indicating "another talisman in the bag") show that the author laughs at herself even as she is careful to ensure that she has enough material objects on display to bring her the good luck on her pilgrimage. The author "radiates" good humor and energy as she speaks of radiating "a certain holiness." At the outset of her journey she shows a willingness to display the trappings of pilgrimage, while at the same time she ironically detaches herself from any deep investment in traditional pilgrim culture. When she draws herself on Day 10 struggling with her backpack attachment, she notes that her breasts look like those of a Madonna of the Flemish primitives. The aligning of a reference to "high art" with a low modality diagram of her uncomfortable situation with the backpack is humorous, at the same time as it underscores Vanistendael's seriousness as an artist, and her facility in making links between high and low culture.

By contrast, Jason uses comic caricature drawing, at the same modality level, throughout *On the Camino*. The eyes of all the characters, which often signify the overall modality of an illustration, are drawn as empty circles and do not give us access to the interior life of the pilgrims. Simple lines around from the eyes sometimes indicate age, but do not emphasize emotional states. Each animal character is drawn simply, and the distinguishing characteristics of each animal are very minimal, e.g., a rounded instead of a curved beak, a black or white body, or a different "hairstyle." Unlike *Pelgrim of niet?*, which only mentions a handful of fellow pilgrims by name, *On the Camino* represents a number of different conversations with named travelers along the way. Because there are so many fellow pilgrims, and they are drawn in this minimal style, the reader finds it challenging to remember the gallery of characters along the way, distinguish them, and recall some of them as they reappear. In this way Jason shows that his priority was to experience authentic, yet temporary *communitas* with a crowd of fellow travelers, rather than to create intense new friendships that would translate back into his everyday life.

Scholars of comic texts warn that Kress and van Leeuwen's discourse on the "modality cues" of a visual text should not be automatically applied to a comic text, because the discourse assumes that photographic realism makes the highest truth claim, whereas the "truth value" of a represented experience in a graphic text is often communicated through an openly subjective, caricatured drawing (which, in Jason's case, represents humans as animals). El Refaie notes that the visual abstraction of a comic text does not necessarily lower its modality or "truth value" (167). Mikkonen notes that graphic caricature of face, gesture and pose, needs to be examined as a form of perception (319). The graphic caricature of face and body can be an important way of understanding an author's way of relating to a character (including their own "character" in the story) and distilling important characteristics into visual form. Groensteen notes that a consistent comic style is acceptable as a narrative convention, a form of graphic handwriting. This consistent graphic handwriting, even where it uses comic conventions of representation, can be understood to give the reader an insight into the personality of the author. A regular, consistent graphic style ensures that emphasis will be on the subject matter, and reinforces a "reality effect"—it gives a narrative credibility. Jason's use of a persistent style and his minimalist representation of the differences between pilgrims, shows his attempt to "distil" the essential experience of his pilgrimage.

While Jason employs a persistent style of comic caricature throughout *On the Camino*, he also employs methods of "narrative digression" that break up the text, heighten subjectivity, and force the reader to focus on certain aspects of pilgrimage. Stewart describes a narrative digression as a "descriptive section" which foregrounds the narrator's control over the material and consequently the narrator's control over the reader's passage toward closure (30). The dense "visual descriptions" in *On the Camino* include wordless sequences of panels, and the interspersing of occasional wordless full-page images among the pages of four panel sequences. Wolk notes that upon encountering a wordless sequence, readers will tend to "hit the brakes," and because there is no language that acts as a "timer" or contextual cue for understanding an image, a reader will stop at every visual change and assess what is happening and how long it is meant to take (129).

The full-page image on page 35 gives the reader a "break" from the rhythm of the narrative as well as showing a rest break for Jason and some other pilgrims, sitting on some steps. As the conventional reading path moves from the left to the right, this leaves the viewer looking at Jason at the middle right of the comic panel, perched at the top of the steps with pen and book in hand. Jason is positioned as an observer but also as embedded within the pilgrim experience: he does not afford himself a "birds' eye position." The image shows "layers" of pilgrim experience, as the top of the image shows two pilgrims with backpacks walking against a backdrop that appears to be a mural of pilgrims and animals from another age moving across in the same direction. The image emphasizes the common experiences and needs of pilgrims (food and rest, for example) across the ages, and even though Jason is writing or drawing, he is not positioning himself as an artistic "outsider." The layout of the picture also suggests that there is an "ideal" pilgrimage schema that forms the mental backdrop for most pilgrims, even in the middle of the messy, tiring reality of the experience. Kress and van Leeuwen note that the "ideal" is often represented at the top of a picture, and the "real" at the bottom (186–193). In this case the "ideal" is not known in detail—it is represented by the shadowy figures of pilgrims and animals—but the "given" is a more chaotic layout of backpacks strewn across the ground, and pilgrims hunched on steps, eating and resting.

On the Camino, page 57.

The wordless sequence of panels on page 57 is the closest that *On the Camino* comes to realizing the emotional intensity that Vanistendael inscribes in *Pelgrim of niet?* (Figure 3). This is achieved by the starker use of digital shading in this layout, and the use of lines to indicate and exaggerate a sense of perspective. The first panels shows Jason on a road between buildings, the short vanishing point emphasizing an incline and the sense of tall buildings closing in, in the shaded darkness of early morning. It is not clear what the second panel shows, but it suggests the stretched, inclining shadows of pilgrims past and present. The exaggerated tilt-forward of these figures suggests tiredness and the slow, drawn-out nature of the pilgrim experience. Jason is walking from right to left in both right-hand panels, which prompts a sense of unease and a suggestion that pilgrimage gives a sense of "to and fro," rather than a clear linear sense of progress. The aggressively cross-hatched fence with its crosses in the last panel is apparently significant for pilgrims, but because readers are not able to decode its significance it is a "heavy" closure to the sequence of panels and leaves the reader with a sense of burden.

The heaviness in this section of *On the Camino* is not present throughout the rest of the text. There is a playfulness in the comic text that lightens the narrative. This playfulness shares Jason's enjoyment at being a storyteller as he lets his imagination run ahead of the "real experience." The text "corrects" his over-imagination, for example, by drawing a giant snail and then correcting its size in the next panel, conceding "well not that big" (27). He shows himself shooting up bedbugs with a semi-automatic weapon, and then notes in the next panel that the pleasure of killing was actually "with my own fingers" (105). The humor is also self-deprecatory, making fun of Jason's desire to turn any misfortune into a good story, with Jason shown falling off a cliff and being bitten by a snake, and wryly noting in both panels "well it's good for the book" (146). In this way Jason "lets readers in" on the post-pilgrimage process of assembling his experience into a narrative and shows it to be an enjoyable experience.

These imaginative "over-reaches" also demonstrate Jason's propensity to locate his own experience within popular culture. For example, he enters Sahagún and imagines *Wizards of Sahagún* as the name for a science fiction series, with a book cover showing action combat. Instead, he concedes in the final panel on the page that the "reality" is *I drank a coffee in Sahagún*, a book of short stories (97). A sequence of panels also shows a couple having a "Woody Allen movie crisis," which Jason then concedes "is all in my head. I'm sure they're very happy together" (94). The implication is that Jason is a compulsive storyteller, always imagining compelling angles, and that the experience of pilgrimage, with its slow walking and slow and often uneventful "plot line" provides ample opportunity and incentive to develop these exciting angles along the way.

Nikolajeva notes that an abundance of detail in an image, or intervisual elements, can slow down the reader's processing of visual information and provide the brain with more time to access stored emotional memories (282–283). Jason's slowing of the text, through playful storytelling and intertextuality, is a way of assisting the reader to "spend time" in the emotional moment of the story, and to become complicit in imaginative over-reach even as it is pared back to what was "real."

Conceptual Blending

Both memoirs "mix up" ideas about pilgrimage with other concepts, and play this out within the visual and verbal text. This is a form of "conceptual blending" described by Fauconnier and Turner. Human beings have the ability and propensity to create new meaning through the "blending" of mental spaces. Mental spaces are "very partial assemblies constructed as we think and talk for purposes of local understanding and action" (Fauconnier 351). When the elements and relations of a mental space are organized as a package we already know, the organization can be referred to as a "frame" (352). Blends are elaborated by treating them as simulations and running them simultaneously. Conceptual blending is an important aspect of how humans interact with each other and their world, make sense of it, and come to new understandings. Indeed, Turner asserts that conceptual blending "is at the root of what makes us human" (378). Both *Pelgrim of niet?* and *On the Camino* open up mental spaces and frames and blend them to create new understandings of the pilgrim experience.

Vanistendael blends mental frames of pilgrimage with frames that relate to a "bubble of isolation" and "rebirth." She struggles to obtain enough privacy and space to undertake her artistic endeavor, and sickness forces her into an uncomfortable "bubble" within pilgrim activity. Vanistendael describes herself as withdrawing into a "*mentale capsule*" [mental capsule] or "*mentale luchtbel*" [mental bubble] when she is sick (Days 34 and 35). She draws herself naked and curled up in a fetal position within a bubble while tourist/pilgrim activity "pulses" around her.

In this way the idea of mental isolation, framed by the concept of a "mental bubble" is blended with an idea of gestation, and perhaps links to ideas of pilgrimage as resulting in a "rebirth." It also blends with the idea of the tourist/pilgrim community as a pulsating body with its own life, however the elaboration of all these mental spaces does not evoke a comradely sense of *communitas*. The drawings of the tourist/pilgrims are carnivalesque, and imply a feverish, rushed drawing (which, perhaps, the drawings are). The people have tourist/pilgrim paraphernalia, including a camera,

Pelgrim in mentale luchtbel, peregrina on ou burbujo
Ongeveer 100 km van Santiago begint de bel. Ce créer een luchtbel om me af te sluiten van de hordea pelgrims die uit het
niets terrorischijn spingen. De strijd om een bed te vinden begint.
De herbergen zitten overvol. On een oorkonde van Compostela

Pelgrim of niet?, Day 35.

staff and wine bottles, and the protective hand over the narrator's head suggests that this is all overwhelming.

The elaboration of these mental spaces gives the sense that Vanistendael operates within this tourist/ pilgrim body, but that she remains isolated while within it, and presumably separate from it after any "rebirth." The mental space for gestation also evokes the sense of being cramped, and the sense that intense physical pain is an inevitable part of the experience. The image in Figure 4 is reproduced in the inner leaves of the book, which suggests that it is of key figurative importance, and also signals to the reader that, once they reach this page in the text, they need to slow their reading because there is significant meaning to be made that will shape understanding of the whole narrative.

On the Camino features panels that blend the mental frames of pilgrimage with those of "actor" or "performer." In one sequence Jason depicts himself as an actor being prompted by the director "Steven" to put "more emotion into it!" by remembering how he witnessed his little brother drowning (114). Jason injects wry humor into this scene by explaining to Steven that he does not have a little brother. Jason also shows his entry to the town Estella by falling to his knees, ripping his shirt off, and a note under the panel references "Marlon Brando in A Streetcar Named Desire." In these blends, the idea of pilgrimage as performance is elaborated, and the sections perhaps betray some concern that the authorial "real-life" experience is not dramatic or emotional enough to be captured in a compelling story, at least for the "audience," and that Jason needs to inject more drama into his "performance."

There are also panels that blend the mental space of pilgrimage with that of "comedic performer." Jason depicts himself sitting in a café, explaining to three other pilgrims that it was "either the Camino or the Porsche" (137). The three pilgrims are sitting a little removed from Jason and the exaggerated "HA HA HA" above their heads brings to mind the laughter track on a sitcom television show, or the laughter at a stand-up comedy show. Jason "performs" his mid-life crisis to comedic effect, suggesting that he is seeking to avoid awkwardness through self-deprecating humor, and also that his companions are happy to grant him a sympathetic audience and accede to the humor. Later, Jason has a conversation with a fellow pilgrim about "the Martin Sheen" film, and a panel that depicts him as a stand-up comedian follows, asking "where's the scene where Martin Sheen hand washes his socks?" (139).

This sequence shows that Jason enjoys engaging with intertextual references to the Camino with other pilgrims, and that this movie's distance from "reality" provokes a kind of solidarity and sense of *communitas* on the Camino. The elaboration of the pilgrim/performer blend also shows how comfortable Jason has become with his pilgrim "material" and suggests

On the Camino, page 40.

On the Camino, page 139.

that Jason (now) feels confident that it has the potential for a much greater "audience" than just his fellow pilgrim traveler.

Beginnings and Endings

This section will consider the extent to which the beginnings and endings of each text frame the pilgrim experience and signpost significance for the reader. In particular, are the motivations of the two narrator pilgrims clearly signaled at the outset? Do the endings of the texts close the pilgrim experience at the same time as they open up new possibilities for understanding it?

Vanistendahl begins the graphic section of the novel with a drawing and text that represent the two-week process of saying goodbye to her children and leaving them with her aunt. The text launches straight into a handwritten journal entry, which is hard to decipher and contains idiomatic language that functions as shorthand to describe somewhat of the emotional "rollercoaster" and anxiety of her children before her departure, and then the eventual calm as she leaves them with their aunt. The visual text is hard to decipher as well, but shows the backs of seats, perhaps train seats on the way to Bayonne, and a person absorbed in a newspaper in front of her. This is "Day 1," and so the reader understands that the pilgrimage has begun, and that the author has successfully disentangled herself from her everyday web of familial relations. However, the journal entries give no detailed description of her motivation and the reader understands that from now on these will be her notes and drawings "on the go." Vanistendael enters a liminal state apart from her everyday life, but her experience (and desire for) *communitas* is muted, compared to Jason.

Jason begins his comic with a panel captured "The Train to Bayonne" (3). He observes fellow travelers with walking poles and big backpacks, and wonders whether they are also walking the Camino. He prompts himself to "Ask them. Are you walking the Camino?," but the sweat beads on his forehead and his decision to look out the window in the last panel of this section (4) indicate that social anxiety prevents him from doing so. This beginning section reflects Jason's motivation to connect with other pilgrims on his journey and that he is on the lookout for the trappings of authentic pilgrimage, but that this is also a source of anxiety that Jason hopes will be "cured" through his Camino experience.

Toward the ends of their journeys, Vanistendael and Jason have awkward interactions with the registration authorities at the Pilgrim's Office in Santiago de Compostela. Vanistendael does not wish to nominate her reason for walking, as she feels the categories do not fit, but the clerk nominates her as a "spiritual" pilgrim so she can obtain the certificate. Vanistendael is upset and "feels forced into a corner." Jason asks the clerk how he is to fill out the form as a "non–Christian" (167). The clerk describes the decision as "as a matter of if you went for spiritual reasons or partied and drank," and in response to this apparent pilgrim spirituality /tourist hedonism dichotomy Jason decides his walk was for "spiritual reasons." Jason's mood in his subsequent tour of Santiago de Compostela seems to tip into ambivalence—his summation of the Cathedral is "Yup. Impressive," and his next thought as he walks around town is mundane: "Ripped jeans have become in again?" (169). By continuing their pilgrimage journey beyond this point, both authors appear to "walk off" their dissatisfaction with the power relations inscribed in these interactions and seek to lay their own meaning-making process over the bureaucratic one.

Jason's travel to Finisterre allows him time to reflect on the significance of his journey, and he encounters the "Camino Cop" at a bar, a fictional, ridiculous "sage" character. When Jason ruminates that he doesn't know whether walking the Camino has changed his life, "like Martin Sheen in that movie," the Camino Cop reassures him that "one degree" is still change ("you talked to a nun, you started conversations" [178]). Jason's concern is that such conversations are more difficult in "real life," but when he asks the Camino Cop for advice about "real life," he is not happy when the advice is the trite "take it easy" (179). Jason's thought bubble reads "idiot" after the Camino Cop observes that he is "not Gandhi," and that Jason should come up with something better himself. The reader understands that Jason's "success" on the Camino has opened up some anxiety as to how/if this success will translate to "real life."

Both Jason and Vanistendael appear to be "soothed" somewhat by their arrival in Finisterre. For Vanistendael, it appears as her most overtly spiritual experience, and she engages in the "magic" of it by burning her shoes, a common ritual, and singing songs on the beach. She feels "*één met het universum*" [at one with the universe], and the soothing nature of the experience is represented in an image where the silvery tones of water and sky seem to merge. Vanistendael references the journey to Finisterre as the "spiritual section" of the pilgrimage in pre–Christian times, and perhaps its relative lack of Christian symbolism and religious bureaucracy make it more appealing for her as a source of *communitas*. This sense of a magical comradeship carries over to her experience on the journey home, where she experiences the theft of her bag but also the help of a fellow pilgrim, her "*reddende engel*" [guardian angel].

On the Camino finishes with a series of wordless panels in the last two openings. These panels show Jason walking through the rain and then the sunshine, his arrival at the beach and his entry into the water. The number of panels give a sense of his actions being slow and deliberate. The lack of text, and interaction with anyone, shows that, at least for this moment,

Jason has put aside any anxiety about his return to "real life." The last panel, with the cloud ripples in the sky mirroring the wave ripples at the shore, gives a sense of Jason being at "one with the universe," as Vanistendael felt on the same beach. He had previously indicated to another pilgrim "I have this image in my head. I've reached Finisterre. I take off my shoes and walk into the Atlantic Ocean. And that's the end of my Camino" (111). By entering the water, Jason is performing a ritual as well as composing a picture of himself that he already has in his mind—it is fitting that Jason, the comic artist, chooses to insert it as the last panel in his narrative of pilgrimage.

Vanistendael closes the narrative with an image from Brussels. It is not outlined in black like the other drawings, thus highlighting that it does not form part of the "one picture a day" enterprise and is a picture from her return to "real life." The picture is hard to decipher, but uses again a strong red color to shade what appears to be water in which the author's feet are soaking. This color revisits the emotional valence of earlier pictures from the pilgrimage. There looks to be a piece of paper resting on the figure's lap. The picture suggests that the author needs recuperation after the journey, but also that the process of creating the memoir will not be painless—it will "stir up" painful memories. A return to a more abstract form also leaves the reader guessing as to what form Vanistendael's artistic endeavor will "translate" to in the future.

These texts crack open the storytelling and artistic possibilities of the pilgrim experience. The sense of fun and playfulness in storytelling within *On the Camino* shows that Jason has enjoyed hitting his stride as a comic "pilgrim storyteller," and that he continues to make enjoyable links with popular culture in the telling, even as he worries that his ability to engage with people on the Camino won't translate into "real life." In *Pelgrim of niet?* Vanistendael is able to display an expert use of painting modalities to convey emotion, mood, her inner "mental bubble" as well as the social interactions of those around her. Completing the Camino offered Vanistendael and Jason the opportunity of hitting their artistic stride, both on the journey, and in its "post-production," and the texts also allow readers to enjoy this sense of artistic possibility along the Way.

NOTE

1. All translations from Dutch to English are mine.

WORKS CITED

El Refaie, Elisabeth. "Reconsidering 'Image Metaphor' in the Light of Perceptual Simulation Theory." *Metaphor and Symbol,* vol. 30, no.1, 2014, pp. 63–76.

Fauconnier, Giles, and Mark Turner. *The Way We Think: Conceptual Blending and the Mind's Hidden Complexities*. Basic Books, 2002.

Groensteen, Thierry. *Comics and Narration*. University Press of Mississippi, 2013.

Jason. *On the Camino*. Fantagraphics Books, 2017.

Kress, Gunther, and Theo van Leeuwen. *Reading Images: A Grammar of Visual Design*. Taylor & Francis, 2006.

Lejeune, Philippe. *On Autobiography*. University of Minnesota Press, 1989.

Mikkonen, Kai. "Presenting Minds in Graphic Narratives." *Partial Answers: Journal of Literature and the History of Ideas,* vol. 6, no. 2, 2008, pp. 301–321.

Nikolajeva, Maria. "Reading Other People's Minds Through Word and Image." *Children's Literature in Education*, vol. 43, no.3, 2012, pp. 273–291.

Sutliff Sanders, Joe. "Chaperoning Words: Meaning-Making in Comics and Picture Books." *Children's Literature*, vol. 41, no.1, 2013, pp. 57–90.

Turner, Mark. "Conceptual Integration." *The Oxford Handbook of Cognitive Linguistics*, edited by Dirk Geeraerts and Hubert Cuyckens. Oxford University Press, 2007, pp. 377–393.

Turner, Victor, and Edith Turner. *Image and Pilgrimage in Christian Culture: Anthropological Perspectives*. Columbia University Press, 1978.

Vanistendael, Judith. *Pelgrim of niet? Een voettocht naar Santiago de Compostella*. Oog en Blik B.V, 2015.

Wolk, Douglas. *Reading Comics: How Graphic Novels Work and What They Mean*. Da Capo Press, 2007.

PART TWO

Experiencing the Camino

Ultreia in Experiential Learning

Is There a Better Way Than "The Way"
of Saint James?

José Domínguez-Búrdalo

Putting on the Boots

That The Way of St. James is a journey like no other to deepen under-standings of Spanish and European cultures (and, by extension, both Western civilization and pilgrimage studies) is something that anyone out of the hundreds of thousands who have done *El Camino* would be more than likely to corroborate.[1] While I suspected that much before starting the study abroad program that led me to *El Camino*, I was certainly able to corroborate it in situ every time I had the honor to command Miami University's (MU) footprints into The Way, between 2011 and 2017. A survey conducted among all MU participants came to prove my impression in non-subjective terms. The survey was distributed by email in the spring of 2018 after having been approved by the Miami University Institutional Review Board. Designed to complement the knowledge acquired all these years through teaching about, and leading *El Camino*, the survey specifically sought to explain, among other things, how and in what capacity, or to what extent, students had indeed benefited from this singular course. Particularly, the survey delved into why The Way is such a wonderful spawning ground to put in practice the principles of experiential learning, additionally expand-ing the academic scope of the course among a variety of subjects, such as art, architecture, sociology, religion, physiology and, above all, history. In this essay, I will analyze and discuss student pilgrims' perceptions of their *Camino* to explore the reasons why it constitutes such a formidable nexus where culture, learning, and personal growth meet. While pursuing this goal, I will also offer some insights to understand why The Way of Saint

James is such a popular destination for so many people from all over the world.

Historically, the Camino was indeed a popular point of confluence for many Europeans already in medieval times, mostly during the 12th and 13th centuries, but its attractiveness decreased clearly from the 14th century onwards. This occurred more markedly around the end of the 16th century, as stated by Ambrosio de Morales, the official chronicler of the Spanish King Felipe II, in 1572: "ni el fervor de las peregrinaciones ni el aprecio del 'Liber Sancti Iacobi' parecían encontrarse en un momento de esplendor" (Bravo Lozano 8–9).[2] The decline was greatest while the remains of the saint were hidden in fear of an English pirate attack. In fact, these relics were left as a hidden treasure until their existence was acknowledged as such in 1879. Despite this acknowledgment, The Way remained an almost forgotten journey until just three decades ago. Thus, we find that as recently as 1985, less than 1,000 pilgrims finished *El Camino* yearly, while more than 300,000 pilgrims collected their *Compostelana* in 2018.[3] This last number is especially surprising if we take into consideration the fact that those hundreds of thousands of pilgrims embark on such enterprise fully aware of its harshness. They will be walking an average of 20 kilometers per day, or biking around 40 or 50 kilometers per day, for a period of time that may go from days to months. In 2018, the last year for which complete data has been recorded, the number of pilgrims reached 327,378, and contrary to the tendency until then, more women than men completed The Way that year. The data available so far for 2019 show that the number of pilgrims continues to grow, and maintains the tendency for a higher number of women pilgrims.[4] Table 1 shows the number of pilgrims for each year between 1970 and 2017. Holy Years in Santiago de Compostela are those in which the day of St. James falls on a Sunday.

Year	Pilgrims	Year	Pilgrims
1970	68	1994	15,863
Holy Year 1971	451	1995	19,821
1972	67	1996	23,218
1973	37	1997	25,179
1974	108	1998	30,126
1975	74	Holy Year 1999	154,613
Holy Year 1976	243	2000	55,004
1977	31	2001	64,418
1978	13	2002	68,952
1979	231	2003	74,614
1980	209	Holy Year 2004	179,944

Year	Pilgrims	Year	Pilgrims
1981	299	2005	93,924
Holy Year 1982	1,868	2006	100,377
1983	146	2007	114,026
1984	423	2008	125,133
1985	690	2009	145,877
1986	1,801	Holy Year 2010	272,135
1987	2,905	2011	183,366
1988	3,501	2012	192,488
1989	5,760	2013	215,880
1990	4,918	2014	237,886
1991	7,274	2015	262,458
1992	9,764	2016	277,854
Holy Year 1993	99,436	2017	301,036

Table 1: Number of Pilgrims by year. Source derived from the Oficina del Peregrino (https://ofici nadelperegrino.com/en/statistics).[5]

A source of syntagmatic and paradigmatic knowledge, that is, both present and past,[6] a source of exogenous (the others) as well as endogenous knowledge ("selfhood as *ipseidad*"), The Way of St. James offers a valuable opportunity of "experiential learning" to anyone willing to become a pilgrim, even if only for a few days. However, if we ponder the attraction toward *El Camino* in the last 30 years, it is perhaps surprising to find that it has not resonated in high culture, that is, in "the works of art, literature, scholarship and philosophy that establish a shared frame of reference among educated people" (Jones).[7] In a study about the influence of the Camino in Luis Mateo Díez's work, M. José Lacarra states that literary novels on this millenary pilgrimage route are not only fewer than expected, but also of a questionable literary quality in many cases (141). José Luis Puerto, in *El Camino de Santiago en la literatura*, finds some traces of The Way in the poetry of Unamuno, Antonio and Manuel Machado, Lorca, Alberti, and in Gerardo Diego's *Ángeles de Compostela*. More recently, he notes the interest of poets such as Gamoneda and Colinas. In prose, I find fair to acknowledge the novels by Jesús Torbado, *El peregrino* (1993), and Basilio Losada, *La peregrina* (1999). Puerto includes some minor texts, and some major works that incorporate The Way only in passing, which confirms Lacarra's opinion about *El Camino* in literature. This limitation in the number and quality of literary texts finds a parallel situation in cinema, where we could highlight a French production by Luis Buñuel, *La voie lactée* (1969), a film that uses The Way to offer a burlesque history of the anathemas and heresies within the Catholic Church. It was not be until *The Way*

(2010), by Emilio Estevez, that the world of cinema was witness to the significance of the Camino in the Spanish, European, and even world cultures.

In this context, I would like to mention two best-selling books that exemplify the tendency to write about The Way through a diary or travel log without (high) literary aspirations. One is the book published by the German television host and comedian Hape Kerkeling, whose *Ich bin dann mal weg* (*I Am Off Then: Losing and Finding Myself in the Camino*, 2006) narrates his experience along 800 kilometers of The Way. This book had record-breaking sales in several languages, especially in German, with more than 3 million books sold. Another record-breaking book, the pseudo-diary by Paulo Coelho, *O Diário de un Mago* (*The Pilgrimage*, 1989) was translated into several languages. Coelho himself referred to the success of his book in the 2001 edition. In that addendum, he contrasted the number of pilgrims that walked The Way in 1986, when the Brazilian writer did it for the first time, and in 2001, when he writes in Saint-Jean-Pied-de-Port the following footnote (*y nunca mejor dicho*): "The year I made the pilgrimage hardly 400 people had done The Way of St. James. In 1999, according to official statistics, 400 people passed, each day, by the establishment mentioned in the text" (15).[8] Even though many may find Coelho's text distressing from a human perspective, and questionable from a literary one, we cannot ignore the influence of this author, one of the 10 best-selling writers in the world, with more than 100 million books sold altogether, ten of which correspond to *O Diário de un Mago*.[9] We can only speculate about the possible impact of this book on increasing the popularity of The Way from the beginning of the 1990s, but we must also admit that, based on his own immense popularity, Coelho may not be too far off when he claims for himself part of the current popularity of *El Camino*.

All things considered, both Coelho and Kerkeling incarnate the tendency to write about The Way from a personal and experiential perspective in the shape of a diary or travel log, and both help to introduce a question that will permeate this essay, namely, why The Way constitutes such an attractive destination today. The magnetism of the pilgrimage route is indeed such that, as Kerkeling writes, many pilgrims repeat their experience every year because they cannot ignore the calling of The Way (83).[10]

Among the reasons to understand the attraction of El Camino among people of all walks of life regardless of their age, gender, nationality or even creed,[11] it is important to recognize the existence of a network of hostels and other lodging places accessible to travelers of all budgets, as well as the care that has gone into the adaptation and signposting of The Way itself. The absence of these amenities was sadly noted by Álvaro Cunqueiro when he decided to do The Way in 1962.[12] However, even if we need to acknowledge the facilitating role of these factors, the question remains of why so many people embark on an enterprise that requires such a physical and mental effort. Even though my study cannot answer this question directly, since it is based on the experiences of a group of students who did The Way as part of a study abroad program (for them, SPN 321 was "another course"), I can state without hesitation that one of the attractions is the wide learning scope that El Camino offers.

Miami in Spain

It is in this context that I created in 2011 a course for Miami University of Ohio as part of the study abroad program "Miami in Spain." Between 2011 and 2018, for approximately ten days in the months of May, June, or July, I led a group of 20 to 40 students along different routes. We walked and biked the North, Primitive, Portuguese, and Sanabrés Ways, and we followed the French Way at different points. We biked between Burgos and León and then walked from Sobrado dos Monxes in 2013, and we walked from Ponferrada in 2014. We also biked between Puente la Reina and León in 2016, walking from Sarria onwards, and we biked again between Burgos and León in 2018, making Ourense the start of the walking section. Since all of this happened as part of a study abroad program, my duties encompassed not just the academic component, but also all logistics. The former included a series of learning goals based on the principles of experiential learning, as defined by Kolb: "Learning is the process whereby knowledge is created through the transformation of experience" (38). Those learning goals were evaluated in a final essay based on student pilgrims' personal experience on The Way, namely, a reflection on their interactions with other pilgrims and local people, cultural tours, and challenges and successes of their journey. Reading these student pilgrims' writings was personally inspiring and left no doubt about how El Camino may be considered the epitome of experiential learning, as "an approach which has students actively engaged in exploring questions they find relevant and meaningful, and has them trusting that feeling, as well as thinking, can lead to knowledge" (Chapman & et al. 18).

The Epitome of a Learning Experience

In the field of education, experiential learning entails a pedagogical approach whose roots can be traced in "the dialectic tension and conflict between immediate, concrete experience and analytic detachment" (Kolb 9). To be more precise, experiential learning theory is usually depicted following a four-stage learning process. First, students must face a *concrete*

The first group of Miami's pilgrims, in 2011, Camino Norte.

experience, that is, a new situation, which in the case of The Way rests upon several layers: a new country, a new culture, a new language, among others. In second place, students are encouraged to engage in a *reflective observation of that new experience*. Because The Way is an enterprise completed during many hours of solitude, there is significant time to reflect on the totality of the experience, which is paramount. From direct observations of Romanic, Gothic or Baroque architecture to personal interactions with pilgrims from all over the world, or from the direct embracement of the surrounding and changing nature to the lives of locals, everything student pilgrims experience works as a powerful force—whether collective or individual, entirely unique—that turns into deep knowledge. Kolb would refer to this third stage as *abstract conceptualization*.[13] Indeed, the study of the survey shows how reflection gives rise to unexpected thoughts and sometimes the modification of pre-existing ideas, in great part thanks to the uneasiness of the milieu in which the students find themselves. The University of Toronto refers to the complete process with these precise words:

> At this point the learner might be experiencing some feelings of "unbalance" attributed to the sense of newness and/or strangeness of the experience—a sense of something unknown, inadequately explained, and/or unexplored— and hopefully, feels curious about areas of further learning. They might be upset about something that has occurred, feel frustrated by the experience, or, quite frankly, feel frustrated about how experiential learning is so different than traditional classroom learning. This could also be referred to as a sense of

"dissonance" or "disequilibrium." This disorienting dilemma is an opportunity to "make-meaning" of both the experience and the observations [University of Toronto].

Finally, among the student pilgrims' answers to the survey, we also encounter an *active experimentation*, a post-reflection, so to say, through which students are able to place themselves in the world thanks in part to the vital learning acquired while being pilgrims.[14]

Needless to say, the process of learning is always more fruitful when accompanied by authentic opportunities for applying knowledge, which is what motivates students (and any kind of learners) the most. In this regard, as we will see in the next section, The Way stands up as a wonderful environment to grow and mature. The student pilgrims that participated in the program achieved that goal thanks to the development of knowledge, skills, and values from direct experiences. This is possible precisely because El Camino encompasses a variety of opportunities for students to take initiative ("do I walk alone?"; "do I talk with that person?"; "I must stop and help this pilgrim") and make decisions ("I am going to rest for one hour"; "I will find out how to prepare that dish"; "I must interview that person"). Being accountable for those *steps*, they learn from natural consequences, whether mistakes or successes. At the same time, learning through The Way is possible thanks to the deep involvement (social, emotional, and physical) experienced by the student pilgrims in an intellectual and creative environment. In fact, when the student is really attached to the experience, when s/he can see that his/her relevance creates a personal corpus that cannot truly be evaluated with a simple grade, the motivation to go on *no matter what* is achieved. Meanwhile, the collusion and resolution of a dual dialectic (action/reflection and experience/abstraction) evolve into a set of meaningful learning transactions that we could frame under the following maxims:

I hear and I forget, I see and I remember, I do and I understand.—Confucius, 450 BCE

Tell me and I forget, Teach me and I remember, Involve me and I will learn.—Benjamin Franklin, 1750

There is an intimate and necessary relation between the process of actual experience and education.—John Dewey, 1938.[15]

Chapman et al. have provided a list of characteristics that should be present in order to define an activity or method as experiential. Out of their ten features of experiential learning, I would like to highlight a few of them, because of their importance to interpret the responses of the survey.[16] Chapman et al. believe that experiential activities must encourage the big picture perspective, and allow the students to make connections between the learning they are doing and the world (22). One could wonder to what extent the experiences of El Camino may be transferrable beyond the place and time where they happen. These connections take place, most fundamentally, in interactions with other pilgrims. The Way constitutes a microcosm where people who otherwise would never cross paths, can establish short-lived but meaningful relationships. This is linked to another of their claims, namely, that an experiential learning activity must incorporate the presence of meaningful relationships.

In a similar way to Kolb, Chapman et al. emphasize also the role of reflection: students should be able to reflect on their own learning, bringing "the theory to life" and gaining insight into themselves and their interactions with the world (22). As we will see below, this is perhaps the most valuable gift of The Way for the student pilgrims of the program—what they learn about themselves—probably because, as they also argue, students must have an emotional investment and be fully immersed in the experience, not merely doing what they feel is required of them (22). As we will see further on, the answers to the survey show, time and again, that the course requirements, or the fact that they are walking as part of a study abroad program, is secondary to what they are doing and what they gain from the experience. In addition, I would like address the claim that learning must happen outside one's perceived comfort zones (23). On The Way, the physical demands of the task at hand are obvious, but the social environment also offers many opportunities to challenge oneself. This could include, for instance, being accountable for one's actions and owning the consequences (20). In particular, I cannot omit a reference to how many students remarked on the value The Way had beyond their academic lives, and on the impact it still has in their professional careers.

Finally, all of the above may lead to a quite natural confluence with the acquisition of global awareness, which is encapsulated by Miami University under these directions for the design of Global Perspective courses: "[it] must begin to penetrate a student's cultural, ethnic, national, and linguistic insularity. A Global Perspectives class will be multinational and comparative, and it will extrapolate global patterns of geopolitical, economic, and historical shifts."[17] In what follows, I present how these principles regarding experiential learning and global awareness are conceptualized in the words of the student pilgrims' themselves.

The Survey

A total of 184 students were sent an invitation to complete an anonymous survey using Qualtrics, and 59 responses were received.[18] The survey consisted of 20 questions (see the Appendix) that combined multiple-choice and open-ended answers. It included questions about experiential learning, but also about specific aspects of the course in the context of the Miami study abroad programs, such as questions about the promotional videos made during these years. These last questions were left out of the analysis, since they are not directly relevant for the objective of this essay.

The quantitative analysis of the survey does not have any statistical relevance with the possibility of generalization, but rather it offers the opportunity of examining plausible patterns that are then explored in more depth in the open-ended responses of the survey. After all, the results are based on voluntary participation, and thus it may be a case of self-selection where those students who had a better experience are the ones who responded. It is important to notice too that this survey reflects the subjective perceptions of the students about their experience, rather than an objective measure of the actual learning that took place, or the success of the course in achieving the learning objectives.

The first thing to notice is that an overwhelming majority of the students consider that The Way has had an overall positive impact on their intercultural and global learning experience. On a scale of 0 to 10 (with 0 being "not at all" and 10 being "very much"), only one student was neutral while 48 students gave the experience at least a B grade (so to speak):

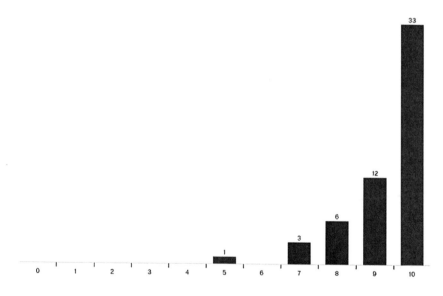

Figure 1: How much do you think The Way helped to improve and/or expand your global and intercultural perspectives? (on a scale of 0 to 10, with 0 being "not at all" and 10 being "very much").

The analysis suggests that part of the perception of an increased cultural competency by the students stems from the fact that the course promoted interactions with people outside the program. As explained above, this is a fundamental part of any experiential learning course, although not all students welcome this type of engagement with equal enthusiasm. At the same time, however, students seem to be aware of the benefits of these interactions. In Figure 2, notice that only the category "Interaction with Other Classmates" was perceived as "not important" by a few students, while interactions with other pilgrims or local people are considered more fundamental for their learning experience:

Looking back on the experience, students seem to value *El Camino* mostly for its cultural component, and for the personal challenge and degree of adventure it presents, as shown in Table 2. More than two-thirds of the respondents consider these three factors "Very Important" in making The Way attractive. Also relevant are history and social interactions, which were considered "Very Important" by more than half of the students. The religious component of The Way, which a priori could be expected to have more relevance, does not appear to be such a crucial part of the attractiveness of this course. This could be due to two reasons. One, these are not individuals who have chosen to do The Way, but participate on it as part of a Study Abroad program.[19] Second, there seems to be more interest in spirituality than in religiousness per se.

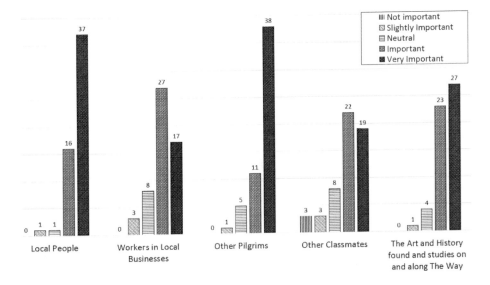

Figure 2: How important have each of the different types of interactions listed below been in expanding your global and intercultural perspectives?

#	Question	Not Important		Slightly Important		Neutral		Important		Very Important		Total
1	Culture	0.00%	0	0.00%	0	0.00%	0	28.00%	14	72.00%	36	50
2	History	0.00%	0	0.00%	0	2.00%	1	42.00%	21	56.00%	28	50
3	Religion	12.00%	6	4.00%	2	20.00%	10	36.00%	18	28.00%	14	50
4	Adventure	0.00%	0	0.00%	0	2.00%	1	24.00%	12	74.00%	37	50
5	Social Interactions with Fellow Students	4.00%	2	8.00%	4	8.00%	4	22.00%	11	58.00%	29	50
6	Social Interactions with Other Pilgrims	0.00%	0	4.00%	2	6.00%	3	32.00%	16	58.00%	29	50
7	Social Interactions with Local People	0.00%	0	2.00%	1	10.00%	5	30.00%	15	58.00%	29	50
8	Sport	12.00%	6	12.00%	6	34.00%	17	24.00%	12	18.00%	9	50
9	Personal Challenge	0.00%	0	4.00%	2	4.00%	2	24.00%	12	68.00%	34	50
10	Tourism	2.00%	1	10.00%	5	26.00%	13	38.00%	19	24.00%	12	50
11	Spirituality (Finding Self, Internal Journey, etc.)	4.00%	2	4.00%	2	18.00%	9	30.00%	15	44.00%	22	50
12	Stops Along The Way, Locations	0.00%	0	2.00%	1	6.00%	3	38.00%	19	54.00%	27	50
13	Stops Along The Way: Down Time For Exploring	0.00%	0	4.00%	2	16.00%	8	30.00%	15	50.00%	25	50

Table 2: Beyond the obvious academic and linguistic component, which other factor(s) would you consider as the greatest attractions of The Way.

Another aspect of experiential learning courses is the ability of students to engage freely, and the possibility of making individual decisions, as we saw before. The results of the survey show that more than half of the students appreciate the possibility of free, individual exploration, and taken together, more than 90 percent consider this "Important" or "Very Important." Finally, the physical component of The Way or its touristic attractiveness, while valued, did not show as high percentages as the other components.

Another question explored in the survey was the role of language in facilitating or promoting experiential learning. While some students believe language (in this case, Spanish) is not crucial for a successful Way, a majority of them (63.5 percent) believe that language is important, as shown in Figure 3. Likewise, a previous exposure to Spanish culture through the students' homestays with host families in the first part of the study abroad program, seems to predispose students favorably toward the learning that takes place during El Camino, as can be seen in Figure 4.

When designing and building a course such as this, it is difficult to anticipate what students will actually learn. After all, it is supposed to be a

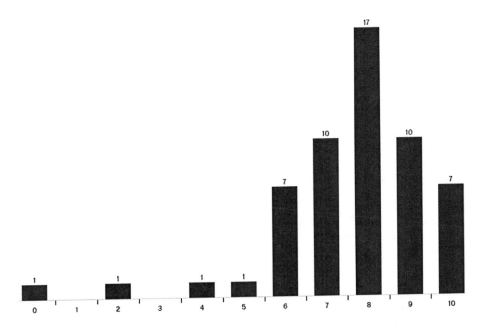

Figure 3: In terms of the potential of The Way for expanding your global and multicultural perspectives, how important do you believe having an appropriate command of the Spanish language is to making the most of that potential? (on a scale of 0 to 10, with 0 being "not at all" and 10 being "very much").

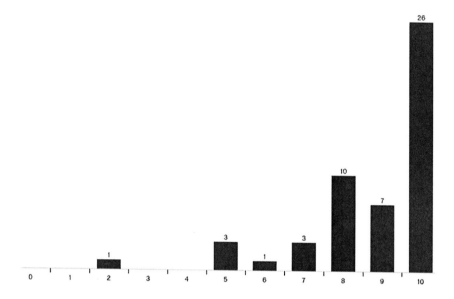

Figure 4: In terms of knowledge of Spanish culture, do you think that living for six weeks in Spain prior to starting The Way placed you in a better position for succeeding both academically and experientially on The Way?

personal and unique experience. Therefore, in the survey we tried to obtain information about two different but complementary aspects: traditional academic learning and experiential learning.

Regarding the academic component of the course, student pilgrims overwhelmingly mentioned history as what they learned most about. Of the forty-nine people who answered Question 15 ("In strictly academic terms, what do you remember as the most important knowledge obtained on The Way?"), twenty-five of them mentioned "history" explicitly, and three more referred to history indirectly. Reproduced below is one of the responses to the question. This particular student is aware of the emphasis on history within the course, but most importantly, the answer is a good example of an abstract conceptualization of the experience that allows the student to achieve a greater global awareness, as defined above:

> [I learned] That many parts of Spain had changed and been home to numerous different cultures over the years. All of these cultures have cumulatively contributed to what is today Spain and the rich traditions it has in the modern era. I think this is an incredibly important point for students, especially American ones, to learn. Europe has centuries more of history than the modern (Anglophone) US, and through those centuries it has played home to hundreds of different cultures and ways of life, all of which contribute to a broader and better whole. It's important to be able to look back at history and see that cultures

different from our own, or from what we currently deem as "correct," can in the end contribute positively and immensely to our overall society and way of life.

Many student pilgrims singled out architecture as a crucial tool to acquire historical knowledge. Observing the material evidence of history is, in fact, one of the crucial elements that facilitates experiential learning on El Camino. Thus, many of the answers to Question 16, ("In which ways do you consider that the learning experience gained on The Way differs from the learning experience gained in a classroom?"), mention actually "seeing" and "visiting" places as a crucial difference. Besides that, respondents underline quite often the fact of having "first-hand experience" or "hands-on experience," or as one student put it, "walking in history in place of hearing about it."

Two other aspects mentioned in relation to academic learning are culture and language. As we saw in the quantitative results, not all students consider knowing Spanish essential to learning from The Way, but some of them (specifically seven students) appreciated how their language skills improved, and how language was the key to access other kinds of experiences, as we will see later. Culture was mentioned in seven cases too, but this is perhaps a term difficult to interpret, since culture seems to be an encompassing word that may mean different things to different people. In fact, all of the open-ended questions include responses that refer to culture, but in a very vague, abstract way. Respondents to the survey write about "the culture of the natives," about "experiencing the culture," or about "cultural differences," but in very rare cases they articulate what that culture or what those differences may be. This is perhaps an area of reflection for those leading groups of students abroad in general, or those undertaking The Way in particular, namely, what we mean by culture, and how we, as teachers or leaders, can facilitate the observation and conceptualization of the vast variety of components of a culture.

When asked about the most crucial component of The Way in terms of experiential learning (Question 14), one common answer links to the acquisition of academic knowledge. Although not the most frequent answer, we often find references to culture as something they *experienced* rather than something they just *learned*. This may be the reason why three respondents make an explicit contrast between the position of a tourist and their own position in relation to traveling and visiting other cultures. As one participant put it, "Appreciating the 'unseen' culture. That is, interacting with locals, observing architectural differences, taking in the unique landscape, etc., beyond what you could do as a tourist."

Aside from getting to know the Spanish culture through El Camino, two elements seem to be mentioned more often than others: the personal, individual challenges of The Way, and the interactions with other people. Although these two may seem contradictory, they do go hand in hand in the experiences of these student pilgrims. As a direct observer of their experiences, I truly believe that The Way transformed them and opened them up to others, and through communication with others, they experienced a personal transformation.

El Camino seems to have been a challenge for many of the student pilgrims, not only because it tested their physical endurance, but because experiencing hardship helped them learn about others and about themselves:

> I think the most crucial part was actually walking and fighting through the pain. It was so fulfilling to walk every step of The Way and I believe that every step added value to The Way and shaped my perspective on the world.
>
> Learning how to be with and by yourself—The Way is physically relatively difficult to go down and while there are many people around you, there's no one WITH you. You're on your own—it's meant to be a spiritual, personal experience.
>
> I learned so much about my physical and mental capabilities. Setting a goal and achieving it is something I have experienced before, but it's never been to the significance that I felt on The Way. Laying down in the street looking up at the cathedral is a "once in a lifetime" feeling and I'm so grateful to have experienced it.
>
> I would say it was a good opportunity to really push myself physically and personally beyond my normal comfort zone. Having to navigate myself and other students in another country is such an awesome experience. I think it's such a unique opportunity that really does challenge you in so many ways and because of that you finish feeling strong and more capable than maybe you realized you were before you started.

As the previous examples show, walking or biking The Way was a new experience for the student pilgrims, but the learning that took place seems to have emanated from a reflection on the challenges rather than by merely partaking in the challenges themselves. This may be one of the reasons why several participants in the survey appreciated the combination of solitary and group moments that El Camino provides:

> The ability to disconnect from the world (i.e., technology) and really focus on the experience and others around me.
>
> This was single-handedly one of the best experiences I have ever had in my life. Really having the opportunity to immerse in the experience, away from distraction, was great.
>
> Being able to travel, communicate, and think independently (while being moderately and safely guided in a group) along our journey was the most crucial component on The Way for me. I was able to lose myself in the history and experience of our pilgrimage as I independently interacted with other pilgrims and explored each location where we stayed, and find myself at the finish line more enlightened.

In contrast with these testimonials, sixteen participants in the survey also remarked on external elements as those promoting most experiential learning, especially interactions with other pilgrims:

The best component in my opinion was talking to other pilgrims. We met people from all over the world and each had a unique story. That was probably where I learned the most on the Camino.

Interacting with the locals was the most valuable part of my experience on The Way. I found that speaking with people that owned or worked at restaurants, cafes, or hostels along The Way gave me the most insight into diverse cultural perspectives—especially because the locals who live along the Camino spend so much of their lives interacting with pilgrims from every corner of the planet, and thus have incredibly unique perspectives.

Personally, I learned the most from interacting with other pilgrims and locals along The Way. By having evenings free to roam the different towns where we stayed, I was able to meet a lot of different people, all with different experiences. I certainly practiced and expanded my Spanish skills (including familiarity with different dialects) but, more importantly, I was able to learn more about how other people saw the world.

Whether internal or external, the answers to the survey show that reflective observation and abstract conceptualization did take place among students, who were able to "live history" ("The physical challenge, though brief, made me appreciate the difficulty of completing the entire pilgrimage earlier in history"), and to experience natural, human, and material components of The Way at a deep level, as illustrated in the following answer:

> I learned so much about the culture and those that participate in The Way in the 10-day time span, much of which I would have never fully comprehended in a classroom or movie. I have a much deeper understanding of the livelihoods of those on The Way, as well as the overall demeanor of many of the locals.

Regarding Question 16, ("In which ways do you consider that the learning experience gained on The Way differs from the learning experience gained in a classroom?"), it is important to remark on the words and phrases chosen to describe the experience on El Camino, which was qualified as "real and living," "first-hand experiences," "real world," "living the lesson," "hands on experience," "authentic way," or "tangible." The respondents often described participating on The Way as "immersing" themselves in the experience, and also contrasted the "reading" of the classroom with the "seeing" of landscapes, towns, etc., as well as with the "speaking" with other people. The idea of learning by doing, explicitly mentioned in several cases, extends not only to history or architecture, but also to language:

> [It] provides a very natural way to practice learning the Spanish language. I learned more Spanish on this trip than I did in my entire history of Spanish class.
>
> On the Camino, other Spanish-speakers are native speakers and challenge one to improve both speaking and listening skills in the language.
>
> In the classroom, language interactions are structured and great for practice; along The Way, they are authentic and you have no choice but to succeed if you really want whatever it is you're trying to communicate.

Although not a frequent answer, the emotional investment of the student pilgrims appears to be a deciding factor in separating how they learn in the classroom and how they learned in *El Camino*. As stated before, there is nothing here about grades, evaluations, or requirements. On the contrary, learning takes place because of the immersion so often mentioned in the survey, and also because it is an individual as well as a group experience.

> HUGE difference. Both are special and unique in their own way, but the learning experience gained on The Way is something that really cannot be learned in the classroom as it was the biggest emotional and physical test I have done. It pushed me physically and challenged me to really tell myself "I can do this."
> There is emotional investment. You are living the lesson and cannot be a passenger.
> Having the chance to speak to locals and other pilgrims. These experiences definitely could not be replicated in a classroom by any means—it was the human interactions that made it such a powerful learning experience.

Another question from the survey asked students to comment on how their experiences on The Way may have had a long-lasting effect on them. Although the respondents were at various points in their college and post-college years, many of them were able to pinpoint specific areas where they had experienced an impact. Taken together, the student pilgrims who answered Question 17, ("Do you feel that The Way made a lasting impact on your life? If so, how?"), indicate four areas of growth: emotional, academic, relational, and skill/ability. In their answers, we find references to specific skills such as "problem solving," "time management," "to be flexible," "people skills," but also to a sense of overall growth:

> I believed it helped me be a more well-rounded human.
> I feel that El Camino did make a lasting impact on my life. It showed me that I could do things physically and mentally that I didn't know I could before.
> I'm much more at peace and know myself better, and I understand spirituality in a way that I never have before as someone who isn't religious.
> The Way has made a lasting impact on my life in a way that I experience daily, and as a lasting change on my character and my personal life long goals. The Way led me to meet many impactful pilgrims, and experiences, that opened my perspective on The Way I view life.
> To this day I try to take time to do a day trek or a few days similar to the time I had on The Way in order to re-center myself. It helped me to realize the important things in life.

In this sense, we see that the experiential learning that takes place during The Way is inextricably linked to a new global awareness that challenges their insularity:

It was so fulfilling to walk every step of The Way and I believe that every step added value to The Way and shaped my perspective on the world.

It definitely made a long lasting impact on my life. I feel like that was one of the most challenging things I've done. It's also so unique to be able to spend that time to reflect while being a part of something so much greater than ourselves.

Yes, I do, because it has given me a new perspective on cultures across the world. Especially from a religious perspective, it helps me understand and gain a greater understanding of people's motivations.

Final Thoughts

From the answers of the student pilgrims who accepted the invitation to participate in the survey, we can see that El Camino can be a true learning experience. For this to happen, the "course" must encourage group and bonding experiences as well as time for individual reflection and observation. This facilitates the achievement of new and deeper views on the encounters with other pilgrims, on their collaboration with other people from the group, on the places they visit, or the landscapes they go through. While the design of the specific course that this essay is based on facilitated both aspects, an additional issue to consider would be to include a somewhat structured time every day to share this reflection.

Active experimentation was definitely encouraged by the requirements of the course, which included a final essay/journal based on the student pilgrims' interactions with other pilgrims, on trying new food, and the myriad of new experiences they had each day. However, within this general requirement, student pilgrims had to make decisions at every turn, which is probably why they experienced such a feeling of growth and accomplishment. Finding a balance between individual decisions and course requirements is an issue that needs to be carefully considered to facilitate experiential learning while maintaining a safe environment. What is truly remarkable in this context is that no respondent wrote about their experience in terms of "course requirements" or even described their participation in The Way as an external imposition. Instead they convey the experience as a personal journey.

Coming back to the question posed at the beginning of this essay, namely, what it is that makes The Way such an attractive undertaking, it would be difficult to give a single or simple answer. While the data and testimonies offered here are linked to a very specific approach to The Way, it may not be farfetched to imagine that many of the pilgrims that walk or bike The Way undergo a similar "experiential learning" process. The intrinsic difficulties of a physical activity such as this, the natural and human landscapes, and the individual circumstances of the pilgrims, all join to encourage or facilitate a growth that takes places at many levels and manifests itself in many different manners. It may be that the profound and long-lasting transformations that likely take place for thousands of people while doing The Way are difficult to translate into a literary or filmic production. Maybe The Way is an ineffable experience one can only know by doing.

Ready to get in your boots?

Appendix

Survey: Quantitative Questions
Scale: 0–10 (0 = Not at all, 10 = Very much)

1. How much do you think The Way helped to improve and/or expand your global and intercultural perspectives?

2. More specifically, how important have each of the different types of interactions listed below been in expanding your global and intercultural perspectives?

3. In terms of the potential of The Way for expanding your global and multicultural perspectives, how important do you believe having an appropriate command of the Spanish language is to making the most of that potential?

4. Do you consider the Miami created movies filmed on The Way, yearly since 2014, help somehow to anticipate and expect of the global and multicultural perspectives you experienced there?

5. If you saw one or more of the movies before doing The Way, to what degree do you consider that those movies provoked in you a desire to widen your global and multicultural perspectives?

6. How do you think this experience enriched your educational and personal growth, particularly towards broadening your global and multicultural perspectives, while studying abroad?

7. In terms of Spanish language fluency, how important do you think your linguistic abilities were towards your success on The Way?

8. In terms of knowledge of Spanish culture, do you think that living for six weeks in Spain prior to starting The Way placed you in a better position for succeeding both academically and experientially on The Way?

9. How important is it to be physically fit for completing The Way?

10. Do you consider you had the necessary physical fitness level to do The Way?

11. If not, would you welcome a mandatory series of training sessions prior to register in The Way?

12. Beyond the obvious academic and linguistic component, which other factor(s) would you consider as the greatest attractions of The Way?

13. Would you like to do The Way by yourself (or with family members/friends) in the future?

Open-ended Questions

14. In terms of experiential learning, which was the most crucial component of The Way for you?

15. In strictly academic terms, what do you remember as the most important knowledge obtained on The Way?

16. In which ways do you consider that the learning experience gained on The Way differs from the learning experience gained in a classroom?

17. Do you feel that The Way made a lasting impact on your life? If so, how?

18. In order of importance, indicate the three most important reasons that motivated other non–Miami pilgrims to embark on The Way.

19. What are some things you wish someone told you before doing The Way and/or what would you tell future participants?

20. In which ways did the faculty who accompanied you during The Way play an essential role in making your experience a positive one?

NOTES

1. Throughout this paper, I will use the expression "The Way" interchangeably with the Spanish original *El Camino*.

2. Neither the fervor of the pilgrimages, nor the appreciation of the "Liber Sancti Iacobi" seemed to be in a moment of splendor (My translation).

3. The *Compostelana* is an official credential issued by the Pilgrim's Office of the Archbishopric of Santiago de Compostela that certifies the completion of The Way. In order to be granted the diploma, the Catholic Church stipulates that all pilgrims must complete 100 kilometers on foot or 200 kilometers on bike. (See https://oficinadelperegrino.com/estadisticas for other options, as well as for yearly statistical information since 2004.) During the years on The Way, we found many people completing those 100 or 200 kilometers in four to six days, but we also encountered many pilgrims walking from northern France, Belgium or Italy, who spent two or three months on their pilgrimage. As an acknowledgment, my best wishes for Klaus, an Austrian pilgrim who planned to spend eight full months walking The Way: Vienna-Santiago-Vienna. We met him at Monte del Gozo, in 2015, right in the middle of his long journey.

4. In 2018, according to the *Oficina del peregrino*, the distribution by gender indicates, for the first time ever, a majority of women, 164,836 (50.35%), compared to the 162,542 (49.65%) men who completed El Camino (data obtained from https://oficinadelperegrino.com/estadisticas. At the moment of reviewing this essay (August 31st, 2019), the above-mentioned web site offers statistical data only until June. These are the numbers for men and women, respectively, in 2019: January, 66% vs. 34%; February, 59% vs. 41%; March, 52% vs. 48%; April, 48% vs 52%; May, 48% vs. 52%; June, 50% vs. 50%. Considering the average distribution of pilgrims by month (https://www.cuatrocantones.com/en/estadisticas-del-camino-de-santiago-2014), we may conclude women pilgrim numbers stay in good shape.

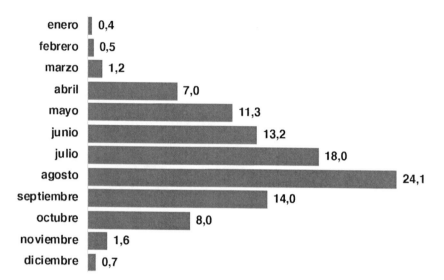

enero	0,4
febrero	0,5
marzo	1,2
abril	7,0
mayo	11,3
junio	13,2
julio	18,0
agosto	24,1
septiembre	14,0
octubre	8,0
noviembre	1,6
diciembre	0,7

5. Somoza-Medina and R.C.L. González offers this statistical table, in which we could graphically verify the exponential success of The Way in the last years (392):

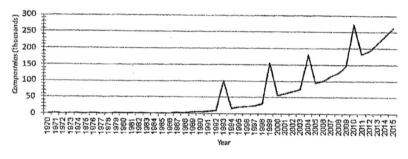

Figure 37.1 Number of pilgrims to Santiago who receive the *Compostela*, 1970–2015. *Source:* Derived from Oficina del Peregrino 1970–2015.

6. After completing her Way, Shirley MacLaine wrote: "As I boarded the plane, I looked and felt like a refugee, a refugee from another time" (299).

7. "While to some degree no absolute universal definition for high culture really exists, it is mostly taken to indicate art forms that are considered the best a culture has produced and that also take some measure of exposure or training to appreciate fully. (…) Thus high culture often appears distinct from popular culture, the latter being those art forms and cultural practices that appear in mainstream media and venues and that take no particular skill, exposure or social position to recognize or appreciate." (www.reference.com/world-view/examples-high-culture-ac60c9cd9c54808e).

8. It is also worth mentioning that the numbers offered by Coelho are a distant approximation. According to data presented by the Catholic Church, the figures are 1,801 pilgrims in 1986 and 61,418 in 2011. That leaves out the many pilgrims (around 80%) that do not pass through Saint-Jean-Pied-de-Port, because they begin The Way at some point in Spain (or in Portugal, or in England) (My translation).

9. Coelho's far reaching popularity is also reflected on social networks. Coelho himself stated in March 2015, in an interview with Ruiz Mantilla: "I already have 26 million followers on Facebook, 10 million on Twitter" (http://elpais.com/cultura/2015/03/20/actualidad/1426851110_279034.html).

10. During my years travelling the Way, I encountered many returning pilgrims, and several of the student pilgrims that participated in Miami in Spain program have done The Way at least once more outside the program.

11. To have a more precise idea of the increasing interest in The Way, readers can visit https://oficinadelperegrino.com/estadisticas, where they will find the complete set of statistics compiled by the Catholic Church since 2004, including the declared motivations of pilgrims who complete The Way.

12. See *Por el camino de las peregrinaciones* (87–89). See also "Improving the Walkability of the Camino," by Xosé Somoza-Medina and Camilo Lois González. In particular, I would like to underscore how public administrations copied the goals of organizations that promoted El Camino de Santiago "(from 1976 to the present day), starting with the Spanish Government, which saw the possibility of justifying the historical Europeaness of Spain at a time of the country's integration into the European Community" (391).

13. Abstract conceptualization is often the most difficult and most obtuse component of the Kolb model to decipher. This is because it requires us as educators and facilitators to explicitly meld the many diverse and divergent experiences of our students (and ourselves) with the ideas of others, who are not present, and which is embodied in theory. This is a process of building connections, but also of engaging in abstraction in order to build deeper connections across and between seemingly disparate experiences (experiential.asc.utoronto.ca/abstract-conceptualization).

14. Kolb (4) summarizes the totality of the learning experience with this diagram:

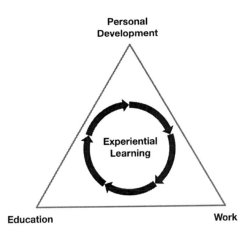

Figure 1.1 Experiential Learning as the Process That Links Education, Work, and Personal Development.

15. An article from Northern Illinois University equates "experiential learning" to "learning by doing," and describes how, before Kolb, educators such as John Dewey (1859–1952) and Carl Rogers (1902–1987) started to build the concept of experiential learning (https://www.niu.edu/facdev/_pdf/guide/strategies/experiential_learning.pdf.). However, for Bill Proudman, "Experiential learning is not simply 'learning by doing.' Often, this is not education, but simply a routinized, prescribed pattern of social conditioning that teaches us to stay in pre-determined boxes of fear of being labeled as outside the norm." (Chapman, McPhee and Proudman 20)

16. (1) Mixture of content and process; (2) Absence of excessive judgment on the instructor's side; (3) Engagement in purposeful endeavors: In experiential learning, the learner is the self-teacher; (4) Encouraging the big picture perspective: making connections between

the learning they are doing and the world;(5) Teaching with multiple learning styles; (6) The role of reflection; (7) Creating emotional investment; (8) The re-examination of values; (9) The presence of meaningful relationships; (10) Learning outside one's perceived comfort zones (Chapman et al. 21–23).

17. https://miamioh.edu/liberal-ed/faculty-staff/mp-proposals/global-persp/index. html. Accessed on April 4, 2019. See also from this page the definition of Global Citizenship: "Global citizenship is a choice and a way of thinking. It means firsthand experience with different countries, peoples, and cultures. It means making a connection between the global and the local. It is also a self-awareness and awareness of others—understanding the interdependence of fellow human beings and having a sense of responsibility towards them. It is also having cultural empathy and intercultural competence."

18. The entire survey could be accessed through this link: miamioh.edu/cas/academics/departments/spanish-portuguese/academics/study-abroad/spain/2018-survey/index.html (no password needed).

19. Although a prominent part of the Study Abroad, by no means was El Camino mandatory. Participation in The Way was always voluntary: no questions asked. However, 98% of MIAMIinSPAIN (summer) students registered for and completed El Camino.

Works Cited

Bravo Lozano, Millán. *Guía del peregrino medieval. Codex Calixtinus.* Centro de Estudios del Camino de Santiago, 2004.

Catedral de Santiago de Compostela. "Oficina del peregrino." oficinadelperegrino.com/estadisticas/. Accessed August 31. 2019.

Chapman, Steve, Pam McPhee and Bill Proudman. "What Is Experiential Education?" *The Journal of Experiential Education*, vol. 15, no. 2, August 1992, pp. 16–23.

Coelho, Paulo. *El peregrino de Compostela. Diario de un mago.* Planeta, 2009.

Cuatro Cantones. "Estadísticas del Camino de Santiago 2014." www.cuatrocantones.com/en/estadisticas-del-camino-de-santiago-2014. Accessed 23 September. 2019.

Cunqueiro, Álvaro. *Por el camino de las peregrinaciones.* Alba, 2004.

Domínguez-Búrdalo, José M. "Miami University Survey on the Way of St. James." https://miamioh.edu/cas/academics/departments/spanish-portuguese/academics/study-abroad/spain/2018-survey/index.html.

Jones, Andrew. "High Culture Versus Pop Culture: Which Is Best for Engaging Students?" *The Guardian*, 20 February 2013, www.theguardian.com/teacher-network/teacher-blog/2013/feb/20/pop-culture-teachinglearning-engaging-students/. Accessed 23 September. 2019.

Kerkeling, Hape. *Bueno, me largo.* Santillana, 2013.

Kolb, David A. *Experiential Learning. Experience as the Source of Learning and Development.* Prentice-Hall, 1984.

Lacarra, María Jesús. "El Camino de Santiago en la literatura contemporánea: El ejemplo de Luis Mateo Díez." *Boletín Hispánico Helvético*, vol. 6, 2005, pp 141–158.

Losada, Basilio. *La peregrina.* Grijalbo, 1999.

MacLaine, Shirley. *The Camino: A Journey of the Spirit.* Pocket Books, 2001.

Miami University. "Global Perspectives Proposals." https://miamioh.edu/liberal-ed/faculty-staff/mp-proposals/global-persp/index.html/. Accessed September 23. 2019.

Puerto, José Luis. *La ruta imaginada. El Camino de Santiago en la literatura.* Edilesa, 2004.

Reference. "What Are Some Examples of High Culture*?" www.reference.com/world-view/examples-high-culture-ac60c9cd9c54808e/. Accessed September 23. 2019.

Ruiz Mantilla, Jesús. "El Camino, una y no más." *El País*, 20 March 2015, elpais.com/cultura/2015/03/20/actualidad/1426851110_279034.html/. Accessed 23 September. 2019.

Somoza-Medina, Xosé, and Rubén Camilo Lois González. "Improving the Walkability of the Camino." *The Routledge International Handbook of Walking*, edited by Michael Hall, Yael Ram and Noam Shova, Routledge, 2018, pp. 391–97.

Torbado, Jesús. *El peregrino*. Planeta, 2001. facdev@niu.edu (University of Northern Illinois.) "Experiential Learning." www.niu.edu/facdev/_pdf/guide/strategies/experiential_learning.pdf/. Accessed 23 September. 2019.

University of Toronto. "ASC Experiential Learning." https://experiential.asc.utoronto.ca/abstract-conceptualization/. Accessed 23 September. 2019.

Paradoxical Pilgrims

Remaking Religion for the Modern World

JOANNE BENHAM RENNICK

In 2010, I walked the *Camino de Santiago* with my family. We followed the French route (*el Camino francés*) that begins in Saint-Jean-Pied-de-Port France, and runs 780 kilometers across the northern part of Spain to Santiago. The journey was motivated by several things: I had a research leave, our daughters were still young enough to take several weeks out of school, and my 78-year-old mother was starting to decline. Our little troupe were paradoxical pilgrims in the sense that, we were walking as a family unit, are not religious, were motivated by togetherness rather than seeking, and were known and cheered on by others who had heard about the family of Canadians walking with little ones and a senior. In December 2018, my mother died after a long, degenerative illness that took every ounce of the strength, independence and vitality that were the hallmarks of her life. The mutual trust, sharing, suffering, beauty, and love we had experienced on the Camino—not because we are religious, but because we were devoted to each other's success and supported each other's journey—resonated as we traveled with her on that final journey toward death.

In this essay, I use autoethnography along with social science theories on modernization to examine my Camino experiences as a significant pilgrimage that continues to resonate for my family and me. I examine the journey itself, and its continued influence as we have negotiated various complexities of modern existence, including attending to my mother in her last months of life.

I consider modern trends including individualization and subjectification, diffuse forms of belief, preoccupation with physical and mental health and well-being, increasing reliance on technology, and the rising interest in thematic tourism. I argue that, because modern pilgrims continue to wrestle with age-old questions of meaning, purpose, and values, they may be remaking religion to suit their needs and interests. Finally, I suggest that the Camino's social, emotional, psychological, spiritual, and physical benefits are so contradictory to the increasingly alienating aspect of modern life, that it holds paradoxical appeal for many who are neither religious, nor spiritual.

Introduction and Methodology

I first walked and began researching the Camino de Santiago in 2010. I have tried several times to produce a scholarly paper but, as a result of my own experiences on the route, I found I could not position myself in relation to the material in a way I found fitting for academic work. This essay is informed by several years of literature review, participant observation, informal interviews and formal surveys I conducted, and secondary statistical analysis of published data but, for the most part, it is autoethnographic.

Anthropologist Clifford Geertz famously noted that good ethnographic research produces "thick description" able to generate nuanced insights into culture (10). Autoethnography pursues the same end, but from a personal point of view. It is oriented to producing "aesthetic and evocative thick descriptions of personal and interpersonal experience" (Ellis et.al n.p.). A breakdown of the term autoethnography is useful for understanding why it is a relevant approach here. *Auto* refers to the personal experience aspect that is explained and analyzed, or *graph*ed. Together this allows us to gain a better understanding of *ethnos*, or cultural experience. Ellis et al. explain, "[A]s a method, autoethnography is both process and product … that acknowledges and accommodates subjectivity, emotionality, and the researcher's influence on research, rather than hiding from these matters or assuming they don't exist" (Ellis *The Ethnographic I* 3).

A reflexive autoethnography, such as this one, goes a step further to document "ways a researcher changes as a result of doing fieldwork" (Ellis *The Ethnographic I* 50). It is partly about my own relationship to the Camino, partly about my relationships with others who walked it with me, and partly about how those experiences intersect with modern life.

Context and Historical Significance of the Camino

Each year, in increasing numbers since the 1970s, thousands of individuals from around the world arrive at one of the numerous entry points to the *Camino de Santiago* or, Way of St. James. They typically walk, but some also cycle, or ride horses for days to months, with a goal of arriving at the Cathedral at Santiago de Compostela in Northwestern Spain, or even further west to where the land disappears into the Atlantic Ocean at Finisterre.[1]

Santiago is the Spanish form of *Saint James* whom the Christian Bible identifies as one of Jesus' disciples. Camino folklore[2] tells that, following the death of Jesus, James went to the "end of the earth" (*Finis Terrae*) to preach and convert people to Christianity. On returning to Palestine (ca. 44 CE), James was taken prisoner by reigning King Herod Agrippa, and tortured to death. James' disciples acquired the body and placed it in a marble coffin on a small boat that was somehow driven by ocean currents all the way to the Spanish coast. There, believers identified it as James', miraculously retrieved it, and sequestered it to a field for secret burial. Several centuries later (ca. 813 CE), the tomb was rediscovered by a local hermit who reported hearing heavenly music and seeing sparkling lights that glowed like a field of stars (*campus stellae*). The bishop commissioned a chapel dedicated to St. James and declared him patron saint of the Spanish empire. In subsequent years, as access to Jerusalem was limited by crusaders battling their way across Europe, the route to Santiago de Compostela became an important alternative pilgrimage route. By the 13th century, the town was declared a Holy City on par with Rome or Jerusalem, and a cathedral was built and pilgrims began to arrive.

The etymology of the term "pilgrim" links the Latin root for the concept "beyond" with the term for "country" or "land" to produce the meaning "foreigner." The term eventually became specific to a religious devotee who travels to a sacred site for the purpose of penitence or divine supplication.

After centuries of disuse, the Way of St. James is increasingly popular with travelers from around the world, regardless of their personal religious beliefs. The Internet provides copious amounts of information for neophytes, and virtual communities for alumni. People start from different points throughout Europe—some as far away as Helsinki and St. Petersburg, but most people start in the South of France (on the *Camino francés*), in Portugal (*Camino portugués*), or on one of several routes in Spain.[3] Extensive supporting infrastructure eases the difficulties of staying on the path, obtaining lodgings, or getting help as needed. Souvenirs and photographic opportunities are abundant along the Way.

Pilgrims can validate their journey by carrying a passbook or *credencial* to be stamped and dated in every town traversed. The *credencial* can be presented to officials in the Pilgrim's Office in Santiago for authentication, and exchanged for a *Compostela* certificate of achievement signed by the Bishop.[4] Pilgrimage along the ancient Way of St. James now takes a modernist form due to the imposition of technological optimization, commoditization, bureaucratization, and changing interpretations of religion.

The Canadian Family

In the spring of 2010, my family undertook a five-week journey through France, Spain and Italy. Our troupe consisted of my husband, our young daughters (eight and eleven), my mother, and myself. After two weeks on the road, my husband left to return home to Canada and the rest of us carried on.

It was a good time for us to undertake an adventure of this sort. After a decade working in the information technology sector during the dot-com boom, I had elected to go back to university and try my hand at a doctorate. On graduation, I became director of an international program that required extensive travel in volatile and challenging regions of the world. My mother played a central supporting role through all of this by living with us part time and helping with anything that needed doing. The year we walked the Camino, I had just turned forty, landed a tenure-track position, and felt the beginnings of burnout. My mother had just turned 78 and, although still active and healthy, was showing signs of slowing down. Our daughters were still pre-teens and having an easy time at school.

I grew up in the gap between a devoutly Catholic mother and atheist father. I remain curious about the role that religions play in society, but reject religious worldviews of any sort for myself. For my mother, the journey was the culmination of a dream to visit the Catholic shrines at Lourdes, Santiago and Vatican City. For me, it was an opportunity to support my mother in this quest and thank her for the tremendous support she had given us over the years. For all of us, it was an enjoyable trek through the countryside, villages and towns of three countries, full of interesting history, culture and nature. It allowed us to step out of our frenetic lives and spend time together at a more natural pace.

The year 2010 had been declared a Holy Year: a year during which St. James' July 25 Feast Day fell on a Sunday. We knew that typically more pilgrims undertake the Camino during Holy Years making it more crowded and sometimes difficult to find accommodation. We flew into Paris in April and headed directly by train to our first stop at the major Catholic shrine in Lourdes. After a few days in Lourdes that allowed my mother to attend Masses and see the various religious curiosities, we headed to our official starting point at St.-Jean-Pied-de-Port. Our arrival aligned with a major strike that disrupted rail travel in France for several days making this busy town unexpectedly quiet and easy to find lodgings. On our first day, we walked across the Pyrenees into Spain to magnificent views and spring-like weather. Arriving in Roncesvalles, we had a dormitory to ourselves and learned of the now infamous eruption of Iceland's Eyjafjallajökull volcano that disrupted air travel across Europe for weeks. My mother interpreted these serendipitous near misses as divine intervention on our behalf. With more skepticism but no less gratitude, I acknowledged we had been fortunate where others were not.

My mother, a physically tiny woman, was a force of nature. Growing up in Scotland during a war that kept adults busy with other things, she experienced a semi-feral childhood full of escapades with her twin brother. Because there were two of them and one was a boy, she had liberties atypical for most girls of her era. I believe this contributed to her fearlessness in the face of hardship and challenge. She and her brother shared a great love of the outdoors and were avid walkers and hikers across their lifetimes.

She moved quickly in everything she did. One of my earliest childhood memories is running to keep up with her as she marched down the road. She was known affectionately among my friends and neighbors as "the white flash" due to her speed and prematurely white hair. She taught me to swim, ride a bike, jump rope and spend as much time outside as possible. If I slept in too late, she'd say, "What's this? Wasting God's good daylight!" and pull the curtains open. Through necessity, she was a great walker. She had grown up in a big city and needed her feet or public transport to get anywhere. She didn't learn to drive until her late forties. Over time, walking became her preferred form of exercise and stress relief. We frequently walked together simply because we enjoyed talking and moving together. In so many ways, the Camino mimicked our lifelong relationship—carrying and sharing our burdens as we moved our bodies across geographic and temporal distances.

When I first proposed walking the Camino together, she was immediately enthralled with the idea. As we spoke about it more seriously, she became doubtful and anxious—would she hold us back? What if she wasn't strong enough? What if she couldn't handle the distances? The feisty little woman, whom I'd always known to outwork the biggest of men while bringing a smile to all those around her, doubted herself. I was astonished. We planned and packed carefully to ensure that she and the children were comfortably equipped with proper footwear, rain gear, and backpacks. None of us had more than 11kg. The plan was not to injure or kill anyone—it was supposed to be fun.

The truth is, although all of us were physically fit and running on adrenaline, the first day was hard. We covered 29km up and over the Pyrenees. It was steep and we frequently moved slowly. My husband and I exchanged several anxious glances as we monitored the progress of the girls and my mother. We stopped early for coffee and breakfast and were greeted with amazed and impressed looks from everyone we encountered. By the end of the first day, we were exhausted but exhilarated. Everyone had survived, the views were exceptional, and we'd made a number of new acquaintances. We *were* having fun.

By the end of the first week, we were hardened in to our packs, had adjusted to the daily rhythm and were enjoying the views. The kids were having the time of their lives. They ran and jumped and danced along carrying their packs like they weighed nothing. People stopped to chat with them and give them chocolates while admiring "*las peregrinas pequeñitas*" [the little pilgrims]. Each morning we'd stop for breakfast and pick up bread, cheese and fruit for lunch. By mid-afternoon, we'd find something more substantial and then try to turn in early to sleep. My mother became a minor celebrity as we journeyed. Local people cheered her up steep hills clapping and calling "*Vaya abuela! Vaya!*" [Keep going Grandma], or would tentatively ask her age. French groups we encountered informed us they'd heard about "*les canadiens courageux*" [the brave Canadians] traveling as a family. To the many Spaniards we met, we were simply, "*la familia*" [the family].

By week two, it was obvious my mother was growing tired. She had developed terrible blisters on her feet but refused to mention them for fear of "slowing us down." She had started to list to one side a little while she walked. On one steep section of trail, she'd tripped on a stone and hit her head when she fell. The large young man behind her lifted her bodily by her pack and put her back on her feet. The woman walking behind him happened to be a nurse. She had an instant cold pack in her backpack that she activated and put on mum's head to reduce the swelling. Although we appeared to be in the middle of nowhere, the next bend of the path brought us to a vending machine with hot tea—my mother's preferred crisis-response beverage. She laughed and cried as she explained that the orange in her pocket had broken her fall. It was terrible and hilarious at the same time and we laughed at the absurdities of the situation that she again attributed to the "goodness of God."

To celebrate her eleventh birthday, our oldest daughter requested cake and a rest day. We turned it into a few days, to give everyone a rest and let mum's feet heal a little. A few days later, we saw my husband off to the bus station as he headed for his flight home. Now we were four, and all of us were feeling his absence. Although the rest days had helped restore mum's feet, we'd all suffered a stomach bug that seemed to hit her the hardest. She endured without complaint, but as we started back on the trail, it was obvious she was struggling. The girls rallied round to encourage her and I started carrying her pack as well as my own. When we arrived at the next town, she sat down heavily at the bottom of a long flight of stairs, completely exhausted.

Unfortunately, I had not confirmed our reservation at the local hostel and the place was now fully booked. When the receptionist understood our situation, two little girls and a grandmother, she went out of her way to assist us and found us a clean, private lodging just up the road. It was ideal for letting my mother, never one to nap, sleep heavily for most of two days. Over many kilometers, our relationships shifted. We, who had always been protected and encouraged by our beloved caregiver, became solicitous caretakers.

Recognition as a "legitimate" pilgrim is given to those who complete a journey of at least 100km to Santiago. From the 100km mark, there is a noticeable increase in foot traffic and horseback travelers on the route. This home stretch was a period of struggle and triumph for my mother. She had suffered and endured. She had encountered interesting people and seen beautiful sights she'd never expected to see. She'd been adopted and admired for her courage and tenacity over several hundred kilometers. When she arrived for the overcrowded Pilgrim's Mass at the Santiago Cathedral, it was standing room only. A Spanish group we'd encountered repeatedly over tens of kilometers took her arm and cleared a space for her at the front of the church by asking others already seated to "please make way for this lady who is a real pilgrim." My mother wiped tears from her eyes and the girls and I stepped outside to do the same. It was a powerful moment of triumph and wonder for all of us.

We continued on to Finisterre, then took a train to Barcelona and sailed from there to Italy where we spent a couple of days in the frenzy of Rome. My mother was satisfied to see the Vatican from the outside. It couldn't compete with the Camino. When we finally returned to our "real lives," we made a coffee table book with the photographs from the journey and often revisited our experiences together while we got on with the ordinary moments of modern life.

Over the next few years, my mother's vitality deteriorated. I have a video from Valentine's Day 2016, of my mother and father waltzing together in their living room. By the next spring, after increasing hints of decline, she was diagnosed with Parkinsonism—a type of degenerative neurological disorder sharing many features of Parkinson's disease—and required assistance to open containers, hold a spoon, and stand. We continued to "walk" together, although she now required a wheelchair. Within months she was bedridden and required 24-hour care. I spent many hours at her bedside talking about her life and our memories and watching her grow weaker.

Although all of her physical strength failed her, my mother kept her sense of humor and gratitude, and rarely complained. She was beloved by her caregivers whom she daily thanked for their work. One day she thanked me for allowing her to be part of our lives. She said that walking the Camino had been one of the greatest experiences of her life and that she couldn't have done it without me. Twice she rhetorically asked me, "What more could a person want than fresh air and a beautiful daughter?" She told me she was happy and that she'd had a wonderful life and that she wasn't afraid to die. She continued to smile and joke until she was no longer able to communicate with us. Two years of watching her steady decline, increasing suffering and transformation from the robustly dynamic person I'd always known to a fragile invalid, was devastating. Unlike our Camino journey, there was no way to ease her burden. I could only be present with her on the journey to the end. When she died, very early on the morning of December 15, 2018, I felt profound relief that she was no longer suffering. Ten days later, on Christmas morning, my youngest daughter gave me a photograph of my mother and I walking across a field, hand in hand.

Who Are the Pilgrims?

The Archdiocese of Santiago's Pilgrim's Office in Santiago compiles and publishes pilgrimage statistics monthly. Data from the last three Holy Years (2004, 2010, and 2018) give insights about pilgrims and their reasons for making the journey. In 2004, nearly 180,000 pilgrims completed the Camino. That number rose above 27, 000 in 2010 and 330,000 from 207 countries in 2018. Since 2004, roughly equivalent numbers of women and men participated (44:56 percent in 2004 and 2010, 50:50 percent in 2018). Walking remains the preferred mode of transit (87 percent in 2004 and 2010, 93 percent in 2018).[5] The majority of pilgrims continue to be 30 to 60 years of age (55 percent 2004, 58 percent 2010, 50 percent 2018), followed by under-30s in a downward trend (37 percent 2004, 29 percent 2010, 26 percent 2018), and over-60s in an upward trend (8 percent 2004, 13 percent in 2010 and 18 percent in 2018) (Archdiocese of Santiago).

Religious motivation for completing the Camino shows a steady downward trend since 2004 while mixed motives and secular motives have drifted upward:

Personal Motivation for Completing the Camino	2004	2010	2018
Religious	75	55	43
Religious and cultural	20	41	48
Cultural only	6	5	9

Sociologist Peter Berger, in his seminal work *The Sacred Canopy*, described religion as a "sacred canopy" holding society together, providing shared meanings and values, as well as protecting society from chaos and disintegration. He and others have argued that religious authority and influence would ultimately fade in the face of scientific positivism. Durkheim, for example, believed that as institutions within a society became more structurally differentiated, religion would take on an increasingly peripheral role and would lose its authority to regulate morality (*Suicide* 389). Weber believed that the collision of religion with rationality would ultimately result in a questioning of religious beliefs as they became less plausible under the intense scrutiny of scientific examination (*Essays* 155). He described the alienation that individuals would experience in modern society as a certain "disenchantment of the world" as magic, meaning and the "uniquely human" were replaced by cold, scientific calculation (*Essays* 148–155). Like Weber, Berger argued that elements of modernization like religious pluralism and scientific rationalism, undermined the monolithic worldview of religion to cause a "crisis of credibility" and create a profound sense of moral anomie as shared values disappeared in the wake of religious thinking and scientific reasoning (127–153). Karl Marx understood religion as a form of false consciousness that obscured the real problems of modern society and oppressed people under the control of capital, the state and the church (28).[6]

The twin forces of globalization and modernization have significantly transformed traditional forms of religious identity around the world (Asad; Casanova; Davie; Hervieu-Léger "The Role of Religion"; Roof; Wuthnow). The word *religious*, remains associated with "membership in religious institutions, participation in formal rituals, and adherence to official denominational doctrines" (Fuller, "Fresh Takes" 5). The term *spiritual* is associated with the more abstruse setting of an individual's private realm of thought and experience. People who call themselves "spiritual but not religious" may reject formal religious organizations in favor of "individualized spirituality that includes picking and choosing from a wide range of alternative religious philosophies" (6). These might include health and wellness projects, practices originating in various religious traditions (e.g., yoga, meditation, particular diets, essential oils), and different ways of viewing the world. Camino statistics related to motivations for participation appear to conform to these arguments. However, Robert C. Fuller states that spirituality and religion are essentially the same thing because they connote a belief in and a desire to connect with a Higher Power or reach a higher state of being ("Fresh Takes" 151). He adds that confusion regarding these terms comes from the gradual association of the word "spiritual" with "the private realm of thought and experience while the word 'religious' is associated more with the public realm of membership in religious institutions, participation in formal rituals, and adherence to official denominational doctrines" *(Spiritual* 5). James A. Beckford further addresses this matter of pitting "religious" against "spiritual" when he writes:

> Medieval and early modern notions of spirituality tended to emphasize personal discipline and the intensification of commitment to institutional teachings and practices. Yet, spirituality has come to refer to the quality of individuals' relations with the divine or a sense of awareness of a suprareality that goes beyond life as ordinarily experienced. Indeed, it is common for Christians to construe their spirituality as a freely chosen expression of their "real selves," thereby accentuating the difference from externally controlled religion. The re-drawn boundary between popular conceptions of spirituality and religion is associated with broad changes in culture and social relationships, including patterns of religious belonging, believing and practicing [72].

In fact, there is widespread evidence of the focus on individualized spirituality even within organized religious communities (Beyer; Bibby; Fuller *Spiritual*; Roof; Stark & Finke; Wuthnow). Even when people who consider themselves spiritual rather than religious do participate in a particular religious tradition, they insist that as individuals, they have the final interpretive authority on religious doctrines they consider relevant to them. This modern twist makes reliance on statistical information problematic for studying religious belief. Robert Wuthnow states that the highly individualized state of modern spirituality means that it is typically:

> …hidden from view except insofar as it is talked about or revealed through personal interviews or indirectly in public behavior…. Spirituality consists not only of implicit assumptions about life but also of the things people talk about and the things they do…. At its core, spirituality consists of all the beliefs and activities by which individuals attempt to relate their lives to God or to a divine being or some other conception of a transcendent reality…. Spirituality is expressed in many different ways. But spirituality is not just the creation of individuals; it is shaped by larger social circumstances and by the beliefs and values present in the wider culture [vii–viii].

My own research, in the form of surveys (n=180) and personal interviews (n=50) conducted between 2010 and 2014 but not previously published, shows that people walk the route for religious, cultural, health, and tourism reasons. In addition to being an interesting holiday, many people describe the Camino as a physical challenge, a rite of passage, and a form of meditation that helped them wrestle with personal transitions. Survey respondents indicated they were motivated to undertake the journey in response to health crises,[7] damaged relationships, changes of employment, transitions between life stages, grieving, lack of self-understanding, religious piety, and other concerns. This subjectification of belief is noted by a number of scholars who examine religion in modern global society. For example, Hervieu-Léger argues that when people link religious tradition with new ways of interpreting meaning they retain the symbolic, ideological, and practical benefits of belonging to a community of believers without diminishing the significance of their personal experiences and interpretations of the meaning behind the beliefs (*Religion* 82). This is why a multi-pronged approach to data collection and analysis is essential if we are to gain helpful insights about the culture of the Camino and its modern pilgrims.

Religion, Spirituality and Personal Growth

The first time I experienced it, the Camino was a curiosity and as a scholar, I hoped to gain insights about why an ancient Catholic pilgrimage route appeared to be gaining popularity in what appeared to be an increasingly secularized global context. Being neither spiritual nor religious, I saw the journey as an opportunity to have a uniquely interesting cultural experience together with my family, allow my mother to fulfill her interests in visiting several Catholic shrines, and collect some data along the Way. On subsequent visits, I was surprised and unnerved by the memories of my family's trip years before. During the last months of my mother's life, I was struck by the subtle lessons and impressions the Camino had left on all of us.

Others agree that even as people are abandoning traditional religion, many have developed new, highly individualized, privatized, and subjectivated ways of experiencing religion (Wuthnow 115; Roof 77–110). Grace Davie describes this approach to religion as "believing without belonging" and both she and Danièle Hervieu-Léger argue that religious "ways of being" are continually reshaped and reformed in the face of social influences that now extend beyond traditional options to more individual and privatized forms (Davie; Hervieu-Léger *Religion* 32). Danièle Hervieu-Léger sees religion as an "ideological, practical and symbolic system" through which a sense of individual and collective belonging is established and maintained through a particular chain of religious belief stored in the memories and traditional associations of individuals (*Religion* 82). For example, she argues that even as groups and individuals create new ways of believing they associate their beliefs and practices with pre-existing traditions. Hervieu-Léger links Durkheim's idea that religion generates social cohesion with Weber's methodology to produce a definition describing religion as a tradition-based (in this case a religious tradition) social construct that generates a sense of belonging and establishes social norms for its members. Relatedly, evidence that people turn to religious resources in times of hardship and stress suggests that religion and religious resources remain valuable sources of comfort and consolation despite individuals' rejection of traditional organized religious forms (Fuller, "Fresh Takes"; Heelas et al.; Hervieu-Léger *Religion*; Lyon; Roof; Wuthnow).

For many people, including those who continue to participate in established religious communities, this subjective outlook takes precedence over established religious doctrines (Hervieu-Léger *Religion*; Roof; Wuthnow). The subjectivation of religion to personal interpretation seems to go hand-in-hand with the notion of religious "seeking" described earlier by Roof and Wuthnow and comes in part as a rejection of traditional ways of believing. Like myself, many of the individuals I met on the Camino are reflexive, aware of religious alternatives, and doubtful of all-encompassing views of "the truth" (Bauman; Beck; Bibby; Giddens; Hervieu-Léger, *Religion*), yet they chose an ancient Catholic pilgrimage route, of dubious authenticity, to investigate and experience their beliefs.

I have been on different sections of the Camino many times since that first walk with my family and I have encountered many pilgrims walking and searching their way to Santiago. Those people have different reasons for walking. Some are indeed doing it as a religious pilgrimage. Others are avid hikers enjoying the convenience of having inns and hostels along the Way as well as beautiful countryside and historically interesting sites all along the route. Others are dealing with burnout from their jobs, their lives, their personal circumstances and simply want to get away from it all. Frequently I've heard tales of a lost job, an illness, a failed relationship, a personal crisis, a sense of not knowing what to do next with one's life. These individuals sought a period of withdrawal, reflection and meditation distinctly different from the fast-paced, alienating aspects of modern society. Some described the journey itself as a results-producing spiritual quest. One Japanese Shiatsu and Reiki practitioner told me she believed her healing practice would improve if she completed the journey. Another woman from El Salvador believed her prayers would be answered if she could make it all the way to the sea at Finisterre. She was walking the journey with agonizing tendonitis in both feet and had been told by two physicians that she should not be walking at all. Another young woman from the Netherlands had just finished university and was "feeling lost." A French group of six, middle-aged friends explained they annually walk a different 100km section during a week's holidays with a multi-year goal of completing the entire distance together. Since one of their members had died the year before, the project had now also taken on a memorial aspect. A Canadian was overcoming a lost relationship, trying to "reinvent himself," and "get back in shape."

These examples reflect Pierre Bourdieu's differentiation between an "objectivated" state directly observable in practices, institutions and objects and a "subjectivated" state that is internal and self-reflexive (Bordieu et al. 89). In the latter framework, self-identifying associations, values and behaviors orient one's actions as opposed to being inspired by the praxis occurring in their environment. Fuller points out that many secular activities serve the same functions and meet the same socio-psychological needs as religion. Based on his earlier distinction between the "religious" and the "spiritual," although walking the Camino is a historically religious pursuit, those who walk it may not in fact have a spiritual dimension, but only *seem* to because they are similar to certain Christian religious activities. However, Fuller goes on to add that spirituality becomes relevant in these activities:

> wherever we struggle with the issue of how our lives fit in to the greater cosmic scheme of things. This is true even when our questions never give way to specific answers or give rise to specific practices such as prayer or meditation. We encounter spiritual issues every time we wonder where the universe comes from, why we are here, or what happens when we die. We also become spiritual when we [are] moved by values ... that seem to reveal a meaning or power beyond our visible world. An idea or practice is "spiritual" when it reveals our personal desire to establish a felt-relationship with the deepest meanings or powers governing life [Fuller *Spiritual* 8].

For me, this was certainly true. I was not practicing or following a religious tradition but my actions were directed by values, associations and behaviors inherited from my mother and subsequently, in relation to my mothers' illness, they became spiritualised.[8]

The surveys and interviews I did with other pilgrims, as well as my own experience support the notion that many pilgrims find traditional religious practice and experience being reshaped and reinterpreted along the Camino. Pilgrims in the past may have walked for salvation, but today cyclists and hikers can be seen traveling together in matching outfits and there are hiking clubs and pilgrimage groups around the world of Camino devotees. Fitness and community seem to be aligned with personal growth and finding inner peace as much as religious accomplishment.

Conclusion

The Camino de Santiago offers intriguing insights to the culture of religion and spirituality in modern, globalized society. It appears to offer a geographic and temporal space for seeking, sampling and investigating some of the big questions of life, individually and in community with others. At the heart of modern religious movements lie the subjective interests of individuals. Health issues, psychological suffering, curiosity, soul searching, pain and loss, penitence, self-discovery, escape, personal challenge, adventure, diversion, all appear on the Camino. Weber foresaw that the regulated nature of modern institutions and the objectives of bureaucratization, to develop and maintain efficiencies, would not only erode culture and undermine traditional values, but also enslave and alienate people in a routinized "iron cage" of modern society (181). The Camino offers reprieve from the iron cage where community and relations are often subsumed by economic obligations, technological distractions and superficial interests. The secularization of society that removes a religious or moral framework of understanding can also result in a sense of instability and un-rootedness known as anomie (Berger; Durkheim; Hervieu-Léger, "The Role"). Yet even as many people reject religion in its traditional forms, others are finding revelation and community on the Camino.

For me, walking the Camino in 2010, was a joyful family journey. In subsequent years, the Camino became a metaphor that sustained us through the final long walk to my mother's death. For others like me, both religious and secular, the ancient Way continues to hold meaning because the modern seeker deals with ageless questions.

Notes

1. Finisterre is believed to have been a pagan site dedicated to fertility and goddess worship. Pilgrims of old who completed the journey frequently also walked the additional 100km to Finisterre to wash away the grime of the journey in the sea and collect one of the abundant scallop shells from the beach demonstrating they had fulfilled their objectives. Many modern pilgrims continue this tradition and the scallop shell remains emblematic of the Camino.

2. There are many sources telling the history of St. James and the Camino. For a concise overview, see Gitlitz, David and Linda Kay Davidson. *The Pilgrimage Road to Santiago: The Complete Cultural Handbook*. St. Martins Griffin, 2000, pp. xiii–xvi.

3. For more information on the various routes visit www.santiago-compostela.net/index.html.

4. Many Spanish and Portuguese youth obtain a *Compostela* to include it on their resumés in the hope of improving their employment opportunities. This practice reflects Max Weber's thesis (*Essays*) that religious affiliation can distinguish a person's integrity and character and improve economic opportunity.

5. Others arrive, in much smaller numbers, by bicycle, horse and wheelchair.

6. He described religion as the "flowers on the chains" that held people under oppressive control.

7. Although all respondents noted the physical hardships including fatigue, strains and injuries, the majority noted that the physical nature of the experience also increased strength, endurance, cardiovascular fitness, and resulted in weight loss.

8. One unexpected finding related to my mother's experiences, and consequently my interpretation of the value of the Camino journey is about the walking itself. Walking has long been a form of spiritual practice in various religious traditions and for my mother, walking was a form of stress relief. Recent studies on stress and the brain show that physical outlets are critical for reducing stress hormones in the body and releasing dopamine and have a direct effect on the progression of Parkinson's and Parkinson-like illnesses (Doidge 2007; 2016; Sapolsky 2006). It is likely that my mother's love of walking, extended her life and increased its quality.

Works Cited

Asad, Talal. *Genealogies of Religion: Discipline and Reasons of Power in Christianity and Islam.* The Johns Hopkins University Press, 1993.

Bauman, Zygmunt. *Intimations of Postmodernity.* Routledge, 1992.

Beck, Ulrich. *World Risk Society.* Polity Press, 1999.

Beckford, James A. *Social Theory and Religion.* Cambridge University Press, 2003.

Berger, Peter. *The Sacred Canopy.* Anchor Books, 1967.

Beyer, Peter. *Religion and Globalization.* Sage Publications, 2000.

Bibby, Reginald. *Restless Gods: The Renaissance of Religion in Canada.* Stoddart Publishing, 2002.

Bourdieu, P., R. Chartier and R. Darnton. "Dialogue à propos de l'histoire culturelle." *Actes de la Recherche en sciences sociales,* vol. 59, no. 2, 1985, pp. 86–93.

Casanova, Jose. *Public Religions in the Modern World.* University of Chicago Press, 1994.

Davie, Grace. *Religion in Britain Since 1945: Believing Without Belonging.* Blackwell, 1994.

Doidge, Norman. *The Brain That Changes Itself: Stories of Personal Triumph from the Frontiers of Brain Science.* Penguin, 2007.

_____. *The Brain's Way of Healing: Remarkable Discoveries and Recoveries from the Frontiers of Neuroplasticity.* Penguin, 2016.

Durkheim, Émile. *Elementary Forms of the Religious Life.* Free Press, 1965 [1912].

_____. *Suicide: A Study in Sociology.* Routledge, 1952.

Ellis, Carolyn. *The Ethnographic I: A Methodological Novel About Autoethnography.* AltaMira Press, 2004.

Ellis, Carolyn, Tony E. Adams and P. Arthur. "Autoethnography: An Overview." *Forum Qualitative Sozialforschung / Forum: Qualitative Social Research* [Online], vol. 12, no. 1, 2011, n.p., Web. Accessed 2 Mar. 2019.

Fuller, Robert, C. "Fresh Takes on a Classic: William James's Varieties Approaches Its Centennial." *Religious Studies Review,* vol. 26, April 2000, pp. 151–55.

_____. *Spiritual but Not Religious: Understanding Unchurched America.* Oxford University Press, 2001.

Geertz, Clifford. *The Interpretation of Cultures.* Basic Books, 1973.

Giddens, Anthony. *Modernity and Self-Identity: Self and Society in the Late Modern Age.* Stanford University Press, 1991.

Gitlitz, David, and Linda Kay Davidson. *The Pilgrimage Road to Santiago: The Complete Cultural Handbook.* St. Martins Griffin, 2000.

Heelas, Paul, and Linda Woodhead. *The Spiritual Revolution: Why Religion Is Giving Way to Spirituality.* Blackwell Publishing, 2005.

Hervieu-Léger, Danièle. *Religion as a Chain of Memory.* Rutgers University Press, 2000.

_____. "The Role of Religion in Establishing Social Cohesion." *Religion in the New Europe: Conditions of European Solidarity,* edited by K. Michalski, Central European University Press, 2006, pp. 45–63.

Holman Jones, Stacy. "Autoethnography: Making the Personal Political." *Handbook of Qualitative Research,* edited by Norman K. Denzin and Yvonna S. Lincoln. Sage, 2005, pp. 763–791.

Lyon, David. *Jesus in Disneyland: Religion in Postmodern Times.* Blackwell, 2000.

Marx, Karl. "Karl Marx Selected Writings." *Economic and Philosophic Manuscripts,* edited by L.H. Simon, Hackett Publishers, 1994 [1844], pp. 54–97.

Roof, Wade Clark. *Spiritual Marketplace: Baby Boomers and the Remaking of America.* New Jersey: Princeton University Press, 1999.

Sapolsky, Robert M. *Why Zebras Don't Get Ulcers: The Acclaimed Guide to Stress, Stress-Related Diseases, and Coping, 3rd Edition.* Holt Paperbacks, 2006.

Stark, Roger, and Rodney Finke. *Acts of Faith: Exploring the Human Side of Religion.* University of California Press, 2000.

Statistics. Archdiocese of Santiago and the Pilgrims' Welcome Office. 2019, oficinadelperegrino.com/en/statistics/. Accessed 2 Apr. 2019.

Weber, Max. *Essays in Sociology.* Oxford University Press, 1946.

_____. *The Protestant Work Ethic and the Spirit of Capitalism.* Scribner's, 1958.

Wuthnow, Robert. *After Heaven: Spirituality in America Since the 1950s.* University of California Press, 1998.

Finding Meaning While Steeping in the Camino Cauldron

Kip Redick

Clearly there is a world of difference between medieval pilgrims and their counterparts who walk the Camino de Santiago in our own age. C.S. Lewis' *Discarded Image* is a study in the difference of world views.[1] Medieval motivations for going on pilgrimage, rooted in the "discarded image," are no longer primary to contemporary pilgrims. Victor Turner writes concerning long established draws to sacred journeys, "One motive for going on pilgrimage is the feeling that a saint's shrine has a sort of 'hot line' to the Almighty" (*Image and Pilgrimage* 16). Though these motives no longer seem meaningful for a majority of contemporary pilgrims, the cultural texts, religious iconography, architecture, and tradition along the Way of Saint James remain rooted in that discarded image. Though some contemporary pilgrims feel this connection, many others no longer live in such a world, and their motives for the trek across Spain are varied.

Given that contemporary pilgrims embark with varied motivations, both religious and secular, how do they interact? In light of the Camino's proliferation of religious cultural texts, how do those whose motivation to hike the trail coming from something other than religion interact with embedded cultural texts which are for the most part religious, that is, when the internal cultural texts have such dense religious meaning? The books of Esther and Ruth are said to be secular texts included in the sacred scriptures of Jews and Christians. Yet, their inclusion in the scriptures brings religious meaning to such texts. Could this same thing be said of secular pilgrims who find themselves surrounded by religious cultural texts along the Camino? In answering these questions, I will show that pilgrim interaction, one with another as well as with cultural texts, is a cooperative hermeneutic practice wherein meaning is discovered, an intertwining of personal and communal meaning. The Camino is the cauldron, the vessel in which pilgrims, cultural texts, and other constituents steep together during the ordeal of journeying to Santiago de Compostela, and in the interaction between these ingredients meaning makes itself manifest along the way.

One overlapping motive between medieval and contemporary pilgrims, even among those who walk for cultural rather than religious reasons, is a feeling of alienation. People leave home for an extended journey, versus embarking on a tourist vacation, in some cases to relieve feelings of alienation. Those with religious backgrounds might describe this alienation in terms of sin. Turner writes, "On such a journey one gets away from the reiterated 'occasions of sin' which make up so much of the human experience of social structure" (7). After piling up such "sins," when the burden becomes unbearable, the pilgrim goes on the journey. Sin is a form of alienation; it separates us from relationship. Pilgrims without religious backgrounds still feel the weight of such fractured relationships, even when manifested beyond the human: loss of meaning in one's profession, feeling disconnected from other meaningful pursuits, even a feeling of unresponsiveness to the earth's ecology.

Pilgrimage offers healing whether one is religious or not. As Turner notes, the ordeal of a pilgrimage breaks the ties of alienation: "these fresh and unpredictable troubles represent, at the same time, a release from the ingrown ills of home" (7). Unlike a tourist vacation, the ordeal provides a spiritual component. Turner writes, "the weariness of the body is submitted to hard, voluntary discipline, loosening the bonds of matter to liberate the spirit" (95). In this way the Camino is a cauldron. The pathway toward Santiago is a container wherein pilgrims steep in their shared ordeal and interact with the various ingredients of the spiritual soup. Everyone walking toward Santiago's tomb experiences this weariness of body, feels the exigencies of discipline, and has the potential for a liberation of spirit.

This shared journey leads to new relationships with fellows along the way. As pilgrims walk together and share one another's ordeals, they form strong bonds. Turner describes this fellowship as *communitas*: "All the writers agree that there is a connection between the pilgrims' discipline and privations and their sense of *communitas*" (133). Turner defines *communitas* as "a relationship between concrete, historical, idiosyncratic individuals. These individuals are not segmentalized into roles and statuses but confront one another rather in the manner of Martin Buber's 'I and Thou'" (*Ritual Process* 131–132). Through *communitas* pilgrims share their encounters with cultural texts. In the sharing of these texts they dialogue and discover common meaning. In dialogue preconceptions may begin to fade and new meaning arises in the process.

I will use a phenomenological and hermeneutical approach to explore pilgrim meaning making. This approach involves discovering meaning in lived experiences rather than through conceptual modes of explanation. I have used this research approach on both the Appalachian Trail and the Camino de Santiago, living as a long-distance hiker and pilgrim in order to better understand the phenomenon of spiritual journey and pilgrimage. This essay incorporates my research along the Camino and involves autoethnography as well as phenomenological description. I will begin with a section outlining phenomenological bracketing of preconceptions as it relates to the way pilgrims interact with cultural texts. I will then explore the hermeneutics of cultural texts as they are framed in the liminality of the journey, as well as through embodied ritual, myth and dialogue. I will then explore the hermeneutics of text and intertextuality as they unfold along the Camino. Finally, I will look at these texts through the lens of idol and icon as described by Jean-Luc Marion.

Hermeneutical Bracketing of Preconceptions

Cultural texts themselves play a constituting role in establishing preconceptions. Such texts focusing on the pilgrimage to Santiago de Compostela have proliferated from the Middle Ages through the current age, from the *Codex Calixtinus* to contemporary documentary films. In the last decades of the 20th century the pilgrimage attracted new attention. Paulo Coelho's 1987 book, *The Pilgrimage*, drew many pilgrims, especially from his native Brazil. Hape Kerkeling's 2006 book, *I'm Off Then: Losing and Finding Myself on the Camino de Santiago*, attracted hundreds of German pilgrims. In conducting research along the Camino since 2008 I have noted a significant increase in the number of North Americans following the film *The Way*, released in 2011. Those pilgrims influenced by these cultural texts come to the Camino with preconceptions formed as they interacted with these texts. In dialoguing with pilgrims through research I have heard many proclaim that the journey did not meet their expectations. Their projections are often shattered in the first days of the walk.

In addition to popular culture texts such as written personal accounts published as books, blog posts, and documentary films, guidebooks of the Camino are abundant. Some pilgrims read through these guides, pour over maps, seek advice on equipment, and plot their intended course. They envision themselves walking the route across Northern Spain, enjoying the villages and views, connecting with fellows, and projecting themselves into particular situations they have imagined in the days, weeks or months of planning. They are, after all, embarking on a pilgrimage that has captured the imaginations of countless Europeans through the late 20th century and now has entered the imaginings of people from Asia and the Americas.

Such preconceptions will begin to fall apart, if not in the first days then later, after many kilometers of trekking through the Pyrenees, the Meseta, the Mountains of Leon, the villages and cities, the weather, and in their weariness, expectations will not meet the reality of the Camino.

In the wake of these varied contemporary cultural texts pilgrims are drawn to the walk with divergent motivations, some religious and some merely cultural. As pilgrims integrate into the age-old route, a cauldron of embedded religious and cultural texts continually bubbling to the surface and manifesting along the way, they experience an ever-evolving inter-textual journey. Sojourners who come to the walk via some interaction with a text prior to the journey must navigate a myriad of embedded texts along the way. Interpretations evolve as the journey unfolds. Early in their journey pilgrims impose their preconceptions and frame embedded texts with virtual experiences derived from prior exposure. But as they steep in the Camino cauldron their interpretations change and the Camino itself becomes a frame of meaning. Those whose interpretation begins to change unknowingly engage in a phenomenological and hermeneutical practice. They do, as Maurice Merleau-Ponty writes in characterizing phenomeno-logical description, "turn back to the things themselves" and "return to that world prior to knowledge of which knowledge speaks" ("What is Phenome-nology" 60). In order to open themselves one to another, to the indigenous people along the way, the artifacts, and the environmental constituents, they must set aside their projections and allow the other to manifest. When pilgrims with divergent motives drop their preconceptions and discover *communitas* one with another they open themselves to meaning not envi-sioned. In their discovery of new meaning, of encountering wonder, they share their interpretations and listen to other's experiences. This dialogue becomes another element in the cauldron.

What follows is a phenomenological exploration of cultural texts along the Camino, focusing on those texts that evidence contemporary pil-grim interaction with embedded texts. Pilgrims interpret texts reflexively and, in doing so, sometimes communicate by responding to and creating texts along the route. These texts manifest as call and response, a liturgy of walking within the rich field of texts. Pilgrims attend to the call, interpret symbols, and create new texts in response. Some examples of these texts will be graffiti, items left at shrines, cairns, shrine fences, and crosses.

Pilgrimage involves a unique approach to encountering cultural texts. As Turner writes, "If mysticism is an interior pilgrimage, pilgrimage is exteriorized mysticism," the journey within unfolds in the exterior encoun-ters with signs during the walk (*Image and Pilgrimage* 7). Reading a tradi-tional sacred text, such as the Bible, and reading texts along the route of the Camino differ in the sensuous encounter, that is in the way texts are experienced through our senses. Whereas reading the printed words on a page of the Bible involves our eyes moving in an ordered fashion across the face of a page, heightening the experience of seeing as understanding and dampening the experiences of other senses such as feeling the leather bound book or the paper as each page is turned, reading the signs in fields, forests, villages, cities, and buildings involves our whole body, all of our senses. Walter Ong shows us the distinction between oral and literate cultures and their approaches to communication, in the sensuous encounter, using the written word versus other forms of communication (*Orality and Literacy*). Reading texts along the Camino is a fully embodied and walking hermeneutic. Merleau-Ponty writes of this kind of hermeneutic, "It is not a surveying of the body and of the world by a consciousness, but rather is my body as interposed between what is in front of me and what is behind me, my body standing in front of the upright things, in a circuit with the world, an *Einfuhlung* with the world, with the things, with animals, with other bodies" (*Nature* 209). A walking interpretation happens in the full environmental surround wherein all of the others, human and extra human, interact. It also happens in the quiet of a church along the way, where the pilgrim is alone in a building filled with religious iconography.

Those who come to the Camino with no religious background are not at a disadvantage. Turner writes, "a pilgrimage is very much more than its theology. It is a field of social relations and cultural contents of the most diverse types, formal and informal, orthodox and heterodox, dogmatic and mythical, often juxtaposed rather than fused, interrelated, or systematized" (106). Whether or not one is religious, encounters happen in diverse social relations and cultural contents. Turner elaborates on this theme noting that such encounters come in the context of more informal than fixed liturgies: "pilgrimage should be regarded not merely as an ideal model but as an institution with a history. Each pilgrimage, of any length, is vulnerable to the history of its period and must come to terms with shifts of political geography. Pilgrimage is more responsive to social change and popular moods than liturgical ritual, fixed by rubric" (231).

Hermeneutics and Cultural Texts

One example of an evolving alternative interpretation of a common Camino cultural text comes from the figure of the *matamoros*, Saint James the Moor slayer. I had encountered the *matamoros* in various locations along the Camino Francés. The largest sculpture was high up on the façade of the *Iglesia de Santiago* in Logroño. There he was riding a war horse, which was rearing up on hind legs, front hooves hovering over the heads of Moorish soldiers who lay prostrate underneath. Saint James himself was dressed in his customary pilgrim robe and wearing the wide-brimmed hat. Scallop shells adorn his garments. Instead of a water gourd on the end of a staff, the typical accouterment of Saint James the pilgrim, this version of the saint wields a sword, which is raised above his head ready to strike at the soldiers clinging to the earth. The image is based on the legend of Saint James' appearance at the Battle of Clavijo where he charged into the fray and led the Christian army against the Moors.

My initial interaction with the image was more critical than anything else. I could not make sense of a Christian saint engaged in killing human beings, of leading any particular nation in battle against another. I saw the image as an idol of ideology and political aims rather than a religious icon. Of course, religion has often been used as a tool of ideology and national aspirations. My critical gaze continued to engage other texts and ideas I encountered along the way. Some pilgrims told me of a new age belief that the power of the Camino resulted from an underlying magnetic field that lined up with the Milky Way.[2] One night, sleeping under the stars, the Milky Way became visible, and I saw that it was perpendicular to the Way. My critique of cultural texts extended to both architecture and manifestations of commerce aimed at the pilgrimage. I found the decadence of some of the larger cathedrals to counter the spartan lifestyle of pilgrimage. As for the commercialism attached to religious aspects of the journey, those cultural texts seemed to thrust the pilgrim into a tourist life.

My critical viewpoint came naturally as an academic. This reminded me of Paul Ricoeur's articulation of the hermeneutical circle: "We must understand in order to believe, but we must believe in order to understand" (351). We start with a pre-critical, naïve belief and often take messages at their surface meaning, a literal interpretation. If we enter the next phase of the circle, we begin to deconstruct the previous interpretation. However, such a deconstruction begs to be resolved by another interpretation, more likely one with more symbolic complexity. This then leads to a secondary belief. Ricoeur notes that the circle "is always directed by a prior understanding of the thing about which it interrogates the text" (351). Preconceptions brought to the Camino drive the circle from initial belief, even if that belief is not directed by religion, to deconstruction and then a secondary belief. Everyone comes to the Camino with some belief. Secular pilgrims believe they will have a previously envisioned experience, or at least the potential for some fulfillment of the vision which motivated the journey.

As I continued along the route toward Santiago de Compostela, my interpretation began to change. Texts such as the *matamoros* are symbols rather than signs. Turner writes, "signs are almost always organized in 'closed' systems; while symbols, particularly dominant symbols, are

The façade of the *Iglesia de Santiago* in Logroño with the *matamoros* in the upper panel.

Closeup of the *matamoros* in the upper façade of the *Iglesia de Santiago* in Logroño.

themselves semantically 'open'" (245). Being semantically open symbols invite participation. The open-endedness, or the excess of meaning communicated by these symbols is magnified because of the *liminality* of the journey. They involve the participant in an interpretative process that is performative. The performance along the Camino, whether one is religious or secular, involves ritual within the context of a particular religion.

As stated earlier in the essay, this ritual is not liturgically rigid but thrusts the participant into a *liminal* journey, a particular pilgrimage focused on a Christian saint.

Liminality as a hermeneutic lens. *Liminality* separates participants from their previous existential situation. They exit the world of structure and enter a world between, or on the edge. Turner characterizes *liminality* as the in-between world happening during religious ritual wherein potentiality dominates and change occurs. Turner writes that *liminality* is a "betwixt-and-between state" and a separation from "the structural arrangements of a given social system," or "voluntarily setting oneself apart from the behavior of status-occupying, role-playing members of that system" (223). I have written that *liminality* facilitates flow and thereby "opens pilgrims and long-distance hikers to heightened encounters and communion with the constituents of the journey" (Redick 48–49). In *liminality* the ritual participants encounter one another as members of a unique community.

Turner uses the term *communitas* rather than community to distinguish "the unstructured and spontaneous bond that forms amongst pilgrims" (Redick 48). He writes that *communitas* "is a *liminal* phenomenon which combines the qualities of lowliness, sacredness, homogeneity, and comradeship" (250). Edith Turner writes, "Almost everywhere *communitas* is held to be sacred or holy because it is accompanied by experiences of unprecedented potency" (183). Rudolph Otto elaborates on this sacred potency, showing that it produces feelings of awe independent of particular religious traditions. Otto refers to this potency as the *numinous* and in his interpretation of sacred experience he proposes to call the human response to the Holy a "feeling of dependence," "'creature-consciousness' or creature-feeling. It is the emotion of a creature, submerged and overwhelmed by its own nothingness in contrast to that which is supreme above all creatures" (10). In Otto's words the Holy as wholly other "is quite beyond the sphere of the usual, the intelligible, and the familiar ... filling the mind with blank wonder and astonishment" (26). The feeling associated with the Holy transcends human capabilities of rationalizing and so must be approached through symbolic language, as in myth (26).

Through *liminality* pilgrims, whether motivated to come on the journey through religious or secular reasons, are opened to this kind of sacred encounter. They have exited the structures of the previous world, secular or religious, and entered the alternative world of the pilgrimage ritual. Edith Turner writes, "power structures tend to kill *communitas*. It is the fact of *liminality*, its aside-ness, its below-ness, that produces and protects *communitas*. These pods are where the domination system of the corporations and state power is not watching and appropriating all loyalty to itself"

(184). Pilgrims have been relieved of power structures that have been in place for much of their lives up to this point. In the opening provided by *liminality*, they are free to shed preconceptions that have been imposed, even when the imposition remains hidden. Edith Turner shows how in this opening, pilgrims of all kinds might encounter sacred power: "their secular powerlessness is compensated for by a sacred power, derived on the one hand from the resurgence of nature when structural power is removed, and on the other from the direct experience of the sacred at the key point, though hardly recognized as such" (183). She points out that participants may not recognize sacred power. This is especially true for pilgrims who have had little to no past experience with such power.

Liminality can also be understood to facilitate phenomenological reduction, or a bracketing of preconceptions in order to enhance an authentic encounter with the constituents of the journey and discover interpretations of cultural texts that transcend expectations. Jean-Luc Marion outlines a "fourth and last formulation of a possible first principle of phenomenology: 'As much reduction, as much givenness'" (*In Excess* 17). In its bracketing of the natural attitude, setting aside the way we interact with things based on preconceptions and thereby take things for granted, the reduction distances us from the usual; that is, moves us away from the way we normally interact with others and things via a prescribed repertoire. Pilgrimage is a potential setting of this reduction, an opening up to an authentic interaction rather than a reliance on prearranged interactions. In the *liminality* of pilgrimage, one is distanced from the usual. A gap forms between the pilgrim and the usual so that texts and persons within the journey both give themselves and are received authentically. They are not organized in a preconceived schema. Marion describes the formation of such a gap as being "between the (appearing, transcendent) thing and (immanent) lived experience (in which the thing would appear)" (55). In this way *liminal* distance facilitates meaning making as it unfolds through dialogue, an authentic and cooperative interaction, during the journey. *Liminality* sets aside the natural attitude, the prescribed repertoire we rely on in everyday interactions, and exposes the pilgrim to an authentic alternative. Flow experiences, that sometimes happen in *liminality*, open pilgrims to this alternative and work to open pilgrims to phenomenological reduction wherein the text gives itself to the pilgrim in the gap (55). Merleau-Ponty, as discussed earlier in this essay, references phenomenological description as turning from conceptual practices in the natural attitude and returning to the things themselves, where they reveal themselves beyond our projection: "To turn back to the things themselves is to return to that world prior to knowledge of which knowledge speaks" ("What is Phenomenology" 60). Pilgrims practice a walking phenomenology and open themselves to encounter, to the given of a world of things preceding their conceptualization, that is to both texts and persons whose meaning preceded the encounter.

In the *liminality* of the journey pilgrims as ritual participants enact a myth, a foray into a mythic reality. Their preconceptions of the mythic reality set aside, they encounter this reality anew, sometimes not being conscious of the mythic nature of the *liminal* world. Ricoeur defines myth as "a traditional narration which relates to events that happened at the beginning of time and which has the purpose of providing grounds for the ritual actions of men of today and, in a general manner, establishing all the forms of action and thought by which man understands himself in his world" (5). The myth associated with the *Camino* fits this definition in every way with the exception of its reference to an event happening at the beginning of time. The event does, however, relate to mythic time through its connection with the Apostle James, through him to Christ, and through Christ to the Christian interpretation of sacred history rooted in the creation and fall narratives of Genesis 1–3. The myth of the Camino then provides ground for the ritual actions of this particular pilgrimage. Through the ritual action of this pilgrimage those who participate by walking to Santiago act in and among a complex field of concrete mediated symbols, cultural texts, through which a particular set of symbolic forms create meaning for the pilgrim and extend from the ritual to the world beyond.

Embodied ritual as hermeneutic lens. Each pilgrim enters this rich symbolic ritual bodily, as Merleau-Ponty writes, "in a circuit with the world" (*Nature* 209), not alone but with companions who for the most part, were unknown to each other prior to the journey's beginning. Drawing meaning from the Camino results from the pilgrim's *liminality* and the interrelation between them and the mediated field of symbols into and through which they walk. Pilgrims use all their senses to gather information for a meaningful interpretation of the journey. Rather than merely reading or hearing, they insert themselves bodily into a sacred narrative, a myth, and thereby identify bodily with the story, even if they have never believed the story to be literally true. Their participation in the walk is a kind of act of faith, with varying degrees of faith, a subjective interaction with the myth that plays out uniquely for each individual. Some identify closely with the details of the story. Others discover the story and approach it curiously as one would read a novel. All are walking toward the purported grave of Saint James.

One way of understanding this complex embodied ritual is through another ritual, the Christian Eucharist and its communication of meaning to the participant. The believer takes bread and wine, the body and blood of Christ, into his or her own body and thereby communes bodily. The myth is enacted at the Mass. The participant enters the church and becomes *liminal* during the liturgy. But in pilgrimage the ritual participant steps into the myth for an extended time and over a vast space, his or her body surrounded by the earthen elements of communion. If we explore this embodied ritual through the metaphor of fertility, we find meaning coming forth in the interaction of male and female cooperating to give birth. The Eucharist presents the sacred as male, the body and blood, which enters the believer, the female whose womb receives the life-giving seed. The Camino manifests the sacred as female, the cauldron, and receives the pilgrim into herself, surrounding the ritual participant with the earthen elements. The pilgrim's life-giving seed, their interpretive interaction, manifests itself in a profusion of artifacts born from the womb of God the Mother. That is, the cultural texts along the way function as sacramentals and the pilgrim responds reflexively, sometimes producing more cultural texts along the way. The very action of walking each day becomes a kind of cultural text akin to music, which resounds into the world and then vanishes into the atmosphere as the sound fades. That is, most pilgrims respond in dialogue and leave no physical trace of a text, yet the dialogue itself is a cultural text which sounds forth in *albergues*, cafes, or along the path and then fades into silence and contemplation.

Ritual and Reflexive Hermeneutics

A clear practice of responding reflexively happens at various places where pilgrims feel called in the presence of a text and then interact by creating new texts or adding to already present texts. There are many examples of shrine fences where pilgrims add to the proliferation of symbols hanging thereupon. One such fence is about ten kilometers beyond Logroño on the climb to Alto Grajera. A typical chain link fence separates the trail from a major highway. Mostly homemade crosses hang on the fence, stretching for nearly a kilometer. Some of the crosses are made from grass pulled up just beside the Way. Others are from scraps of wood. Still others are made from rubbish. In some cases flowers adorn the crosses. The same type of shrine fence called the *Via Crucis* is located on the upper slopes of the Mountains of Leon about two kilometers before Rabanal del Camino. This is a livestock fence and shorter than the one near Logroño. It is also in an oak forest rather than along a busy highway. The crosses are made of the same material on both fences, but the forest and earthen trail tread give the *Via Crucis* a more rustic appearance. The quiet under the shade of the trees creates a contemplative atmosphere. There are some rock shrines along the fence as well. In addition to crosses, I have also seen a rock mosaic, yin and yang symbol. Shrine fences and rock cairns exemplify the call and response of the liturgy in walking the Camino.

Shrine fence on the outskirts of Logroño at Alto Grajera.

Closeup of crosses on the shrine fence at Alto Grajera.

Shrine fence on the approach to Rabanal del Camino.

Closeup of crosses on the shrine fence near Rabanal del Camino.

Another closeup of crosses on the shrine fence near Rabanal del Camino.

Rock mosaic at the shrine fence near Rabanal del Camino.

The interplay between the pilgrim and Camino that manifests meaning in this context also rises out of the daily walking and rhythm of the ritual action: rising early each morning and preparing for the day's journey; eating and drinking; walking in fields, villages, towns, cities, and forests; stopping at cafés and chatting with fellows and local people; checking into *albergues*; showering and washing clothes; preparing a meal; sleeping.

Gerardus van der Leeuw writes that dance is naturally ecstatic, placing the participant in a position of being beside him or herself. The pilgrim, similar to the dancer, is lifted "above life and the world," and all of their "earthly existence perish[s] in the maelstrom" (29). The spiritual journey is such a dance. In *liminality* the pilgrim is lifted above the world. The ecstasy is partly produced by unfamiliar landscapes, or in places that rise above or separate the pilgrim from the rest of the world. Sometimes the rhythm of walking for hours each day becomes a dance wherein preconceptions are shattered in the maelstrom, opening them to a new interpretation of their own life.

Mythic and Dialogic Interaction as Hermeneutic

Each pilgrim comes to the Camino with a different understanding of the Camino's foundational myth. Some will be conscious of the primary myth, believe without question its veracity, experience its symbols from the standpoint of this first belief and incorporate its etiological function into their ritual journey; they will practice a ritual rooted in what Ricoeur refers to as "the merely semantic understanding" (9). Other pilgrims, though still conscious of the primary myth, will have a secular orientation to myth in general. These pilgrims will most likely have already deconstructed the Camino myth and its explanatory function through demythologization. Ricoeur writes of contemporary persons, both religious and secular, that they "are in every way children of criticism" (350). But to maintain this critical orientation seems unlikely for the person who continues to walk several hundred difficult kilometers all the while surrounded by cultural texts that sing the myth. Their critical orientation gives way to the myth revealing "its exploratory significance and its contribution to understanding," as opposed to its etiological or explanatory function (Ricoeur 5). Put another way Ricoeur writes that "we seek to go beyond criticism by means of criticism, by a criticism that is no longer reductive but restorative" (350). The pilgrim's first belief gives way to understanding, which in turn leads to a second belief informed by an interpretation of cultural texts rising from the ritual of the walk rather than a conceptualization preceding the journey.

The interactive dialogue between pilgrims is integral to considering a hermeneutic of the journey to Santiago. Pilgrims exchange understanding and share their beliefs one with another. The process of exchange is indicative of the hermeneutical circle, the movement from initial belief, through change, and into a secondary belief. Through the exchange belief is modified and understanding grows. As pilgrims share their new-found belief in the myth, in whatever form that takes, and exchange critical views of the myth, they walk over particular landscapes that also communicate meaning. They cross the Pyrenees and walk through the mountains and hill country of Navarra. They spend many days traversing the Meseta, a seemingly flat high plain in north central Spain. They climb the great mountain range west of Leon and descend into the wet, green hill country of Galicia. In each of these distinct landscapes they walk through villages, towns, and great cities. Scattered about the landscape artifacts peculiar to the Camino connect pilgrims of the present to those who walked and lived along this way in the past. Artifacts that are explicitly religious, and many seemingly non-religious, speak to those whose attention is arrested.

Looking back at my own interaction with the image of the *matamoros* in light of the ritual transformation, I started by asking myself what this image of Saint James could mean to people and pilgrims who have attempted to release themselves from the hold of an alliance between religion and the state. After the trip I discovered that the *matamoros* located within the cathedral in Santiago de Compostela had been altered. The heads of the Moorish soldiers beneath the war horse were covered by flowers as a way of erasing the legend, or at least part of it. Yet, Saint James still wields a sword! I continued to question, what existential meaning does this warring saint have hundreds of years after the Moors were driven from the Iberian Peninsula? The walking continued, the ritual unfolded, a transformation of thought began to bubble up along the *Camino* cauldron. Turner writes of ritual as a "transformative performance" working to constructively change culture: "it holds the generating source of culture and structure…. Hence, ritual is by definition associated with social transitions, while ceremony is linked with social states" (244). Walking the Camino is an embodied ritual rather than a ceremonial act. Participants are more likely transformed than established in a social state. Their interpretations are subject to change through transformative interactions.

My participation in the cauldron involved encountering other texts that interacted with the *matamoros*. I saw many images of Saint Michael slaying Satan, as well as some of Saint George slaying the dragon. I recalled Saint Paul's words in his Epistle to the Ephesians, "For our struggle is not against enemies of blood and flesh, but against the rulers, against the authorities, against the cosmic powers of this present darkness, against the spiritual forces of evil in the heavenly places" (*New Revised Standard Version* 6.12).

I began to see the parallel between walking here in Spain, pilgrimage, and the inner struggle all pilgrims experience during the journey. Each of us, whether religious or not, have dragons to slay, personal demons to banish. The daily battle my body endured became meaningful in the exteriorized mysticism of the journey. Any preconceptions of dualism between spirit and body, or mind and body, evaporated and every bodily pain was also spiritual. Turner writes that in pilgrimage "the weariness of the body is submitted to hard, voluntary discipline, loosening the bonds of matter to liberate the spirit" (95). In this case the body represents the tangibility of personal struggles. This example is not Gnostic, the body not evil. The walk is an integration of body and spirit, a recognition that the body has limits and needs discipline. This discipline transfers to the whole of one's life. A new interpretation of the Camino began to take shape. The *matamoros* became a vision of the saint who comes along side and helps in my personal struggle. He struggled to the death, was beheaded by Herod, and laid in a grave. Pilgrims are all walking toward a grave, and there will be struggles along the way. With discipline and courage, we can help one another till death meets us all, just as death meets us at the tomb of Saint James.

Text and Intertextuality

My own account of interacting with the *matamoros* shows an intertextual play in the Camino cauldron. An example of intertextuality that comes to the Camino from beyond the tradition of religious pilgrimage occurs in an instance of graffiti on the concrete wall of an underpass on the outskirts of Logroño. The image includes the aphorism "smiles not miles," and the intertextual message comes from the Appalachian Trail community. In addition to the written word, an Appalachian Trail logo appears, contextualizing the message. The text of the graffiti message communicates a meaning wherein the journey happens in the adventure unfolding each day.

There is clearly a goal for the Appalachian Trail thru-hiker. For the north-bound, hiker it is summiting Mount Katahdin in Maine, and for the south-bound, hiker it is finishing at Springer Mountain in Georgia. Thru-hikers, like those who walk the Camino from St.-Jean-Pied-de-Port to Santiago de Compostela, complete the route in one long, continuous journey. But rather than focusing on the end, "smiles not miles" points to being present in each mile and enjoying the journey along the way. One cultural text on the Appalachian Trail, which is inscribed on a plaque at the southern terminus of the trail, reads, "For those who seek fellowship with wilderness." Many who thru-hike the Appalachian Trail become focused on finishing rather than fellowship. This causes such hikers to attend to their

Graffiti on the outskirts of Logroño with Appalachian Trail logo and reference to hikers on that trail.

daily mileage rather than the relationships with fellows, both human and extra-human, along the way. There is such a strong urge to complete these miles each day that hikers miss opportunities for fellowship. Some Appalachian Trail veterans come to the Camino with the same approach. This focus on the daily distance is easily adopted by anyone who uses guidebooks, which lay out the journey in prescribed stages. One popular guidebook has the pilgrim complete the Camino in roughly thirty days.[3]

"Smiles not miles" sets a different tone. Hikers who emphasize the joy of the journey highlight a possible difference between medieval pilgrims and contemporary sojourners. Many who have walked both the Appalachian Trail and the Camino repeat their walk in subsequent years, unlike those medieval pilgrims whose journey could not be repeated so. Those contemporary pilgrims who do repeat the journey are not wealthy tourists who indulge themselves in a diversion. Some of those who continue to involve themselves in these journeys live on a limited budget. They have decided that hiking such trails brings more meaning than a career in some corporation. They often cite the authentic community that forms along these routes, what anthropologists such as Victor Turner reference as *communitas*. This graffiti artifact is an example of an intertextual message underscoring the power of *communitas*.

Another graffiti image that appears on the *Camino primitivo*, on a concrete retaining wall just before Bodenaya, depicts a stylized, stick figure, pilgrim, with staff and hat, walking just above the symbol for infinity. The lines of the symbol are not set forth in a closed loop but depict an arrow that forms the infinity figure, the beginning of the arrow leading into the loop and the end leading out. The stick figure clearly references the many images of Saint James, or medieval pilgrims wearing the typical robe, hat, and carrying a staff. The infinity symbol has its roots in the *ouroboros*, the serpent eating its own tail, indicating several possible meanings including eternal return.[4] The graffiti image lacks any overt religious meaning, but its placement along the *Primitivo* gives rise to possible religious interpretations. Those pilgrims who come to the Way without any religious background may interpret the symbol as referring to a continuous and never-ending journey. Whatever the interpretation, the message seems to be consistent with the "smiles not miles" image. The journey continues, don't let the goal overshadow being present each moment in the walk.

Graffiti on a concrete wall near Bodenaya on the Camino Primitivo.

Text as Idol and Icon

Jean-Luc Marion, in distinguishing between idol and icon, helps us further clarify pilgrim encounters with texts along the Way. In exploring hermeneutical bracketing of preconceptions we saw that pilgrims come to the Camino projecting an already formed interpretive frame of meaning. Marion's distinction between idol and icon illuminates two ways of approaching cultural texts along the Camino. The text as idol receives an already established meaning and does not participate in meaning making. The text as icon gives itself as pilgrims open themselves to receiving a meaning that originates beyond themselves. The text as icon opens pilgrims to a cooperative hermeneutic where fellow constituents of the journey contribute to meaning making. He writes, "The icon and the idol determine two manners of being for beings" (*God Without Being* 8). Interacting with idols versus icons shows that pilgrims approach texts in two ways of being-in-the-world. On one hand, their being-in-the-world situates them so that they project preconceived meaning upon the other, whether the other is a text or a person. In this case the pilgrim does not engage in cooperative meaning making, discovering with others the meaning being given in the texts. Approaching the texts of the Camino cauldron as idol is to resist the action of steeping with those texts and fellow pilgrims, of not allowing the flavors of the other ingredients to infuse and thereby transform. Marion continues, "the idol and the icon are distinguishable only inasmuch as they signal in different ways, that is, inasmuch as each makes use of its visibility in its own way" (9). That is, texts appear or are visible in different ways.

Pilgrims whose preconceptions prevent them from encountering the other as an alterity, a stranger,[5] as one whose differences cannot be subsumed or colonized, experience these texts as idols. The way the idol appears keeps the pilgrim in control, their preconception does not allow disturbance: "The idol fascinates and captivates the gaze precisely because everything in it must expose itself to the gaze, attract, fill, and hold it" (10). The idol gives the one gazing upon it the feeling of being in control because the experience is theirs, or as Buber writes, "Those who experience do not participate in the world. For the experience is 'in them' and not between them and the world. The world does not participate in experience. It allows itself to be experienced, but it is not concerned, for it contributes nothing, and nothing happens to it" (56). There is no encounter with the other as an alterity, a stranger, everything exists "in them" and is a construction of their own isolated aesthetic imagination. The textual and personal constituents of the pilgrimage are colonized or domesticated projections of the pilgrim who experiences them. Marion shows this writing, "The idol thus acts as a mirror, not as a portrait: a mirror that reflects the gaze's image, or more exactly, the image of its aim and of the scope of that aim" (12). Pilgrims who experience texts as idols only find the meaning that is already there in the preconception.

Pilgrims who encounter texts as icons are addressed by the icon envisaging them. That is, the textual icon is an Other who remains beyond the pilgrims personal orbit or propensity to colonize. This textual alterity gazes back at the sojourner who in turn discovers that they share this journey with others. Marion writes, "The icon does not result from a vision but provokes one. The icon is not seen, but appears, or more originally seems, looks like" (17). The icon as other, text or person, appears and announces itself as another and not the self-same, not the one in the mirror. That is, it appears like that of the face of another who is not me nor my projection. Marion writes, "Whereas the idol results from the gaze that aims at it, the icon summons sight in letting the visible ... be saturated little by little with the invisible" (17). The other who shares the journey with the pilgrim is invisible in that the mystery of their experiences can only be shared through ongoing dialogue.

Another way of exploring the mystery of the other is through Emmanuel Levinas' description of the face. For Levinas the face transcends my self-same enclosure, my colonizing of the world, my placement of everyone and everything else in my own orbit. The face of the other does not look back at me in a mirror. He writes, "the other as transcendent presents herself and exceeds 'the idea of the other in me'" (50), "The face of the Other at each moment destroys and overflows the plastic image it leaves me, the idea existing to my own measure and to the measure of its *ideatum*—the adequate idea" (50–51). The invisibility of the other, transcending my preconception, appears in the face, in the gaze of the icon. The meaning of the text that transcends the pilgrim's preconception appears in the invisibility of its gaze, in the manifestation of its mystery. The text as icon presents an excess of meaning, bursting the limits of any imposition of meaning.

The excess of meaning presented by the text as icon slowly saturates the senses of the pilgrim, who surrenders and so receives the hospitality of the other. Hospitality requires the recipient to receive from the host. The host gives without condition. In such hospitality there is a mutual sharing of meaning, a cooperation through dialogue in the discovery of meaning. Marion writes:

> such a gaze here belongs to the icon itself, where the invisible only becomes visible intentionally, hence by its aim. If man, by his gaze, renders the idol possible, in reverent contemplation of the icon, on the contrary, the gaze of the invisible, in person, aims at man. The icon regards us-it concerns us, in that it allows the intention of the invisible to occur visibly [19].

The text as icon and host draws me to its mystery, and I glimpse that which envisages me. My own primordial essence, my being-in-the-world that has always already encompassed me is manifest. That is, my essence that preceded any formation of imposed meaning comes forth so that I might receive new meaning in the exchange of hospitality. I reimagine a cooperation, and in this happening, I encounter the icon, which can also be my fellow pilgrim.

Buber refers to this as spirit writing, "Spirit in its human manifestation is man's response to his You.... Man stands in language and speaks out of it—so it is with all words, all spirit. Spirit is not in the I but between I and You" (89). Buber understands experience as happening within the self rather than between self and another. He continues:

> It is not like the blood that circulates in you but like the air in which you breathe. Man lives in the spirit when he is able to respond to his You. He is able to do that when he enters into this relation with his whole being. It is solely by virtue of his power to relate that man is able to live in the spirit [89].

Contemporary pilgrimage fosters this relational dynamic; pilgrims discover communion in the Camino cauldron. In the encounter, the happening between pilgrims and their interaction with texts along the route, the sacred sometimes manifests and the life-world is invested with sacred meaning.

Conclusion

The ruins of the convent of San Anton provide another kind of cultural text, transcending both medieval and contemporary pilgrims. Its gothic architecture is just recognizable, though the roof is completely vacant, and the sky appears above the still standing walls. Glass windows have long

View from inside the ruined church at San Anton.

Another view from inside the ruined church at San Anton.

View of the ruin of San Anton as the pilgrim approaches from the east.

gone, but they too open to the trees. All of the recognizable iconography and religious symbols no longer appear. Yet, every time I visit this place I am haunted, I feel something deeply spiritual, religious. The barren and rustic walls seem to sing, interacting with the sky. In this place the mirror play of Heidegger's fourfold presences (173). On my last Camino I spent the night in the ruin and responded reflexively and intertextually, writing a poem. This poem represents one way of approaching this pilgrimage in our own age. The poem brings all of the constituents of the Camino together from across time and gives them voice. Medieval or contemporary, pilgrims share fellowship and respond to a call and engage cultural and religious texts in a reciprocal and cooperative hermeneutic.

Ruined Church

Shaped stone sentinels
in conversation with the ancient ones.
Those grand petriarches looming in the distance,
from whose very body these walls have been drawn.
Wind, rain, fire, and ice carved pinnacle and gnarled slope,
selected boulder, calved cliff face,
dashed pieces falling to the valley below.
There in the sheltered place
we gathered up fragments,
quarried other precious stones
and shaped them to conform to our imagination.
Yet, they remain kin to the ancient ones,
bearing the outward form of an alien race
and becoming ambassadors.
As the etchings fade
there appears a wisdom,
rooted in the elemental form,
a petroglyph fashioned again by weather,
the play of atmosphere and earth.
The truth, beauty, goodness you seek
unfolds in the play,
the sharing of our essential being,
a continuous conversation.

Notes

1. Lewis writes concerning the Medieval Model, "every particular fact and story" held sway as it turned the mind of the Medieval person back to the Model as a whole. He differentiates the Medieval "genius" from the "modern successor" in that the modern has no handle on the significance of reality as a whole, "or even a reality such that the very question whether it has a meaning is itself a meaningless question. It is for him, by his own sensibility, to discover a meaning, or, out of his own subjectivity, to give a meaning…But the Model universe of our ancestors had a built-in significance" (204). This Medieval Model is the image which

has been discarded in modernity. Those who walked the Camino from its beginning until the Modern age inherited this "image." Currently that image has been discarded.

2. There are several variations of this new age belief. Shirley MacLaine outlines one such belief in her book, *The Camino: A Journey of the Spirit*. She writes that the Camino "lies directly under the Milky Way and follows ley lines that reflect the energy from the star systems above it" (4).

3. John Brierley's *A Pilgrim's Guide to the Camino de Santiago: Camino Francés* lists 33 stages. Anna Dintaman and David Landis list 31 stages in their guidebook, *A Village to Village Guide to Hiking the Camino de Santiago: Camino Francés: St Jean-Santiago*.

4. Carl Jung explores this symbolism writing, "In the age-old image of the ouroboros lies the thought of devouring oneself and turning oneself into a circulatory process." He continues, "The ouroboros is a dramatic symbol for the integration and assimilation of the opposite, i.e., of the shadow. This 'feedback' process is at the same time a symbol of immortality, since it is said of the ouroboros that he slays himself and brings himself to life, fertilizes himself and gives birth to himself" (Adler 365). Erich Neumann devotes an entire chapter to the "Ouroboros." He describes several important symbolic meanings, including, "the creative impulse of the new beginning" (18), which is relevant to pilgrimage. Concerning the relevance of such ancient symbols for the contemporary world he writes, "all these symbols with which men have sought to grasp the beginning in mythological terms are as alive today as they ever were; they have their place not only in art and religion, but in the living processes of the individual psyche, in dreams and in fantasies" (11).

5. The New Testament translates the Greek term *parepidémos* as stranger indicating the sojourner as being beyond their home. The other as alterity is a stranger in that their being is grounded in another place. Pilgrims are strangers one to another in that they sojourn beyond their home and symbolically transcend themselves as they step beyond the familiarity of home (Arndt 625).

Works Cited

Adler, Gerhard, et al. *Collected Works of C.G. Jung*, vol. 14. Princeton University Press, 1963.

Arndt, William F, et al. *A Greek-English Lexicon of the New Testament and Other Early Christian Literature: A Translation and Adaptation of the Fourth Revised and Augmented Edition of the Walter Bauer's Griechisch-Dutsches EWorterbuch Zu den Schriften des Neuen Testaments Und der Ubrigen Urchristlichen Literatur*, 2nd ed., rev. and augmented/ed., University of Chicago Press, 1979.

The Bible. New Revised Standard Version, HarperCollins Publishers, 1989.

Brierley, John. *A Pilgrim's Guide to the Camino de Santiago: Camino Francés*. 16th ed., Camino Guides, 2019.

Buber, Martin. *I and Thou*. 2nd ed., Scribner's, 1958.

Coelho, Paulo. *The Pilgrimage*. Harperaudio, 2009.

Dintaman, Anna, and David Landis. *A Village to Village Guide to Hiking the Camino de Santiago: Camino Francés*. Village to Village Press, 2019.

Heidegger, Martin. "The Thing," *Poetry, Language, Thought*. Translated by Albert Hofstadter. New York: Perennial Library, 1971.

Jacobus: Codex Calixtinus de la Catedral de Santiago de Compostela.

Kerkeling, Hape. *I'm Off Then: Losing and Finding Myself on the Camino de Santiago*. Free Press, 2014.

Lévinas Emmanuel. *Totality and Infinity: An Essay on Exteriority*. Translated by Alphonso Lingis, Duquesne University Press, 1969.

Lewis, C.S. *The Discarded Image: An Introduction to Medieval and Renaissance Literature*. Cambridge University Press, 2012.

MacLaine, Shirley. *The Camino: A Journey of the Spirit*. Pocket Books, 2000.

Marion, Jean-Luc. *In Excess: Studies of Saturated Phenomena*. Translated by Robyn Horner and Vincent Berraud. Fordham University Press, 2004.

Marion, Jean-Luc, Thomas A. Carlson, and David Tracy. *God Without Being: Hors-Texte,* 2nd ed., University of Chicago Press, 2012. 0-ebookcentral proquestom.read.cnu.edu/lib/cnu/detail.action?docID=951112.

Merleau-Ponty, Maurice, and John F. Bannan. "What Is Phenomenology?" *Crosscurrents*, vol. 6, no. 1, 1956, pp. 59–70.

Merleau-Ponty, Maurice, and Séglard Dominique. *Nature: Course Notes from the Collège de France.* Northwestern University Press, 2003.

Neumann, Erich. *The Origins and History of Consciousness.* Princeton University Press, 1970.

Ong, Walter J. *Orality and Literacy: The Technologizing of the Word.* Routledge, 1991.

Otto, Rudolf. *The Idea of the Holy: An Inquiry Into the Non-Rational Factor in the Idea of the Divine and Its Relation to the Rational.* Oxford University Press, 1966.

Redick, Kip. "Spiritual Rambling: Long Distance Wilderness Sojourning as Meaning-Making." *Journal of Ritual Studies.* University of Pittsburg, vol. 30, no. 2, 2016.

Ricœur, Paul. *The Symbolism of Evil.* Beacon Press, 1967.

Turner, Edith L.B. *Communitas: The Anthropology of Collective Joy.* 1st ed., Palgrave Macmillan, 2012.

Turner, Victor W. *The Ritual Process: Structure and Anti-Structure.* Cornell University Press, 1977.

Turner, Victor W, and Edith L. B Turner. *Image and Pilgrimage in Christian Culture: Anthropological Perspectives.* Columbia University Press, 1978.

Van der Leeuw, G. *Sacred and Profane Beauty: The Holy in Art.* Oxford University Press, 2006.

The Way. Directed by Emilio Estevez, 2010.

Women Walking

*Purpose and the Poetics of Life Along
the Camino de Santiago*

Nicol Nixon Auguste

For my Camino sisters, Rencia, Susanne, and Anne-Mari

Everything that happens to you is a form of instruction if
you pay attention.
—Prayer scroll, Parroquia de la Immaculada
Concepción. Hontanas, Spain[1]

Wicking *what*? I'm not a hiker. Prior to encountering the 800-kilometer (500-mile) Camino de Santiago's French Route stretching from St.-Jean-Pied-de-Port, France, to Santiago de Compostela, Spain, I knew very little about hiking or navigating regions reaching elevations of 1530 meters (over 5,000 feet or almost a mile high). I didn't even own any essential gear: hiking boots/shoes, trekking poles, a backpack, a proper hat. My Camino began as my summer university sabbatical, one that proposed to collect women's narratives along the Way of St. James. Over forty days I spent listening to and sharing stories with other *peregrinas*[2] and women working at various places along the Camino I learned many meaningful lessons about hiking and life. These teachings fostered personal growth in many new ways that brought both pleasure and pain—blisters and shin splints are rites of passage on the Camino! The daily physical act of hiking, mental act of listening, and spiritual act of reflecting produced a unique discourse: the female Camino. This significant woman-storied Camino is one I aim to tell. My research includes over one-hundred women I encountered during my Camino—hikers from all walks of life, languages, and cultures as well as women working in hotels, pharmacies, museums, and information centers. Not all the women's stories are presented here. My

178

reasoning regarding the stories selected for this piece is two-fold: either the story is representative of a collective of similar stories or the story is extremely unique in its experiential account. For example, I met pharmacists in almost every large town along the Camino, but the story I chose to tell for this piece is Ana's, an orthopedic pharmacist from Ponferrada, Spain, who produces her own YouTube channel. I chose her story because of her compassionate attitude toward pilgrims and because her knowledge in medicinal treatment of a plethora of injuries can greatly benefit the reader, especially those planning to hike the Camino. My greater goal for this piece is to offer the reader an authentic voice representing the women of the Way, relating how and why we choose to hike or live life on the Camino de Santiago.

Structurally, this essay begins with a description of my research methodology, comprised of gathered data, categorical classifications, and an interview process. In examining the data, I discuss three prominent reasons why women hike or work the Camino; these motives all center around relationship: communion with God, communion with self, and/or communion with others. I conclude with an explanation of the meaning I extrapolated from these observations and my placement as both participant-observer and *peregrina*.

Methodology: Organic Participant Observation

> Sing if you will,
> In my own tongue, Galician,
> ……………………………………
> Oh dark lovely girl… [Sing Out 27, 28]
> —Rosalía de Castro

Born in Santiago de Compostela, the end point of the most traditionally-hiked Camino,[3] the *Camino francés* [French Route]—poetess Maria Rosalía de Castro (more popularly adored as Rosalía) composed her poetry in Galician,[4] the language of her people. In her translation of *Galician Songs*, Erin Moure celebrates Rosalía de Castro's ability to bring voice to the everyday people of Galicia: "Rosalía's voice respects those she writes of and acknowledges their agency; de Castro does not just write 'about,' but alongside them, with them" (10). Writing "with them," she situates herself within her community, creating a space for women's discourse reflecting daily Galician life: nature, relationships, economy, labor, love, faith, sexual desire, birth, death.

Rooted within this spirit—one that celebrates women's discourse through "writing with"—I attempt to explore a rhetorical narrative I call the female Camino. Borrowing from Rosalía de Castro's self-situating act, I position myself as a participant-observer: I *hike with* in order to *write with* the women of the Camino. In this context, I become both *peregrina* and participant-observer. This kind of positioning allows me to enjoy both roles: researcher and researched. Here, I include myself within the Camino community. I can observe life on the Camino while also reflecting upon my interaction with God, self, and others along the Way.

My methodology is rooted in the framework of ethnographic researchers and authors Elizabeth Chiseri-Strater and Bonnie Stone Sunstein. Their several-decades collaborative work in ethnographic fieldwork stimulates my process of becoming part of the Camino culture as a participant-observer. Fieldworking is a trinity of rhetorical aims of research and writing, experiential observation of another culture, and self-analysis emerging from the study. In their text *FieldWorking: Reading and Writing Research*, they explain that while fieldwork prompts researchers to "observe, listen, interpret, and analyze the behaviors and language of those around them … [they can also] develop a greater understanding of the 'self'—their own habits, biases, assumptions—as they read, write, research, and reflect on their encounters with the 'other'" (vii). Standing on the shoulders of these women's superlative scholarship, I took to the Camino in order to understand the women of the Way as well as myself. My process diverged from the typical path of formal interviews and archival appointments mostly due to nature of the Camino, as discussed below; this departure resulted in my study becoming a reflection of the Camino itself: organic, authentic, and unpredictable. Yet, the data analysis remained true to my initial aim to tell the (sometimes surprising) stories and perspectives of the women I met while hiking the Camino.

I interacted with and interviewed over one-hundred women during my forty-day Camino. They encompassed two main groups: The women hiking the French Way and the women serving those hiking the Camino. The *peregrinas* included women from seventeen countries: Argentina, Canada, Denmark, England, Finland, Germany, Hong Kong, Ireland, Netherlands, New Zealand, Peru, Poland, South Africa, South Korea, Spain, Switzerland, and the United States of America. Their professions ranged from active or retired teachers and nurses to business owners of employment agencies or retail stores and corporate consultants. The 17–25 age group either just graduated from high school or college or were taking a break from the stresses of college, as many of them were pre-med or medical students. The women I engaged with working to serve pilgrims hailed from France, Spain, Italy, the Philippines, and Venezuela. Working women's roles included Catholic religious Sisters, pharmacists, orthopedic specialists, museum docents, information center employees, volunteers, and hotel and *bar*[5] workers and proprietors.

I intended for my interview process to occur organically. Because of the nature of the Camino, I decided the most respectful approach would be to avoid an intrusive journalistic ethos, as not to offend or vulture other women. We women like our space. My process began with light conversation, initiated with a question about the purpose(s) behind hiking the Way. Using a direct and honest approach about my intentions both as researcher and *peregrina* prompted women to more readily disclose their thoughts and feelings. Once they revealed their purpose, I could ask other questions or just listen—many women were quite willing to discuss their burdens, their joys, their lives with me. When translating, I used the SayHi app,[6] this technology helped tremendously with clarification when encountering the many varied languages women spoke along the Way. This kind of personal interaction served to confirm what Henriqueta (real name),[7] a volunteer from Portugal working at the Pilgrim's in St.-Jean-Pied-de-Port, France, said to me prior to starting the Camino: "In life, we don't speak what we feel. On the Way, we speak what we feel."

Findings: The Relationship Factor

The most prevalent common thread I found when asking women about The Way concerned relationship. Women desired or enjoyed a deep connection with God, self, or others. These three types of relationships categorize the sections below. Even though women spoke mostly about these three types of relationships, not all women fit cleanly into one of these groupings; in fact, many women cross categories, engaging with two or even all three areas. For example, although many religious Sisters (nuns from various Catholic orders) enjoy a personal relationship with God, their main goal is to serve others in the name of Jesus. For the sake of this readership, though, I will include them in the "Relationship with God" section because it is God that prompts their actions to serve others. Also, each section offers data concerning the percentages of women interviewed.

Relationship with God

I know not what I seek eternally
on earth, in air, and sky;
....
it dwells in all I touch and see (I Know, Wordpress.com)
—Rosalía de Castro

The Camino allows us to see the un-seeable.
—Fr. Manny, Pilgrim Mass, Feast of St. James,
25 July 2019. Pilgrim's Office Chapel.
Santiago de Compostela, Spain

The Way of St. James is a historically religious pilgrimage and is included in the top three Christian pilgrimages worldwide—the other two sites include Rome and Jerusalem. The earliest of pilgrims began walking at their front doors; they traversed rugged terrain, treacherous mountain passes, green rolling hills, and wide flowery fields in order to reach the Cathedral of Santiago de Compostela. Upon arrival, they paid homage to the relics of the martyred St. James the Great and earned a plenary indulgence. For Catholics, an indulgence can lessen time spent in Purgatory, the sphere of purification after death prior to entering Heaven. Because of this historical tradition, I expected to encounter a fairly large number of women walking the Way to gain a closer connection with God. This was not the case. In fact, only 11 percent of all women interviewed gave any kind of religious reasoning for hiking or working the Camino. Though a small percentage, these women showed deep devotion to God.

Of the women who hiked for religious reasons, I observed an interesting commonality: The majority of this *peregrina* group was comprised of millennials, mostly between the ages of twenty to thirty. They possess a very intimate view of their relationship with God—it is personal, relational. Arizona, a twenty-one-year-old college graduate (technically a post-millennial), was one of the youngest women hiking the Camino. Having traveled outside of the United States for three years and bilingual in Spanish and English, she felt she was ready to hike the Camino by herself. Standing at 5'2" her backpack engulfed her small, but sturdy frame. Her quiet demeanor somehow glowed with maturity; her personality most likely stemmed from her traveling experiences and her upbringing. Arizona spoke openly about her Camino as a pilgrimage. She had been thinking about hiking the Way for a couple of years. Then, to her surprise, her final college course requirement—a course focusing on travel—included the Camino de Santiago on the list of places where students could travel for credit. She said she felt this course listing option served as a sign from God; He was encouraging her to hike the Camino. More deeply, she desired to hear from God during her pilgrimage. She added, "The Camino is my offering to God." Because she owned few possessions and little money, she gave God the one thing she held precious: time. This time on the Camino served as her love offering to God.

Arizona and I found each other on the Way several days in a row; she became one of my Camino daughters. Let me pause and make an important point about the rhythm of the Way: The Camino is a road where people walk and rest, walk and rest. Save for leaving early each morning, time is not to be rushed on the Camino—it is cherished, respected, loved. Everyone eventually finds her own tempo and this individual pace is part of the beauty of the Camino. This unique rhythm allows *peregrinas* to see each other for a while, walk ahead, rest behind. I might see someone I had not seen in days while walking by an *albergue*[8] bar or resting in the forest on a large rock. Interestingly, there were times I thought I would see someone the next day, but never saw that person again.

Monica was another young millennial walking alone. After sharing time with her, I realized she did not believe that she was walking alone, instead she believed that God was always with her. An extremely joyful 23-year-old practicing Catholic from South Korea, Monica loves life and God. From her personality, it would seem Monica's Camino intended to be a joyful jaunt to absorb all the Camino offers: natural setting, food, travel. But her reasoning was much more thoughtful, touching upon a core element of the human experience: trust. She walked the Camino not only because she is Catholic, but also because her Camino was a two-fold act of following God and learning to trust herself. Monica understood that trusting God first was essential; this divine confidence initiated the process of trusting herself and her own decision-making. She explained that her life is grounded within her religious faith. I met her at the gate of the Roman route outside of Sahagún and again at the *Santuario de la Virgen Peregrina*,[9] now a modern museum of art where pilgrims with the correct documentation can obtain a halfway certificate. Pilgrims need both their official passports from their country of origin and their pilgrim passports credentials. The *Credencial del peregrino*, also known as the Pilgrim's Passport, is a small book that must be stamped at least once each day from the starting point in St.-Jean-Pied-de-Port, France, and two times a day from Sarria, Spain, to earn the Compostela. The Compostela is an official certificate of completion obtained from the Pilgrim's, near the Cathedral of St. James. Stamps come from a variety of places: municipalities, *albergues*, bars, churches, even food trucks!

"I'm going hairy!" Reda cheerily laughed. A 68-year-old South African pharmacy owner, Reda was the first woman I interviewed before my Camino even began (or, maybe this was the beginning of my Camino). By "going hairy," Reda meant that she was traveling alone on the Camino, without her husband; therefore, there is no need to shave. I met Reda at a bus station café in Pamplona, headed for the Camino de Santiago starting point in France. That morning, we sat at a small table talking about the Camino. I told her about my project; she told me what to expect: "Every day, don't expect anything." She believes in the Camino and in God. She explained her belief in God strengthens the Camino. Three years prior, Reda survived a brain aneurism. Her doctor told her to start walking. She did—and now she is hiking her second Camino. She understands one outcome of the aneurism was God prompting her to view life totally differently: life is not about work. Before she endured the aneurism, Reda dared not leave work for any reason. Now, if she leaves for several weeks, it is okay. Her business will be there when she returns. Her Camino is about strengthening her relationship with God and Camino—they create a helix where she can live life freely, both connecting and disconnecting with others.

Religious sisters served as the largest portion of women felt motivated by God to work on the Camino. While in Carrión de los Condes, I attended a special pilgrim's Mass at Santa Maria Church. A pilgrim's Mass is usually offered every evening at a local Catholic church. A blessing is given to the pilgrims at the end of Mass. Sometimes, pilgrims are asked to approach the alter or a side chapel for a blessing from the priest or Sisters. At some churches, special gifts are given to pilgrims to help them keep the faith during their Caminos. At this Mass, I met two sisters from the Convent of Saint Clare: Sr. Marie and Sr. Mary. During the Mass, pilgrims were asked to approach the alter for a blessing. Sr. Marie translated the priest's blessing into English. Then, several of the nuns sang and presented each pilgrim with a small, almost weightless, colorful paper star to carry in our back-packs. They explained these stars serve as a reminder God created light, a source that has always been with us. And just as the stars are with us as we travel on the Way, God is also with us. After the Mass, I had the opportunity to share time with Sr. Marie. She confirmed my other findings about the small number of believers on the Camino as well as in Spain. She said only a minor portion of pilgrims staying at the *albergue* that her order manages believe in any kind of deity. Also, in her line of work—ministry— the number of women has greatly declined with approximately forty-seven Sisters remaining. She said this decrease is due to a couple of different factors: women now have options to work in professions unavailable to them in previous generations and Spain is now mostly atheist—a relationship with God is not at the forefront of people's lives.

Relationship with Self

> If I am not my body, if I am not my mind, if I am not my job, who am I?
>
> —Abby, *peregrina* from South Africa

Thirty-five percent of women walking and working engaged with the Camino in order to relate to the self. *Peregrinas* view a sense of self in various ways: they want to test themselves mentally or physically; they need time to consider their futures; or, they hike to celebrate a personal life event. Many of the *peregrinas* approached the Camino as a mental or physical challenge; these trials provided women training for a future hike, liberation from self-doubt, or a break from everyday life. While Amber's goals were extremely intentional—she used the Camino as preparation to face the Appalachian Trail in the United States—Lynda, a 50-year-old self-proclaimed non-hiker, desired the mental and physical challenge the Camino offers. Lynda's story (like several others in this category) include overcoming feelings of self-doubt—she wanted to see if she could meet the Camino challenge. For example, climbing mountainous inclines gave her a profound sense of accomplishment. Another area of doubt, traveling alone, produced a fair amount of anxiety for Lynda; she was concerned she would get lost, missing the yellow arrows marked along the Way. The morning I interviewed her, she chose to confront this doubt: upon starting her 25-kilometer day, she noticed two South Koreans heading in what she thought was the wrong direction. She yelled to them, telling them to turn back. Once they reached her, they thanked her, telling her, "God sent you to be our Way." Fortunately, she was correct when they all soon came upon a yellow arrow. This story depicts the beauty of the Camino: Lynda gained her confidence—she could correctly navigate the Camino after all and helped others while doing so. Straying from the path can be detrimental and even deadly on the Camino. I met Lynda on a 100-degree (38 Celsius) day under one of the few shade trees lightly peppered along the center stretch of the Camino, one that offers beautiful fields and landscape, but very little cover and no place for miles to stop for water. Like at the peak of the Pyrenees mountains, the body is exposed to the elements, meeting waves of heat and cold, pinching rain, and eye-watering wind. Some sections of the Camino can be desolate; depending on the conditions, the route, and time of day and year, a *peregrina* can walk for hours and not see another soul. The Camino reveals both inner and outer strength and weakness. The Way teaches that listening to the body and the will differ: too much will can, at times, deplete and injure the body. Therefore, pace on the Camino is extremely important in surviving the sometimes-harsh conditions.

Abby, the retired South African high school teacher quoted above, represents many women I met who desired a change in life. These women used the Camino to reexamine their lives and determine who they desired to become. Hiking the Camino for the first time, Abby said she repeatedly heard about the Camino from other women; she soon realized these female voices served as signs: she needed to hike the Camino. She prepared herself by reading several books on the subject, including Shirley MacLaine's *The*

Camino: A Journey of the Spirit. Her Camino represented the nascent phase of her retirement. She decided to open a business that empowers women. She wants women to know life need not be all about work—there is more to life. I saw Abby the day I arrived in Santiago. She was still thinking. Still hiking. She planned to take the extra route to Finisterre.

Many women used the Camino as an instrument of healing and enlightenment: they moved away from taxing pasts into futures where they grew in relationship within themselves. I met Chicago the first day of my Camino as I headed out to climb the peak of the Pyrenees mountains. She was a machine, like many other hikers passing me along the Way. Last year brought Chicago several challenges: a hike on the Inca Trail to Machu Picchu, a broken relationship, and a stressful job experience requiring an unhealthy number of hours on the clock. Chicago needed change. She decided to leave her job, hike the Camino, and then move to Vietnam to teach. Before leaving home for the Camino, she experienced a very emotional moment—one of confirmation. Looking through her jewelry box, she found a pair of shell earrings she had owned since she was a little child. Her parents could not recall who gave them to her. Telling me this story, her eyes started to well-up; she took these tiny treasures as a sign she should walk the Way (other than the yellow arrow, the scallop shell is an important Camino symbol). After the first day, I would not see Chicago again—that is, until 40 days later upon entering the hotel in Santiago; we were staying at the same seminary/hotel after finishing the Camino! She looked rested and ready to start her new life in Vietnam.

And then there's Disney. When I met Disney, I knew she had a story to tell, but she seemed a bit closed off—and for good reason. Sometimes it just takes the right question. "Are you carrying any rocks?," I asked the young teacher while she waited to meet Natalia, her college roommate she had not seen in at least two years. A Camino tradition includes carrying small stones from either a pilgrim's place of origin or picking them up while walking along the Way. These stones represent life's burdens, ultimately left behind on the Camino. Many people select carefully; for example, Woodstock—a *peregrina* who developed large blisters and a bacterial infection—chose several, writing inscriptions on each to leave on the Camino. Sites ranging from kilometer markers and the Iron Cross to small piles of stones and grave markers provide a plethora of poignant places for people to stop, reflect, pray, and leave their stones/burdens behind. Then comes the difficult part: planning a new life. As one priest at the Pilgrim's Office in Santiago de Compostela put it, "The real Camino begins after the hiking is done."

"Do you want to see some *rocks*? I'll show you some *rocks*!" Disney carefully looked around, and then at me again. Smiling, she slowly unzipped her backpack, exposing three extremely large, exquisite diamond engagement rings. Each ring represented a failed engagement. She intended to bury these glistening jewels along the Camino. Momentarily in shock, I stood amazed. Taking a breath, I congratulated her, sharing with her my own story of previous engagements that thankfully did not end in marriage. Once we parted ways, I thought I would never see her again. And yet, the Camino gives (this saying is normally intended for finding much needed essentials—trekking poles, knee tape, band aids, the last empty bed at an *albergue*): I met up with Disney the morning she buried her precious stones. A peaceful, unpopulated site, the only sounds surrounding us were our hiking boots scraping the ground and Disney's slight, soft sniffle. She said a few choice words, made her peace, and then walked away. The sound of her boots faded in the distance. Her form became less and less recognizable. As I watched Disney leave her burdens behind, I remembered my own moments of mourning and liberation so many years ago. Silently, I prayed for Disney—that her future would be filled with wisdom, discernment, and joy.

Speaking of joy, many women trek the Camino to celebrate personal accomplishments, everything from milestone birthdays to cancer remission. Willie was one such woman. This American bible study teacher had hiked the Camino six times; she hiked with family, friends, and alone. This time was different, not because she brought along her 13-year-old grandson—with whom she loved sharing this experience—but because she had a very specific goal: to spend her 70th birthday atop the Pyrenees mountains, 4,688 feet high. There is no other place she would have rather spent the start of her 70th year and planned her hike accordingly. After six Caminos, she shared with me much wisdom during our short time together. The most important advice I gleaned from Willie is the Camino is not a race: "You go at your own pace, just like in life. You have to make the Camino your own." Fortunately, I met Willie very early on during my Camino; I took her wisdom to heart. After about a week or two of trying to keep up with marathon runners from Los Angeles (USA) and athletic machines from Finland, Germany, and South Africa, I needed to find my own pace. My growing blisters, muscle aches, and shin splints screamed at me. One morning, I finally understood Willie's words: Upon observing several small mollusks slowly but surely traveling across the path below me, I realized I need not "keep up" with everyone else. I found my pace, my rhythm. And in their honor, I gained a nickname, one I fully embraced: *La Caracol Americana*.[10]

Women working the Camino do so for basic survival and educational experiences. Neelie, a hotel owner living in a small, beautiful village on the way to Cruz de Ferro (otherwise known as the Iron Cross, a welcome sign that Galicia is not too far ahead), informed me, "We depend on the pilgrims for our survival. They [pilgrims] can tell if the owners like them or not."

She spoke truth, as I encountered several owners and workers in the tourism industry who did not hide their disdain for pilgrims. Neelie's attention to detail demonstrated her love for her work and for pilgrims hiking to Santiago de Compostela. Her hotel provided private rooms with private bathrooms (a luxury on the Camino), an outdoor eatery, a piano for playing and singing, and even door handles and room keys carved in the shape of a pilgrim.

Another hotel entrepreneur, Sophia, worked as a translation instructor in the corporate world prior to entering the hospitality business. Originally from France, she had heard of the Camino many years ago; her growing interest in the Way prompted her to change professions. Now in her eighteenth year of serving as a hotel proprietor, she has determined three reasons people make the pilgrimage to Santiago: "The young ones want relationships; the older ones are true pilgrims; and, then there are those who love the gastronomy. I love them all." Sophia's greatest difficulties as an owner include the harsh winters and being a woman sustaining a business in a man's world. Because the season lasts from April until October, the winters in her region are very difficult to manage economically. One must store up for the winter. Also, "making a furrow amid all the men in the village is difficult, as their mindset is different about women than other places in the world." She suggested women are doing better overall, but there remains a lot of work to be done. Fortunately, her male neighbors are extremely supportive of her and her business.

Not one negative woman did I encounter at any tourist information center. These helpful, joyful women took pride in showing pilgrims how to navigate the trails and towns. Sari, a young woman working at a pilgrim information center in a very tiny village told me an inspiring story about the women in her town. When I asked her why she worked there, she launched into a story about an anonymous benefactor who created a grant of sorts for working women. Now, only women operate the tourist office, *albergues*, hostels, and restaurants. She explained this grant allows women in her community to make a life for themselves, helping them to thrive; otherwise, women would have very little opportunity, a common economic condition I repeatedly heard about while interviewing working women living in both France and Spain.

Relationship with Others

When we look at each other's feet, our suffering binds us.
—Finland, *peregrina*

Women share relationships and share stories. The largest category of all three classification, 54 percent of women interviewed said they primarily engaged with the Camino for the purposes of sharing relationship with others. On the Camino, these stories (and storied relationships) involve all aspects of life—celebrations, limitations, births, deaths, desires, regrets— as well as Camino-related topics regarding bodily aches and injuries: cuts, blisters, shin splints, wounds, muscle strains, sunburns, welts, ear aches, torn ligaments, stress fractures, broken bones—all of it. Suffering binds us, as Finland, a first-time Camino *peregrina*, suggests. I met her during one of my most arduous, yet victorious moments along the Way: a day involving a 35-kilometer hike, including a steep descent down jagged shale, loose pebbles, and river rock. Ireland accompanied her; the two could pass for biological sisters: light blonde hair, blue-eyes, fair skin, same height and body type. Our discussions revolved around purpose, language, colloquialisms, and goal-setting. They met the night before at an *albergue*; within a matter of hours, the two became what I call Camino sisters. A Camino sister is one who travels the Camino with another woman or women; they stick together through thick and thin, triumphs and injuries, never leaving each other's side. Natalia, Disney's college roommate, is a fine example of a Camino sister: she spent her time selflessly supporting a friend who needed to literally bury the past.

Like Finland and Ireland, Disney and Natalia, and so many others I met, Texas and New Zealand became Camino sisters along the Way. These two sisters reflected a mentor-mentee type relationship. Seventeen years sober, Texas knew herself well. A barely 20-year-old New Zealand was finding herself after a bitter break-up with her boyfriend. Every time I saw these two (four times total over forty days), they appeared joyful in their conversation and expression; even in their silence, it seemed, they bonded. During one of our encounters, a moment when five of us took a short break to catch our breaths, hydrate, and enjoy the little morning coolness we had left before the heat of the day would rise up to oppress us, Texas came to the realization, "we all are small parts of a bigger experience called the Camino." New Zealand smiled, soaking in her words. It was in this moment I realized there are more than just Camino sisters: The Camino creates mothers, daughters, aunties, and nieces. I saw these two sisters later, quickly moving through the busy streets of Logroño making their way back to the quiet Camino.

Another inspiring pair of women I met teach in Germany. Both Americans, Sheila teaches kindergarten and Amelia, also a blogger, teaches second grade. Although they originally planned to hike the entire 800-km French Way, they decided to start from Sarria, the shortest distance from which pilgrims can earn a Compostela. Sheila recently learned her cancer had returned for the second time. She would face treatment next month; for her, now was the time to hike the Camino. Her determination to finish showed both on her face and in her voice. After asking her Camino sister Amelia why she was hiking the Camino, she looked at Sheila, then back at me: "I'm along for the ride." Although she answered with a light tone, I knew she truly cared about Sheila—she sacrificed to make her friend's dream a reality.

While many women hike to support others' journeys—in some cases, ones that could be their only or final Camino—other women hike with groups or spouses as a means of celebrating relationship. On the way to Fromista, I met a spirited group of six women from Madrid (the seventh friend would be joining them later that day). They hike a short portion each year until they complete the entire Camino. Because many of them teach they hike during the summer. Next year, their fifth year, they will finish the final 111 kilometers from Sarria to Compostela de Santiago. Espie, one of the teachers, informed me this group has grown each year, from a couple of friends the first year to seven women this year. They share a common goal: to achieve the Camino and have fun doing it. They take the Camino slowly because they want to relish each other's company as well as savor the cuisine along the Way.

Couples from South Africa, Germany, the United States, and Portugal hiked to celebrate their marriages and families. Ironically, the South Africans and Germans both celebrated 38 years of marriage, their anniversary dates only days apart. Utah (a couple from the States) celebrated twenty-five years; and, the Portuguese couple could still be considered newlyweds. Hiking and sharing meals with these couples allowed me to observe how they interact as married people. I noticed several common threads in all four couples: they show equity in familial decision-making; they take time to celebrate their marriages; they value family; and, they actively worship and praise God. Some practices they shared included planning their upcoming months and years; vacationing together; celebrating marriage milestones with their children (as a family event); and, in some cases, working together. On the way to Castrojeriz, Utah shared with me her husband's decision to retire early to support her essential oils business; he now serves as one of her trainers. Utah's celebratory Camino was two-fold: she walked for her marriage and her health. Born with Limb Length Discrepancy,[11] Utah faced a painfully hard hiking path. In addition, she recently endured an agonizing hemorrhage episode; her uterus formed a protective outer layer, somewhat like a shell, sealing her body from an interior infection during a previous C-section. After a complete hysterectomy and recovery, she finally healed. Through this experience, she learned two lessons: prayer works and she needs to celebrate life because illness is unpredictable.

The couple from Portugal, tour guides by trade, had planned the

Camino to celebrate their new marriage. What they did not anticipate was the third person who would be accompanying them along the Way. Three days prior to leaving for the Camino, they discovered they were pregnant! While they have two daughters from Gabriel's (the husband) previous marriage, the 42-year-old Sarah was ecstatic to be carrying their first baby together. They decided to take the Camino slowly, enjoying the trail between the three of them. Sarah believes in signs; she thinks signs are easily seen and heard for those who look and listen. Also, she lives by a popular Portuguese adage told to people of busier cultures like mine: *You have watches, we have time.* This moment prompted me to consider my own choices: do I live by my watch (in my case, a Fitbit) or do I enjoy the time I have on Earth?

By and large, women working for the purposes of connecting with other people truly enjoy their work. Women who had worked in other fields shared with me that, once they had joined the tourism industry, their quality of life improved. Reece, a young woman working in guest services in a small settlement had previously worked as a hair stylist and a restaurant server. She is much happier in the hospitality business; she can meet new people and learn new languages. She eventually wants to open her own hotel or *albergue* in a larger city with her new husband. Keelie, a woman who both cleans and serves meals at a different hotel, has worked in tourism for about seven months. She finds the tourism industry much more exciting than other jobs she has worked. Like Reece, she enjoys meeting people from all over the world; in doing so, she can better understand other cultures and learn their beliefs and customs. Another worker, Landa, enjoys her work tremendously—meeting so many people, she learned, "Whether good or bad, every person leaves you marked in some way. These marks contribute to a greater memory, a greater story."

The several docents I met along the Way enjoyed the pilgrims' excitement and interest in the museums and sites where they worked. Several mentioned how much these captive audiences [pilgrims] made their positions more meaningful. In Atapuerca, a site that has unearthed some of the oldest human remains in Europe, I met Marina (real name), who attends college at the University of Burgos and works at a natural history museum in the quaint outpost. She understands the local history to be extremely important to the globalized fields of art, history, and archaeology. She carved out this position for herself as the site's docent. This position provides her with the necessary experience both in content knowledge and practical skills dealing with the public she will need after graduation. Apparent from the interview, Marina's passion exists in teaching others the importance of history and art and why people should study both.

Ana (real name) works as an orthopedic pharmacist in Ponferrada.

She secured a job in the pharmacy when she was much younger. Over the years, she grew to love assisting and caring for pilgrims. So much so, she decided to return to school for orthopedics. In collaboration with local physicians, she helps heal hurting pilgrims. This position has brought her great joy—and brings relief to pilgrims in pain. She was the only pharmacist I met who was familiar with shin splints—she said the reason why is that she listens and learns from the pilgrims. Working in the profession of orthopedics for twenty-six years, she even has her own YouTube channel.[12]

The Participant-Observer Pinnacle

> Who you are matters more than what you do. You need to
> create a space for yourself.
> —America, *peregrina*

I imagined the climax of my Camino sabbatical experience would include arriving at Santiago de Compostela, and standing at the tomb of Rosalía de Castro, reflecting on her identity as a voice of the Galician people—just as I have attempted to be a voice for women hiking and serving along the Way. I was mistaken. The pinnacle of my participant-observer experience occurred one afternoon upon reaching Triacastela, a congratulatory point for many pilgrims because the region both welcomes pilgrims into Galicia, the birthplace of St. James's legend, and ushers them over the Camino's final mountain pass. This afternoon, I observed a conversation I will not soon forget between three sets of mothers and daughters: Argentina, Denmark, and America. For the sake of clear storytelling, the daughters will be referred to as Jr. For example, Argentina is the mother; Argentina Jr., is the daughter.

These three mother-daughter groups had met early in the Camino and had been traveling together for a few weeks by the time of our encounter. Argentina and America booked *albergues* together to share time and cost. When this afternoon session occurred, I had already briefly met two of the three groups: Argentina and Denmark. I met Argentina Jr. at a church in León where I stopped in for a credential stamp. Argentina (her mother) was born in Argentina; her children were born in America. She teaches Spanish and takes her children to a Spanish-speaking country every year so they can practice their mother's first language. Argentina Jr. attends an ivy league college near Boston, majoring in neuroscience. Her mother explained that Jr. "looks" Argentinian. Her other children do not have the flowing dark hair and glowing olive-toned skin. Jr. fully embraces her ancestral culture and language more so than her lighter-skinned siblings. I saw Denmark and her daughter for the first time at a hotel during a quick breakfast but could not interview them due to time constraints. Denmark Jr. is a carbon copy of her striking Nordic mother: pure blonde, thin, healthy. I had yet to meet America and her daughter. They are natural beauties: earthy, dirty blonde, fit, tattooed.

Again, it was a single request that opened the conversation: "Tell me about your tattoos." 28-year-old America Jr. immediately teared up, looking to her mother for support. And then the conversation began. They both sported tree tattoos representing concepts of life, death, and the importance of seasons. Both mother and daughter referred to Hillsong lyrics from "Be Still" and "Seasons" to explain their ink. About two years ago, their son/brother died in a tragic hiking accident. They endured the winter of death and were attempting to grow and heal through this spring of life while staying rooted in God's Word (they are Christians). They spoke about their grief, the love they shared for him, and their healing process.

Their open honesty prompted Denmark Jr. to begin her story, one that commenced with a confession about her mental illness, a condition she believes stems back to a gymnastics injury that stole her identity during her teenage years. After her accident, she felt like she lost everything. With nothing left, she turned to alcohol, partying, and weekend public acts she would later regret. She admitted she felt worthless. I watched on as America, Denmark, and their daughters openly wept. Then, America prompted an interesting exchange: each mother and daughter in the group told Denmark Jr. the positive traits they noticed in her since meeting her. I silently observed as each mother and daughter praised this young wounded woman's strength, perseverance, friendship, mentorship, and joy. Denmark Jr.'s tears flowed freely down her face as she listened to what the others saw in her that she could not see. America Jr. told her she is worthy and valuable in the sight of God and them—she can be whole. The hearts of these women poured out that day as we sat in small metal chairs eating chips on the side of the *albergue* building, in the shade of the afternoon heat. Tears streamed down seven faces that day. Hearts opened. Trust earned. I sat in silence as each woman hugged the young Denmark. And then America turned to me, "thank you for creating this space." Still silent, my eyes smiled back, thankful that I had experienced this moment of care, love, and liberation.

A couple of days later, I saw the group of six at a small bar enjoying a snack and obtaining a stamp. Denmark Jr. wore a completely different countenance—she beamed. After a quick bite, Argentina, America and their daughters headed out to the Camino. I felt called to reach out to Denmark Jr. that morning. Every day while hiking the Camino, I wore a special Miraculous Mary Medal I was given at St. Mother Theresa's mission in Rome, Italy. I knew I was supposed to gift this medal to someone on the Camino, but the opportunity never presented itself until this moment. After requesting Denmark's permission (even though her daughter is well into her twenties I felt the need to ask out of respect), I removed the medal from my neck and gave it to her daughter, reminding her that healing is a reality. She thanked me and hugged me, holding me tight for some time. Somehow, I knew I would not see her again.

Dénouement

> stay on your path—Iglesias 1.

These four single-syllable words appear alone on the first page of Michael Matynka Iglesias's guidebook, *The Camino Francés: A Wise Pilgrim Guide to the Camino de Santiago from St.-Jean-Pied-de-Port to Santiago de Compostela*. Missed by many *peregrinas*—including myself until Rencia (real name), one of my South African Camino sisters, pointed them out— these four short words provide tremendous insight. I interpret this imperative as an instruction to listen: to my instincts, to my body, to others, to my surroundings, to God. As both *peregrina* and participant-observer, I found the Camino encourages relationship. My findings helped me understand my Camino experience and they have brought me closer to God, to myself, and to others.

Arizona, Monica, Reda, Sr. Marie, and Sr. Mary taught me to more closely listen to God through spending time alone on the Camino, much like a hermit under the stars—reminders God is always with me. The small fraction of young women who hiked for pilgrimage purposes demonstrated the intense nature of relationship between woman and God. They taught me the Camino is divine poetry: it has its own rhythm and rhyme. Its cadence comes from the cock-a-doodle-doo of morning roosters, the mooing of mountainside cows, the bark of bored dogs, and the buzzing of black flies swarming in circles inside the rooms. The Masses provided a home away from home. Attending Mass in France and Spain is like attending an opera: even if I cannot fully understand the language, I know the priest's message.

Amber, Lynda, Abby, Disney, and Chicago share a place of realization: they look at their lives in the mirror of reality and push forward into a new life. That is called courage. Their example helped me to realize a relationship with myself brings about depth and wisdom. Women like Willie who know where and how to celebrate her 70th birthday is a testament to female ambition. Situating myself within this context, I, too, will look toward the future, and plan accordingly. For now, my future is "writing with" these women, sharing their voices as I share my own. Self-examination is imperative when successfully writing the book of life.

Women need relationship. Finland and Ireland, Disney and Natalia, Texas and New Zealand, Sheila and Amelia, the South Africans, Germans, Portuguese, and the mothers-daughters all understand we must hold each during times of suffering and success. We carry each other's burdens. As a participant-observer, I carried stones for myself and others. And yet, I experienced some unexpected surprises—much like Reda said in the beginning: "Every day, don't expect anything." My social media community, friends, and family started reaching out to me. They posted praises and words of encouragement, especially during times of hardship and struggle. When I developed an aggressively painful case of shin splints, many women posted links and advice to aid me. Anne-Mari, a talented, skilled Finnish nurse I met on the Camino, and Jordyn, my massage therapist back in the States (both real names), knew the perfect stretches and remedies that would bring me healing in just two days. Providentially, two days later I met a young student barely walking, afflicted with shin splints; I now had obtained the knowledge he needed to heal. Other surprises included the women who contacted me to carry stones and pray for them. Many days I selected stones along the Way, hiking and praying until I felt led to lay them down. This kind of intercessory prayer helped to keep me focused on a Camino truth: the Camino is a selfless path—one requiring compassion, thoughtfulness, and an eye (and ear) toward other women's needs.

> I sing out, I sing, I sang,
> It wasn't very graceful,
> ....
> Giving it a whirl (I Sing 170)

—Rosalía de Castro

I might never be an accomplished hiker. Ever. But by the end of my Camino, I knew enough to supply advice to others about trekking poles, hiking down a mountain (a much more difficult task than ascending), shin splints, and blisters. As I stood at the foot of Rosalía de Castro's final resting place, located in the Pantheon of the Illustrious Galicians at the Convent of San Domingos de Bonaval in Santiago de Compostela, I recognized, like de Castro, I am common folk: I share this status with my Camino sisters. We sing—sometimes not so well—but we sing! Our stories create a common trail. As Utah's voice rings in my memory: "We create a country all its own called the Camino." Our stories, our languages, our cultures, our bodies— we are the female Camino.

Notes

1. Church of the Immaculate Conception Parish Pilgrims.

2. A female pilgrim. Following the common Spanish usage of this word on the Camino, I will use this word to refer to female pilgrims in this essay.

3. In addition to the French Way, other popular Caminos include the Portuguese Way, the Coastal Portuguese Way, the Primitive Way, the Northern Way, the English Way, Via de la Plata, Le Puy Way, and the Finisterre Way.

4. Gallego (Galician) is a language spoken in the Galician region of Northwestern Spain and is related to Portuguese and Castilian Spanish.

5. Bars are small eateries where pilgrims can purchase food and, on occasion, supplies such as band aids, ointment, and water. They can be connected to *albergues* or hostels.

6. The SayHi translation app allows both speaker and listener to immediately hear language translation. For example, if I set my languages for (USA) English and (Spain) Spanish, I can speak English into my phone and then instantly read and hear the Spanish translation.

7. Unless otherwise noted (as in Henriqueta's case), I use what I call Camino names for identification purposes. These names are meant to protect the identity of women due to the delicacy of their stories, their employment, or for other reasons. Also, while hiking the Camino, I found many people called each other by their place of origin—state, region, country—or another name in order to remember them.

8. An albergue is an overnight accommodation. They are very inexpensive, ranging from donations to 20 Euros a night, depending on the type (municipal, parochial, association, or private). Pilgrims share rooms, amenities, and meals.

9. Sanctuary of the Pilgrim Virgin.

10. The American Snail.

11. LLD is a condition when a person is born with one leg differing in length from the other.

12. See anafarmacéutica at www.YouTube.com/channel/UCCAmQU01VrRdDuuDKs OM9hw.

Works Cited

AnaFarmacéutica. YouTube. https://www.YouTube.com/channel/UCCAmQU01VrRdDuuDK sOM9hw.

Chiseri-Strater, Elizabeth, and Bonnie Stone Sunstein. *FieldWorking: Reading and Writing Research*. 3rd ed., Bedford/St. Martin's, 2007.

de Castro, Rosalía. "I Know Not What I Seek Eternally." Translated by Muriel Kittel. *The Ink Brain: Literary and Other Thoughts*. 2 February 2012.

_____. "I Sing Out, I Sing, I Sang." *Galician Songs*. Translated by Erin Moure. Small Stations Press, 2013.

_____. "Rosalía de Castro: Selected Poems." https://theinkbrain.wordpress.com/2012/02/02/ rosalia-de-castro-selected-poems/. Accessed 8 August. 2019.

_____. "Sing Out, Girl." *Galician Songs*. Translated by Erin Moure. Small Stations Press, 2013.

Iglesias, Michael Matynia. *The Camino Frances: A Wise Pilgrim Guide to Camino de Santiago from St.-Jean-Pied-de-Port to Santiago de Compostela*. 2nd ed., Wise Pilgrim Guides, 2019.

Designing Pilgrim Guide Training in a Secular Time

A Case Study from Switzerland

TERRY INGLESE

Where does the Camino de Santiago de Compostela actually start? According to the Swiss non-profit organization called "jacobsweg.ch," which focuses on providing pilgrims all the necessary and complete information in order to start and conduct a fulfilling pilgrimage experience, the Camino starts directly on the doorstep of our homes. It might start first with one envisioning undertaking a pilgrimage, as a personal development mission or as a beginning of a new life chapter. In order to promote more "guided and accompanied" pilgrimage experiences, the Centre for Pilgrimage of the Evangelical Reformed Church of Zürich, Switzerland, has been offering special training modules for pilgrim guides for over a decade. We suggest that these new guides are like "spiritual bricoleurs," which promote a space and ritual replica of the Camino, a phenomenon defined as "Caminoization."

This essay is divided into four parts: firstly, we first investigate the motivation of the 21st century pilgrim, and then introduce the concepts of the migration of the aura, the "Caminoization" and the replica, combined with a reflection about rituals. We then briefly describe the first Swiss Pilgrimage Day Event, which took place in 2017, connected to the training programs of the Evangelical Reformed Church of Zürich. Thirdly, the concept of "bricolage" (Lévi-Strauss) will be used to analyze and interpret twenty future pilgrim guides' projects, through a textual content analysis of these projects to review how the future guides structured their pilgrimage projects. A taxonomy of ten macro-categories, containing the 845 pilgrimage micro-activities extracted from twenty projects, will be visually summarized and commented. Finally, we will provide a couple of suggestions for future training, based on the analysis. Our thesis is that, pilgrim guide training can be interpreted as a "bricolage process," because as bricoleurs they create a pilgrimage experience based on their own spiritual background practices, replicating and reinterpreting rituals with new meanings.

Pilgrimage in Secularized, Postmodern Times

According to recent estimates of the United Nations World Tourism Organization (UNWTO) around "330 million tourists are visiting the most important world-renowned religious sites every year," even if the statistics and the economical worth of the combined religious, faith-based, spiritual tourism, pilgrimage "niche products" are difficult to know (Griffin and Raj ii). More specifically, Bowman and Sepp reported that over 300,000 people completed the Camino de Santiago in 2017, and the phenomenon increases steadily every year (75).

One reason for this trend is summarized by Filep and Laing who highlight that future directions in tourism, combined with positive psychology, focus on the so-called *eudemonic experience*, meaning the pursuit by tourists-pilgrims of feelings of well-being, combined with a search for deeper meaning in life (Filep and Laing 1). In addition to this trend, new mobility and social media offer a new way of understanding the nature of the postmodern pilgrimage phenomenon, where places are becoming *dynamic* and the praxis of spirituality is expressed as a "fluid search for the sacred" (Coleman and Bowman 3).

Recently, Damari and Mansfeld analyzed pilgrim identity from a postmodern perspective (2016), identifying four stages of the pilgrim identity: the first one is the traditional self-centered stage, where the pilgrim is separated from their environment. In the second stage, the modern pilgrim interacts with the environment through a one-directional purpose, such as a religious one. In the third stage, pilgrims allow the environment to influence their experience with new meanings. Finally, in the fourth and last stage, multiple layers of meanings concerning the pilgrim experience, identity and role, develop and evoke a hermeneutic, self-interpretation of the whole experience. The missing link, however, is the conceptualization of the pilgrimage experience as a holistic phenomenon. For the scholars, the postmodern pilgrimage "is created from a sort of socio-cultural and economic chaos … becoming an individual trip … their experiences stem from much closer encounters with fellow pilgrims and with host communities … pilgrimage tours often (are) inspired by more than one faith, or by no faith at all" (213–214). Damari and Mansfeld define the pilgrim as a *borderline pilgrim*, as "one that looks for experiences, which may either foster or weaken his or her faith. The pilgrimage aims at raising more questions than answers" (213). Therefore, postmodern pilgrims are confronted with more uncertainties and are looking for inclusive experiences, interacting with the local community, seeking to understand the sacred and profane representations of the inhabitants. As Margry puts it, "being a pilgrim is being in transition" (35).

Moreover, Farias et al. conducted an interesting and novel study, measuring six types of motivations for going on a pilgrimage (closeness to nature, community, religious growth, and search for life direction, sensation seeking and spiritual seeking) comparing atheists with Christians. Using a social psychological and quantitative-based approach, they found that there are no statistically significant differences between the two groups related to four of six motivations goals: spiritual seeking, the search for life direction, closeness to nature and sensation seeking. As expected, atheists scored lower on religious growth and community. To better grasp this tendency, Perez and Vallieres tried to understand the reasons why and how religious people become atheists, proposing an analytical model of "religion deconversion." Studies are currently being conducted in this direction, but there is still little research on postmodern pilgrims.

"Beyond the Sacred" through the phenomena of Caminoization. Recently, scholars like Coleman, Bowman and Sepp defined the phenomenon of "Caminoization" as the reproduction of rituals and activities experienced while doing the Camino de Santiago, but in other geographical places. From a historical point of view, Coleman and Bowman recall that long after the Middle Ages, interrupted by the Reformation, during the 20th century there was a sort of reanimation of the Camino (Frey 237). Particularly in the 1970s, its routes were reconnected thanks to inspired communities of pilgrims, who spiritually, esoterically and ideologically gave new meanings to the Camino de Santiago (Margry 30). The Camino's renaissance was sustained by the Cultural Route of the Council of Europe in 1987, and later, in 1993 by UNESCO. The Camino became the European magnet of a new awareness through the valorization of European transnational journeying (Bowman and Sepp 80). Chemin recapitulates this phenomenon as:

> The change in semantics, from a pilgrimage to a Camino (a word that simply means the Way or the Path), placed emphasis on the route rather than the shrine of St. James, and the journey element has since become the focus of the modern pilgrimage. The emphasis on the cultural significance of the routes exposed the rich historical roots of the pilgrimage to a wider public. This change is generally accepted as a move from religious pilgrimage to a more secular version of its pious medieval predecessor—a fairly reinvented ritual based on notions of the past that reflects the mentality of the presence [213].

In their definition of "Caminoization," Bowman and Sepp describe:

> the process whereby various aspects and assumptions of the contemporary Camino, particularly as encountered by non-traditional pilgrims, are transplanted and translated to other pilgrimage sites, routes and contexts ... a proliferation of material culture manifestations, such as pilgrim passports and Compostela-like certificates on completion of the pilgrimage, and "branded" way makers [75].

A new lens for understanding who postmodern pilgrims are, how they interact with the geographies of pilgrimage and what motivates them in undertaking pilgrimage experiences might be the "beyond the sacred" concept. In fact, Di Giovine and Choe reflect on how new geographies of religions, spirituality practices and pilgrimage activities are currently spreading beyond the officially defined and accepted "sacred spaces and sacred places." Through diversity of forms, the unifying features of all these experiences are expressed as "hyper-meaningful travels," promising "some sort of personal and social transformation ... it is travel out of the profane world into that of the sacred ... as an acceptable form of engagement with sacrality, which varies according to contexts" (Di Giovine and Choe 362). The concept of *sacred* is in contrast to the concept of *profane* and is also *variable*. In fact, sacredness is a matter of context. According to Van Gennep, "The presence of the sacred is variable. Sacredness as an attribute is not absolute; it is brought into play by the nature of particular situations" (12–13). However, "the variability of the sacred" is problematic for institutionalized religions, because it is difficult to control. Pilgrimage may operate "beyond" the officially sacred. DiGiovine and Choe explain three official processes of authorization: firstly, through tradition; secondly, through canonical text; and thirdly, through institutional norms (366). However, the decline of Western religions is fostering new searches for spiritual meaning, through novel forms of ritual and secular destinations. In this context, I consider the new role that pilgrim guides might have, promoting more "emic, popular, ritualistic performances and quality" types of pilgrimage experiences (Badone; Badone and Roseman), where places and rituals are newly reinterpreted and afresh replicated anew.

The migration of the Aura and its Replica. If postmodern pilgrims are defined by their mobile and fluid qualities, the question arises whether spaces and places also demonstrate these qualities. Interestingly, Latour and Lowe prompted the concept of the *aura*, going back to Benjamin, who theorized that through the mechanical reproduction of a piece of art, it would inevitably lose its *aura*, because of the never-ending potential of its reproduction through copies or replicas. However, Latour and Lowe in revisiting the etymology of the words "copy" and "copious" reflect that "we are moved so much by the unlimited fecundity of the original Ur-text

… in performance art, (and that therefore) the aura keeps migrating and might very well come back suddenly … or disappear altogether" (5–7). In our concrete case study, the aura of the Camino de Santiago is migrating in a new, fluid, fragmented form through the phenomena of "Caminoization." This consists of a sort of sacredness replica of the Camino de Santiago, "beyond" the French and Spanish geographical borders, in other places, such as Switzerland. These replicas also promote "rites … experiential possibilities, open spaces and open places of spiritual possibilities" (Coleman and Bowman 84; Theos 50). This renewed popularity around the Camino is enhanced through novel activities, beliefs and spiritual practices, as well as by the presence of the Cathedral of Santiago de Compostela.

Coleman and Bowman analyze the historical and spiritual impacts of cathedrals in the UK and around Europe, juxtaposing what they define as "sacred space" and "common ground," trying to understand how cathedrals embodied—and are still embodying today—and encouraged—and are still encouraging today—material and liturgical forms of "replication" (1). They explain that "cathedrals not only contain history, they still have the capacity to produce it. Cathedrals express identity as 'heritage' and therefore trace the politics of replication within and across cathedrals" (2). Moreover, Coleman and Bowman focus attention on how and why cathedral spaces and locations promote interest in investigating pilgrimage phenomena related to the presence of cathedrals. According to Cannon, in medieval times, cathedrals, such as the one of Salisbury, were considered institutions, as a city within the city, embodying multi-purpose functions such as religious, educational, legal, business and social services, "with some of the characteristics of the modern commercial mall, union hall, courthouse and amusement park, as an influx of both industry and prestige for urban inhabitants" (Bercea, Ekelund, Tollison 455). Likewise, for Barral I Altet medieval cathedrals promoted the intensification of pilgrimage practices, because pilgrims were traveling from one holy location to another, with the goal of reaching cathedral shrines. These buildings embedded also political goals of defending Christianity from inter-religious competition and invasions, functioning as colony spaces of territories of European Christendom (Coleman and Bowman 6).

Today, pilgrimage spaces as "sacred space" and as "common ground" embed what Barley (84) defines as the "adjacencies' qualities." "Adjacency" refers to concepts of "being close and near" (Coleman and Bowman 139). *Adjacencies* are represented by the fact that cathedrals offer to spiritual pilgrims a wide range of activities around a variety of temporal rhythms, ritual intensities and ideological expectations, a tolerated co-presence of vicarious religious forms, performed by an active minority on behalf of a less committed and knowledgeable majority. Davie describes this further:

the various *adjacent* relations made available in cathedrals involve more complex forms of ritual.... In effect, the tourist, passer-by, or undecided semi-believer may move in and out of the rhythms and spaces of conventional liturgy, even as they may cross from common ground into sacred space and vice versa—or invoke on realm while located in the other [14].

These "adjacencies" are the expressions of:

the tensions, ambiguities, and complexities that manifest around and within cathedrals, as multiply-framed and multiply-claimed spaces of behavioral fragmentation, adjacency and articulation, in equally complex relationships to the urban spaces around them. In any given day, a cathedral may play host to hundreds of unplanned and unpredictable visitors of many or no religions, before switching quite suddenly towards the drawing up of a tight liturgical frame required by a service, before accommodating an expected or unexpected pilgrimage group whose members may range from the devout to the deeply skeptical [Davie 15].

Replication implies reproduction, mimesis, appropriation, and cathedrals, as authoritative models of the sacred, are embodying a standard for other churches, providing "a feasible model, or emblem, for smaller constituents of religious practice … ways in which cathedrals are each other materially and ritually in processes of mutual borrowing or competition … become subject to a redistributive economy of sacred objects that diffuses sanctity across other religious spaces" (Coleman and Bowman 17–18). If cathedrals promote this standard, also the Cathedral of Santiago de Compostela can do it for other churches spread all over Europe. Coleman and Bowman write "as in all forms of replication, there are questions as to whether the copy can ever reproduce fully the power and authenticity of the original, but also whether the existence of such copies also reinforces the legitimacy of such an originating source" (18). The scholars reflect on the phenomenon of heritagization:

where sacralized history is turned into more secular, commodifiable forms.... As we shall see, examining the varied practices within and across cathedral spaces causes us to expand our understanding of these important contexts where religion still takes place, and where orthodoxy and tradition may persist precisely because of their ability to adapt to new regimes of value [18].

For Bowman and Sepp, the tendency of replicating the Camino experience, particularly where pilgrimage traditions were ruptured, has aided the phenomenon of Caminoization, which "has been instrumental in the creation and re-creation of pilgrim paths, whether linking a number of significant sites or focused on a particular destination. While walking with intent and meta-movement have emerged as central to Caminoization, it has also had an impact on the sites encountered on the ways, and particularly those at the start and end points" (83). Moreover, mobility is part of the European heritage and replication appears to be a consistent feature of Christianity. The new pilgrims, through a form of heritagization of religion, feel that they are walking in other people's footsteps, where the places and spaces are open to new spiritual possibilities, enabling to feel at home and in touch with the past (Theos 50). For Eriksen, "anything can become heritage, as long as somebody declares him or herself its heir" (149). The Camino enables people to feel heirs to it, through the taking part of a long tradition of spiritual travelers (Bowman and Sepp 80).

Case Study: *The Camino de Santiago in Switzerland Through the 2017 Swiss Pilgrimage Day Event*

The "Caminoization" phenomenon is fast spreading in several countries in Europe, including the United Kingdom, Denmark, Sweden, Norway and Switzerland. One Swiss example took place in 2017 when, for the first time in the history of Swiss pilgrimage, the Dachverband Jakobsweg Schweiz, the Swiss umbrella organization for eleven Swiss Jakobsweg Associations, organized a single-day pilgrimage event (the Swiss Pilgrimage Day), under the title *Following the Scallop—In One Day Across Switzerland through the St. James Swiss Caminos.*

On this one Saturday, the 27 of May 2017, both experienced and inexperienced "pilgrims" walked forty-six routes throughout Switzerland. More than six hundred people took part in this unique event. We, the author of this essay, together with the organization team, organized the marketing and the media coverage of the event. This included creating a booklet-flyer that highlighted the forty-six trails available for walking and contact information for the "pilgrim guides." From Basel to Geneva, from Rapperswil to Einsiedeln, or from St. Gallen to Ticino, pilgrims, together with forty-six selected pilgrim guides, walked in a common spirit. These guides "structured" the walk, but also the spiritual experience, with moments of reflection, walking silently, singing songs, praying, reading texts, engaging in conversations and other types of group activities. More than half of them (25) were trained pilgrim guides. The other half were experienced wanderers and hikers, who "gained" a pilgrim guide preparation through a half-day training course, organized by the Dachverband Jakobsweg Schweiz and by an association called jakobsweg.ch (n.d.), in collaboration with the Center for Pilgrimage of the Evangelical Reformed Church of Zürich.

The Evangelical Reformed Church of Zürich and Pilgrim Guide Training. As previously mentioned, more than half of the pilgrim guides (25 out of

46) were trained as such at the Pilgerzentrum (Center for Pilgrimage) of the Evangelical Reformed Church, based in Zürich. The Evangelical Reformed Church has been offering a training course consisting of three-modules to be completed within a one-year timeframe, in order to become a pilgrim guide. During the last decade, 140 new pilgrim guides received their certificate. Approximately half of them (70) are currently organizing different types of pilgrimage experiences in Switzerland. These may be a single day or multiple days or weeks in length and occur in European countries, like Germany, Austria, Lichtenstein, Denmark, Spain and even in in Israel and Palestine.

Because of the well-known Swiss tradition of *wanderung* [walking, hiking], a pilgrimage version of hiking is a natural shift. Swiss people love hiking, and adapting this passion into a spiritual version is a great fit to become a certified pilgrim guide. In 2018, twenty future pilgrim guides, coming from the German-speaking areas of Switzerland, Germany and Liechtenstein, were trained. This special training, which is offered every two years, is called *Ausbildung zur Pilgerbegleiterin/zum Pilgerbegleiter EJW, Europäische JakobsWege*. The initiative of starting such trainings has been warmly welcomed by countries like Germany, Switzerland and France.

Elsewhere we described in detail the course, which involved three modules, covering a theoretical and theological background of what it means to be a pilgrim, and what the characteristics of a European St. James pilgrimage are, together with the concept of spirituality (Inglese 338). Practical aspects were also taught. The participants were divided into groups of four, and had to apply the learnt aspects to a short pilgrimage experience of several kilometers. The groups then compared and contrasted their own work with the others and gave constructive feedback. In the meantime, each participant selected and designed their own pilgrimage project, doing on-site reconnaissance, designing a series of so-called inputs, as spiritual activities, staying at least one night in a monastery or in a pilgrim hostel, creating a flyer with a budget, writing up the project, and presenting it during the last module. In the next section, we will explain the concept of "bricolage," as the construct used to analyze the twenty future pilgrim guides' projects and their role as *spiritual bricoleurs*.

Bricolage—A concept for defining future pilgrim guides. In his pivotal work *The Savage Mind*, the French anthropologist Lévi-Strauss used the term *bricolage* to describe the characteristic patterns of mythological thought, as opposed to engineers' thinking. Mythical thought attempts to re-use available materials to solve new problems. He explains the mythological thought process of the bricoleur:

> unlike the engineer, he does not subordinate each of them to the availability of raw materials and tools conceived and procured for the purpose of the project…. The bricoleur always puts something of himself into it … by using the

remains and debris of events ... builds up structures by fitting together events, or rather the remains of events... [Lévi-Strauss 11–15].

In societies adopting mythical rationalities, the meaning making processes mirror a bricolage process, as more flexible, fluid and open-ended (Rogers 3). A meaning-making bricoleur performs diverse tasks, by combining the imagination with whatever knowledge tools she/he has in the repertoire: rituals, social practices, observations, past experiences, and whatever artifacts she/he has in a given context: discourses, institutions, stories, texts, and so on. In order to understand the process of bricolage, we take into account how bricolage has been interpreted from the discipline of education. In fact, creativity, flexibility and empowerment are typical values of teachers. More specifically, in the educational context, Campbell defines teachers as pedagogical bricoleurs, because of their agency, which promotes a culture of creative professionalism. She explores how knowledge is constructed and shared by teachers, as agents of transformative learning, and uses the bricolage concept as a productive model for their professional behavior, as agents of transformative learning and for promoting in learners a social and personal change. The bricoleur and the engineer, each has a different form of agency. The bricoleur's attributes are: "subjective, aesthetic, disorderly, playful, experiential, individualistic, free, moral, perceptive and innovative." The engineer's attributes are: "objective, scientific, systematic, precise, methodological, authoritarian, controlled, amoral, concept-led and procedural" (Campbell 34). She explains that "the bricoleur uses subjective and aesthetic formations of knowledge ... searches for practical methods to solve problems making use of what is available or ready to hand, developing strategies, adapting materials and creatively interpreting a possible outcome from the heterogeneous objects of which his treasury is composed" (33). The difference lays in the quality of resources accessed, the level of complexity and abstraction. For both, the creation of a solution is the main goal.

Research Method

As mentioned, in 2018 twenty future pilgrim guides (six men and fourteen women, with an average age of fifty), coming from the German-speaking areas of Switzerland, Germany and Liechtenstein, were trained as pilgrim guides. We consider Levi-Strauss' concept of bricolage to define future pilgrim guides as *spiritual bricoleurs*.

Collection of data. The training required attendance and active participation in three modules, as well as the completion of several prescriptive elements. For the individual project, each future pilgrim guide needed to choose a pilgrim-path in Switzerland, and adapt it for a two to four day pilgrimage experience, with at least a one-night stay in a monastery or pilgrim hostel. The project template required documentation of understanding of the geographical places, together with the planning of spiritual activities, distributed over time and over space on the chosen path. In addition, a flyer of the individual project, together with the total budget and the calculation of the costs for each pilgrim, was delivered by a given deadline. In the next section, we analyze the types of micro-activities that occurred in the twenty projects.

Data analysis and results. We did a content analysis of the twenty projects, using Krippendorff's method, by listing all the micro-activities that the future pilgrim guides wanted to experience. A taxonomy of the 845 micro-activities was then created, divided into ninety-six different types of activities, repeated and spread over the timeline of the twenty projects. We classified these 845 micro-activities in ten macro-categories, according to the verbs used by the twenty future pilgrim guides. Below, we present a graphical summary of the data set.

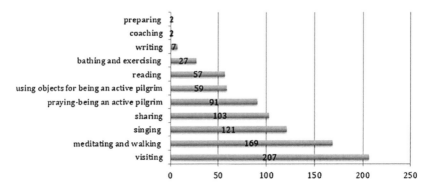

Figure 1: Ten Macro-categories of the 845 Micro-activities of the *Spiritual Bricoleurs*.

The ten macro-categories were: visiting (containing a total of 207 micro-activities), meditating embedded in "walking with meaning" (169), singing (121), sharing (103), praying-being an active pilgrim (91), using objects for being an active pilgrim (59), reading & writing (64), bathing & exercising (27), preparing oneself before the pilgrimage (3), coaching (2) and preparing (2).

The role of ritual. Before commenting on each macro-activity, we would like to add a reflection about *ritual*, as one of the major components of the spiritual micro-activities encountered in the data. In the twenty projects, ritual and ritual activities represent one of the main practices. According to Smith, "ritual is a mode of paying attention ... (it) provides an occasion for reflection ... and sacrality is a category of emplacement" (103). Grimes summarizes Smith's theory of ritual, while also adding his own perspective:

> Ritual is by definition sacral or religious; the domain of ritual is incongruous with that of non-ritual activity; the where—place and location—of ritual is more definitive than its what or how, for the same reason that system is more determinative then performance; place acts; it is not a mere passive, empty receptacle; place is both geographical (literal) and metaphorical (conceptual and social): metaphorical emplacement is more determinative than geographical place; emplacement implies social hierarchy [266].

Moreover, Grimes adds that "ritual is a kind of action, that it inevitably occurs in a specific place, and that such places vary in their importance to the rites they ground" (261). Grimes privileges rite as action, and not—as Smith—as a form of routine and repetition embedded in a specific space/pace. It is multidimensional, through its components: actions (dancing, walking, kneeling), places (shrines, sanctuaries), times (seasons), objects (icons, costumes), groups, figures and roles, qualities and quantities, language (myths, stories, texts), sounds (music, songs, chants), beliefs, attitude, intentions and emotions (ritual efficacies, thankfulness) (267). In addition, geographical place merits attention. Grimes writes, "The logic seems to be something like this: ritual and place do the same thing: therefore, they are the same thing" (268).

Macro-category: Visiting. The twenty projects were planned to be performed in Switzerland; therefore, the future pilgrim guides focused on pathways and "Caminos," reaching churches, chapels and big monasteries, like the Benedictine Monastery and Abbey of Marienstein in Solothurn, the Benedictine Monastery and Abbey of Einsiedeln and Marian Shrine in Schwyz and the Benedictine Monastery of Fischingen in Thurgau. The *visiting* category, with its 207 micro-activities, was the most repeated one. By *visiting* we meant the spiritual activities projected toward reaching a cathedral or a church, along the way. However, on the different paths, there are also many churches and chapels, as well as botanical gardens and labyrinths. These places also involved pedagogical church activities, like entering into the church and exploring their frescos. Often, these paths involved visiting a city or suburbs of cities, together with the allotment gardens, or reaching other ecumenical centers, crossing lakes with boats or crossing bridges. *Visiting* also meant engagement with touristic explanations and sharing historical information, and exploring the natural beauty of the regions, in the form of church and monastery gardens and labyrinths. This category also involved meeting local people, like farmers, producers, city guides, beekeepers, and parsons, as testimonies of the places. A clear replica of the Camino pilgrimage, with its activities, "adjacencies" and rituals, can be considered in this category. Pilgrimage paths were designed by the "spiritual bricoleurs" around a cathedral, or if a big cathedral was not in the path, the activities were designed around churches and chapels.

Macro-category: Meditating or "Walking with Meaning." This key category (169) implies *walking with meaning*, being silent during a certain amount of time, doing reflection exercises, with questions or quotes, distributed on paper before starting to walk. The quotes included pieces from Psalms, the Bible or other religious authors, like Saint Benedict of Nursia, non-religious writers, like Saint-Exupéry, Coelho, Chaplin, and others. Also, proverbs were used. Walking was introduced with a short instruction about the duration of the walk and how to walk, mostly in silence. Sometimes walkers were instructed to consider the environment, mostly woodlands, but also urban areas, with an attentive focus on nature, the presence of bridges, trees, rivers, waterfalls and the environment as a whole.

Macro-category: Singing. The *singing* category (with its 122 micro-activities, 122 songs) implied singing a song, in different settings; in church; while walking; before and/or after an important activity; before starting the day and/or at the end of the day. The trainers organized a special song booklet, which was adapted by the trainees and/or created from scratch. Singing a song was one of the recurrent micro-activities, designed by the future pilgrim guides.

Macro-category: Sharing. The *sharing* category, spread over 103 micro-activities, implied sharing practical information about the pilgrimage projects, orientation maps, ideas, thoughts, suggestions, life mottos, experiences, stories, songs, cards with small quotes, testimonies and so on, either in the big group and/or in smaller groups of two to four participants. Rules and times of activities were shared, together with goodbye gifts (a Compostela shell, a jar of honey, a coffee or cake). The sharing was mostly done in nature and in circles, or around a fireplace. Someone proposed meeting after the pilgrimage, as an extended shared experience. Sharing was also embedded in carrying the heavy rucksacks of others, as a physical metaphor for sharing the weight of the other person.

Macro-category: Prayer. With its 91 micro-activities, *praying* was experienced in different ways: praying a specific pilgrim-prayer/s, lighting a candle, starting with the morning prayer, closing the day with evening prayers, taking part in the church service, talking to God, doing the Via Cruces, praying with the rosary, sharing the pilgrim blessings.

Macro-category: Using Pilgrim Objects and Replication of Material Culture. In addition, typical "*Caminoization objects*," such as the Compostela shell, a pilgrim stamp, stones, small bells, nametags attached to the rucksack, bread and water, several types of pictures, a walking stick, images of

Saint James, incense, and also a special pilgrim soup, were used for conducting spiritual micro-activities (59). For example, a great success was the clothespin, with a specific message: when the pilgrims do not want to share any comments with anyone, the clothespin signaled a request of silence. Together with the "Caminoization," the replication of the material culture of the Camino was clearly designed, including the use of pilgrim passports and Compostela-like certificates, as well as pilgrim blessings, the St. James shell, and diversified ritual activities.

Seventh: The Reading and Writing Categories. The *reading* (57) and *writing* (7) micro-categories implied using a pilgrim's notebook, writing exercises, reading texts, using verses from the Bible and pictures, giving out cards with questions or citations, reading Psalms, or the Bible or quotes from a diverse collection of authors, from more religious authors, like Saint Benedict of Nursia, and quotes from less religious ones, like Saint-Exupéry, Coelho, Chaplin, and many others.

Macro-category: Bathing and Exercising. The care of the pilgrim's body, through 27 micro-activities, was expressed through activities including taking a bath in a river or in a lake or washing feet in a fountain. Other such activities included, breathing exercises in a monastery garden, tai-chi exercises in the morning and laying under the sky to watch the evening or the morning stars.

Mein Pilgerheft

Dieses persönliche Pilgerheft soll dir ein Wegbegleiter sein und dich mit Texten und Gebeten inspirieren, die dir Kraft und Zuversicht geben. Es lädt dich zur Achtsamkeit gegenüber den Menschen und der Schöpfung ein.
Nimm an die Gastfreundschaft, die dir geschenkt wird, und gib, was du geben kannst. Sei als Pilger/in ein/e Botschafter/in des Friedens auf diesem Pilgerweg und lass andere an deiner Freude und Zuversicht Anteil nehmen.

Vorname, Nachname   Geburtsjahr

Adresse

PLZ, Ort

E-Mail   Telefon

Pilgerstrecke   Datum

Besinnlicher Tagesbeginn

1 Begrüßung
2 Gebet

Herr meiner Stunden und meiner Jahre,
du hast mir viel Zeit gegeben.
Sie liegt hinter mir und sie liegt vor mir.
Sie war mein und wird mein,
und ich habe sie von dir.
Ich danke dir für jeden Schlag der Uhr
und für jeden Morgen, den ich sehe.
Amen.

3 Psalm oder Text
4 evtl. Gedanken zur Lesung
5 Stille
6 Übung/Ritual
7 Lied
8 Bittgebet evtl. Unservater
9 Segen
10 Lied

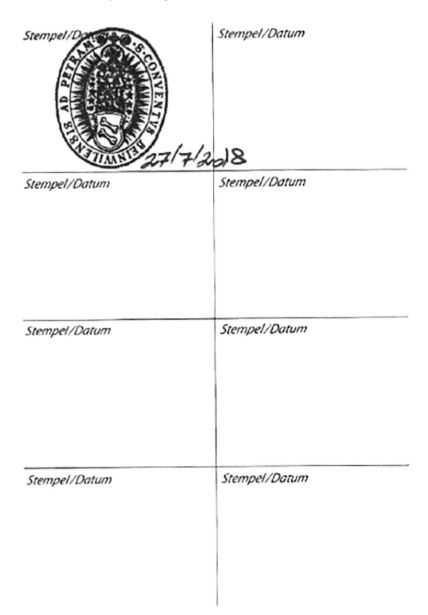

Figures 2 (*previous page*) and 3: The Camino replicas for the Swiss National Pilgrimage Day event in 2017. The *Pilgerheft* or the pilgrim booklet, created by jakobsweg.ch (n.d.), with a list of pilgrim activities and space for collecting the stamps—a nice example of Caminoization, a replica with a pilgrim stamp from the Abbey Mariastein in Solothurn, Switzerland.

Macro-category: Self-preparation. The *self-preparation* (2) category implied sharing explanations about pilgrimage traditions, the project, turning off cellphones while doing certain activities, and reading or writing before the experience as preparation.

Macro-category: Coaching. *Coaching* (2) was offered during the pilgrimage experience as a special type of sharing, with expert coaches. In fact, one of the trainees was also a trained coach. He implemented several coaching sessions during his project, on an individual basis.

In summary, the future pilgrim guides acted as *spiritual bricoleurs.* They planned and designed spiritual experiences, considering their own experience, the environment, landscapes and buildings such as churches, chapels, monasteries and abbeys. They embedded natural spaces, including woods and urban places, gardens and labyrinths, together with formal tourist activities and pilgrimage visits. They used the environment to plan spiritual walking, combined with moments for meditation. All these activities were musically enhanced by singing (mostly by hymns, but also by well-known melodies), and verbally shared between the bigger groups and/ or in small groups. They incorporated prayer, the use of different types of objects and texts to amplify the pilgrim experiences. Moreover, intellectual activities, like reading and writing, together with bathing and exercising, complemented the balance between body, mind and spirit. In addition, preparatory activities were important, but not intensively planned.

Self-reflection: My Individual Project. Because such trainings are not offered within the Catholic Church, my own faith, I appreciated the opportunity to conduct an individual project through the Evangelical Church and the chance to create my own bricolage *Weltanschaung.*

My project was about offering a pilgrimage experience, following in the footsteps of the Icelandic Benedictine monk Nikulás von Munkaþverá, who in the year 1149 and until 1154 started on a four-year pilgrimage from Iceland to Jerusalem, crossing all the European countries, including Switzerland. Through research incorporating a variety of sources, such as his written annotation of the pilgrimage, I designed a project that combined Saint Benedict of Nursia's "Rule," and a spiritual project dedicated to management education, specifically for stressed and burned-out managers. The three-day pilgrimage experience, covered approximately sixty kilometers, beginning in Basel and finishing in Delemont (Switzerland); an intense weekend pilgrimage. The connection with *management education* was inspired by a training, which is still held in Italy, specifically designed for managers and summarized in a book by Folador. Therefore, my bricolage work involved the reinterpretation of Swiss landscapes, imagining Nikulás von Munkaþverá crossing Switzerland searching for Benedictine monasteries, looking for places to stay and spaces to rest and to start a personal development process, where nature might have had an important impact.

What tools were available to me for designing my project? My bricolage elements included: the Saint Benedict of Nursia Rule book, together with a modern reinterpretation of his Rule as seen through Folador's ideas of management education, the historical reinterpretation of contemporary scholars who studied Nikulás and the monastery of Mariastein, a Benedictine building, constructed approximately 400 years after Nikulás's pilgrimage. These bricolage elements became my meaningful collection of tools for designing the project.

In addition, the important element of nature and its landscapes promoted what Bielo defines as "the sensualisation of a new religious pedagogy." In fact, in studying the role of biblical gardens as devotional and pedagogical places and spaces, Bielo argues that biblical gardens enhance visual experience for a more sensual experience, exploring the role of sensuous materiality in religious pedagogy, through the immersion of the visitor in a "particular kind of immersive experience, a metonymic immersion, in which a part (botanic nature) is used to represent a whole (biblical history)" (32). The communion with nature, which can be represented by a biblical garden or just by nature, "might promote a direct encounter with God's creation, as a sort of special access to divine intimacy and understanding" (37). Bielo analyzes how sacred texts are not just read, but are embedded in creative usages and formative ways, committing to textual authority and intimacy through processes of religious mediation and sensory channels, mediating religious experience, communication and learning. The garden-nature pedagogy is mainly experiential, because it "mobilizes bodily experience to foster an intimate relationship with tradition" (36). Bielo contextualizes the sensual pedagogy of biblical gardens, tracing the ritual back to scriptures and to monastic traditions, where gardens fostered a spiritual vitality, promoting an everyday spiritual discipline, as a parallel between the care of garden and the care of self (41). These gardens were also transformed into prayer labyrinths and later private gardens and public places. For Bielo (45) "Gardens supply a pedagogical experience for visitors through their promise of direct access to the biblical past through the senses, and metonymic immersion into the world of the Bible through the flora of the Bible." The gardens work as an embodied experience, grounded in an ideology of sensual indexicality and the strategy of metonymic immersion, "in which tactile, aromatic, audible, and visual capacities are entangled" (50). The feeling and the experience is like being immersed into the sacred past, because as Bielo summarized, "in the garden, the gaze, the touch, the sniff, and the attuned ear are mutually reliant and equally enhanced" (51). More recently, researchers (Lopez) are starting to interpret the Camino de Santiago pilgrimage from the five senses' point of views, through a so-called "geo-literacy analysis" of the Camino, becoming a "sensuous Camino geography."

Discussion and Conclusion

Credibility of a facilitator and storyteller. It is important to reflect on the role of "spiritual bricoleurs" as facilitators of practical theology. According to Pienaar and Müller, the engagement with different audiences, implies a rationale for combining: (a) practical theology and (b) the role of facilitator, thus enhancing credibility. A facilitator is a person that "contributes structure and process to interactions so groups are able to function effectively and make high-quality decisions ... is a helper and an enabler whose goal is to support others as they pursue their objectives." This occurs through practical theology interpreted as a *Handlungswissenschaft* [science of action and of practice] (Bens 3). The role of autobiography and life stories, as "story theology" (McClendon) are means through which we build our experiences and our realities, through a sort of narrative therapy (Combs and Freedman 1996). Social constructionism is shaped by stories, which are means for defining our experiences and are taking concrete forms. Day Scalter defines three important aspects of narrative as identity; firstly, the moral aspect of sharing a personal story; secondly, the story as a social and interpersonal construct, engaging the self with other selves; thirdly, as human beings we take responsibility, and ownership of our story/stories. The storyteller enters into the realm of transitional space, "in which the self continually negotiates its position in the world, inscribes itself in relation to the available cultural scripts, integrates past, present and future through acts of remembering and telling, in a safe, but fragile public space, because it is risky to find a balance between the private and the public" (321–327).

The future pilgrim guides in a secularized time are like *spiritual bricoleurs.* Their projects reflect ways of incorporating spiritual activities, according to their own personal and spiritual search for meaning. They are interpreters of the Caminoization phenomenon, through the replica and the migration of the aura. Using a case study model that examined pilgrim guide trainees' projects, we extracted ten macro-categories of activities. Through these projects local landscapes became the stage for new rituals, activating the valorization of local geographical areas and the development of new trends in heritage culture. The sacredness of the Camino de Santiago has been translated through the migration of its aura and the Caminoization phenomenon, together with its material and immaterial replicas. This has been enhanced through rituals, near religious centers, which offered a variety of collective spiritual experiences, involving fluid and mobile post-secular pilgrims.

So, where does the Camino de Santiago actually start? It does not matter where. The moral geography of each of one of us does not have a specific geographical center; *we start when we are ready to start* searching for our life meaning/s. The pilgrim guide can become an inspirational travel companion, a "spiritual bricoleur" that shows us how to start!

Buen Camino!

Works Cited

Badone, Ellen. *Religious Orthodoxy and Popular Faith in European Society.* Princeton University Press, 1990.

Badone, Ellen, and Sharon Roseman, editors. *Intersecting Journeys: The Anthropology of Pilgrimage and Tourism.* University of Illinois Press, 2004.

Barley, Lynda. "Stirrings in Barchester: Cathedrals and Church Growth." *Church Grown in Britain: To the Present,* edited by David Goodhew, Ashgate, 2012.

Barral I Altet, Xavier. *The Romanesque: Towns, Cathedrals and Monasteries.* Taschen, 1998.

Benjamin, Walter. *Illuminations.* Schocken Books, 1969.

Bercea, Brighita, Robert Ekelund and Robert Tollison. "Cathedral Building as an Entry-deterring Device." *Kylos,* vol. 58, no. 4, 2005.

Bielo, James. "Biblical Gardens and the Sensuality of Religious Pedagogy." *Material Religion,* vol.14, no.1, 2018, pp. 30–54.

Boto, Gerardo, and Justin Kroesen. *Romanesque Cathedrals in Mediterranean Europe.* Brespol, 2016.

Bownman, Marion, and Tiina Sepp. "Caminoisation and Cathedrals: Replication, the Heritagisation of Religion, and the Spiritualisation of Heritage." *Religion,* vo. 49, no. 1, 2019, pp. 74–98.

Campbell, Louise. "Pedagogical Bricolage and Teacher Agency: Towards a Culture of Creative Professionalism." *Educational Philosophy and Theory,* vol. 51, no. 1, 2018, pp. 31–40.

Cannon, Jon. *The Great English Cathedrals and the World That Made Them 600–1540.* Constable, 2007.

Chemin, Eduardo. "The Return of the Pilgrim and the Seductions of the Way: The Road to Santiago as a Liminal Space." *The Seduction of Pilgrimages,* edited by Michael Di Giovine and David Picard. Ashgate, 2015, pp. 211–232.

Coleman, Simon, and Marion Bowman. "Religion in Cathedrals: Pilgrimage, Heritage, Adjacency, and the Politics of Replication in Northern Europe." *Religion,* vol. 49, no. 1, 2019, pp. 1–23.

Combs, Geen, and Jill Freedom. *Narrative Therapy: The Social Construction of Preferred Realities.* Norton, 1996.

Damari, Claudia, and Joel Mansfeld. "Reflections on Pilgrim Identity, Role and Interplay with the Pilgrimage Environment." *Current Issues in Tourism,* vol. 19, no. 3, 2016, pp. 199–222.

Davie, Grace. "Vicarious Religion: A Methodological Challenge." *Everyday Religion: Observing Modern Religious Lives,* edited by Nancy Ammerman. Oxford University Press, 2007, pp. 21–36.

Day Scalter, Shelley. "What Is the Subject?" *Narrative Inquiry,* vol. 1, no. 2, 2003, pp. 317–330.

De Ascaniis, Silvia, and Lorenzo Cantoni. "Pilgrims in the Digital Age: A Research Manifesto." *International Journal of Religious Tourism and Pilgrimage,* vol. 4, no. iii, 2016, pp. 1–5.

Di Giovine, Michael. "Apologia Pro Turismo: Breaking Inter- and Intra-disciplinary

Boundaries in the Study of Tourism and Pilgrimage." *The Journal of Tourism Challenges and Trends*, vol. 6, no. 2, 2013, pp. 63–94.

Di Giovine, Michael, and Jaeyon Choe. "Geographies of Religion and Spirituality: Pilgrimage Beyond the 'Officially' Sacred." *Tourism Geographies*, vol. 21, no. 3, 2019, pp. 361–383.

Eade, John, and Dionigi Albera, editors. *International Perspectives on Pilgrimage Studies Itineraries, Taps and Obstacles*. Routledge, 2015.

Eade, John, and Michael Sallnow, editors. *Contesting the Sacred: The Anthropology of Christian Pilgrimage*. Routledge, 1991.

Eriksen, Anne. *From Antiquities to Heritage: Transformations in Cultural Memory*. Berghann, 2014.

Farias, Miguel, et al. "Atheists on the Santiago Way: Examining Motivations to Go on Pilgrimage." *Sociology of Religion: A Quarterly Review*, vol. 80, no. 1, 2019, pp. 28–44.

Filep, Sebastian, and Jennifer Laing. "Trends and Directions in Tourism and Positive Psychology." *Journal of Travel Research*, vol. 58, no. 3, 2018, pp. 1–12.

Folador, Massimo. *L'organizzazione perfetta. La regola di San Benedetto. Una saggezza antica al servizio dell'impresa moderna*. Guerini Editore, 2016.

Frankl, Viktor. *The Feeling of Meaninglessness*. Marquette University Press, 2010.

_____. *Man's Search for Meaning*. Beacon Press (original work published in 1946), 2006.

Frey, Nancy. "Pilgrim Stories." *On and Off the Road to Santiago*. University of California Press, 1998.

Griffin, Kevin, and Raj, Razaq. "The Importance of Religious Tourism and Pilgrimage: Reflecting on Definitions, Motives and Data." *International Journal of Religious Tourism and Pilgrimage,* vol. 5, no. 3, 2017, pp. ii–ix.

Grimes, Ronald. "Jonathan Z. Smith's Theory of Ritual Space." *Religion*, vol. 29, no. 3, 1999, pp. 261–273.

Hunter, Dale, et. al. *The Art of Facilitation: The Essentials for Leading Great Meetings and Creating Group Synergy*. Jossey Bass, 2007.

Inglese, Terry. "Becoming a Pilgrim Guide for Postmodern Pilgrims in Secularized Times." *Church, Communication and Culture*, vol. 3, no. 3, 2018, pp. 335–361.

"Jakobsweb." www.jakobsweg.ch.

Krippendorff, Klaus. *Content Analysis; an Introduction to Its Methodology*, 3rd edition, Sage, 2012.

Latour, Bruno, and Adam Lowe. "The Migration of the Aura or How to Explore the Original Thorough Its Facsimiles." *Switching Codes*, edited by Thomas Bartscherer. The University of Chicago Press, 2010.

Lévi-Strauss, Claude. *The Savage Mind*. University of Chicago Press; Weidenfeld and Nicolson Ltd, 1966.

Lopez, Lucrezia. "A Geo-Literacy Analysis Through Human Senses: Towards a Sensuous Camino Geography." *Emotion, Space and Society*, vol. 30, 2019, pp. 9–19.

Louvel, Severine. "Understanding Change in Higher Education as Bricolage: How Academics Engage in Curriculum Change." *Higher Education*, Springer, vol. 66, no. 6, 2013, pp. 669–691.

Margry, Jan, editor. *Shrines and Pilgrimage in the Modern World: New Itineraries Into the Sacred*. University of Amsterdam Press, 2008.

Margry, Peter. "Imagining an End to the World: Histories and Mythologies of the Santiago—Finisterre Connection." *Walking to the End of the World: Heritage, Pilgrimage and the Camino to Finisterre*, edited by Christina Carretero-Sanchez. Springer, 2015, pp. 32–52.

McClendon, James. *Biography as Theology: How Life Stories Can Remake Today's Theology*. Abington Press, 1974.

Perez, Sergio, and Frederique Vallieres. "How Do Religious People Become Atheists? Applying a Grounded Theory Approach to Propose a Model of Deconversion." *Secularism and Nonreligion*, vol. 8, no. 3, 2019, pp. 1–14.

Pienaar, Elmo, and Julian Müller. "The Practical Theologian as Decentered but Influential Facilitator." *HTS Theological Studies*, vol. 68, no. 2, 2012, pp. 1–10.

"Reformierte kirch kanton zürich." www.zhref.ch/angebote/pilgern.

Rogers, Matt. "Contextualizing Theories and Practices of Bricolage Research." *The Qualitative Report*, vol. 7, no. 48, 2012, pp. 1–17.

Schaar, Michael. *Immer der Muschel nach—Weg der Wandlung. Handreichung für Etappe leitende am Samstag, 20. Mai 2017.* Reformiertes Pilgerzentrum St. Jakob www.jakob swegschweiz.ch/Documents/20170520%20Broschure%20Weg%20der%20Wandlung-d. pdf, 2017/ Accessed 1May. 2018.
Smith, Jonathan. *To Take Place: Toward Theory in Ritual.* University of Chicago Press, 1987.
Taylor, Edward. "Epilogue: Pilgrimage, Moral Geography and Contemporary Religion in the West." *Gender, Nation and Religion in European Pilgrimage,* Edited by Willy Jansen and Catrien Notermans. Ashgate, 2012, pp. 209–220.
Theos and the Grubb Institute. *Spiritual Capital: The Present and the Future of English Cathedrals.* Theos and the Grubb Institute, 2012.
Van Gennep, Arnold. *Rites of Passage.* University of Chicago Press, 1960.
Zittoun, Tania. "A Sociocultural Psychological Approach to Religion." *Integrative Psychological and Behavioral Science,* vol. 53, no. 1, Springer, 2019, pp. 107–125.

Footprints of the Camino in Slovenia

Three Ethnographic Vignettes

Nataša Rogelja Caf
and Špela Ledinek Lozej

El Camino comienza en su casa *[The Camino Starts at Home]*

El Camino, as it is known and referred to today, is primarily a link to the Iberian Peninsula, and even more specifically with Galicia in Spain, where the route ends. In the following text we aim to reverse this view and reflect on the beginnings of the route from the perspective of Slovenia, a post-socialist country born in the context of the Yugoslav conflict in the 1990s, and a current member of the European Union. We argue that focusing on the starting point(s) highlights various local perspective(s) and variations and, at the same time, highlights the interconnected heritage(s) of a wider European network of military, merchant and pilgrim routes in the region. Highlighting the Slovenian perspective fills the gap between Anglophone and non–Anglophone research on pilgrimage. More specifically, several authors have emphasized the dominance of the Anglophone literature on pilgrimage and discussed the weak link between Anglophone and non–Anglophone scholars (Eade and Katič; Hann; Yamashita, et al.). In the light of these gaps and weak links we begin our route at the threshold of the southern Slavic region and in the context of the newly born state of Slovenia, almost 3000 km from Santiago de Compostela.

The heritage of pilgrimage routes in Slovenia has a long history but it found new expression in the context of the more self-assertive appearance of Christianity in the post Yugoslav period, within an enlarged Europe striving to rediscover a common European identity (Welz), and within the context of tourism and a neoliberal economy aiming to link heritage and pilgrimage routes into the rationale of a "product" (Bambi and Barbari). Regardless of these recent developments, remnants and stories from footprints of Santiago de Compostela and the Camino[1] can be found in local toponyms, folk song and literature, as well as in churches and chapels dedicated to St. James. However, in the context of (more) recent political and other developments, these historic traces have merged with tourist, recreational, cultural and new-age spiritual efforts and imagery. In the first vignette, we highlight past traces (and contemporary life) in order to discuss the historical interconnectedness of a wider European network of military, merchant and pilgrim routes and their footprints in toponyms, churches, folk songs and legends and how they found their way to contemporary web pages. The second vignette focuses on the development and achievements of the Society of Friends of the Way of St. James in Slovenia (Slv. *Društvo prijateljev poti sv. Jakoba v Sloveniji*), their connection with other European initiatives and their impact in cultivating the cult of St. James. This story goes back to 1999 when the founders of the society undertook the French Way, and a year later established the Society of Friends of the Way of St. James in Slovenia with the aim of reviving the tradition of pilgrimages, following the example of other nations, countries and cities in Europe.[2] The third vignette reflects on books and films written, or available, in the Slovenian language, as well as on Slovenian Facebook groups related to the Camino. The track record of authors translated to the Slovenian language, Slovenian authors writing about the Camino, as well as the statistics on book lending figures, will be discussed together with more contemporary virtual material that reveals the growth of cultural and recreational tourism related to the Camino. Methodologically the text builds upon desk-top research related to historical sources, on an analysis of the Slovenian COBISS.SI[3] library catalogue and the IZUM[4] database, as well as in interviews with the members of the Society of Friends of the Way of St. James. Although the three vignettes refer to different historical moments and different materials, they all are embedded in the context of late (Slovenian) modernity,[5] where the Camino also finds its unique expression due to increased global connections, infrastructure development and digital technology.

Vignette 1: Is Galicija in Slovenija?

Yes, a Galicija does exist in Slovenia. It is the name of a local community within the municipality of Žalec in the north-eastern part of the country and looking at the map it may feel like we have already arrived, even though we had never left. There are several etymological and other explanations as to why it was named Galicija. A local topography, the *Krajevni leksikon Dravske banovine,* states that "in the church tower there is a statue of the apostle and patron St. James, who is buried in Galicia, Spain; this is why the place was named 'Galicija'" (105). On the other hand, Davorin Trstenjak (1817–1890), a Slovenian Catholic priest, historian and etymologist claimed that the roots of this peculiar local name are much older and are of Slavic origin: "Places dedicated to the God of Sun, to the musician and dancer, were called Galicije by the old Slavic people. They had dances in the summertime, and with the appearance of Christianity, St. James the Apostle replaced the God of Sun" (Trstenjak 25). The web pages from the local community of Galicija (Parežnik) use different sources, from Trstenjak to topography, also adding a chronogram carved above the entrance to St. James Church and pieces from local oral tradition: "in the old times a Polish man from Galicia, Poland used to live here. If someone visited him, he would say, 'I am going to the Galicijaner,' so the place where he lived was later called Galicija" (Parežnik).

There are sixty-seven churches, dedicated to St. James but only one Galicija in present-day Slovenia; globally, however, there are several Galicias found across Europe and Asia Minor, most probably in relation to Celtic roots, following the etymology dictionary ("Galicia"). But our purpose here is not to solve the etymological riddle. Our aim is to reflect on the variety of footprints left by the Camino in Slovenia from a contemporary perspective. By following the logic of contemporary footprints, we also discover from the local community website of Galicija that its name is connected with Spanish Galicia "since the nobility from our region also made pilgrimages to this [St. James] grave and brought home the cult and the name of St. James, to whom the church was later built" (Parežnik).

The noblest and probably the most famous pilgrim from the territory of present-day Slovenia was Count Ulrich II of Celje (1406–1456), the last member of an influential medieval dynasty. Count Ulrich II traveled to Santiago de Compostela around 1430 in the company of sixty knights and his journey is detailed on various web pages (e.g., Jevnikar). His pilgrimage is also "recognized" due to his visit to Spain having been recorded in the Spanish chronicle of the Castilian kings (Rossell). The text was published by Ignacij Voje: "From Astudillus the king went to Amusco for Easter, and a great German lord, the nephew of Emperor Sigismund, Count of Celje, was there; for he came to this kingdom to go to Santiago, and was accompanied by sixty horsemen, richly equipped nobles" (225–226). According to Voje, there might be an initial religious motif for the pilgrimage but it was probably more a knight's journey as the young Count Ulrich undertook this pilgrimage as a chivalric undertaking (225–226). As Mlinar emphasizes, the pilgrimages at that time replaced previous war campaigns and served as acts of initiation for medieval noble youth on their way to becoming knights (62). At the same time, these became political journeys in order to make connections with Kings Alfonso V of Aragon and Juan II of Castille (Voje 229).

Ulrich II of Celje was not the only noble pilgrim from the region. Even the earliest testimonies of pilgrimages from the territory of present-day Slovenia are related to Santiago de Compostela. Namely, Countess Richardis of Lavant also undertook this pilgrimage and died on the way back while her husband, Sigrid of Speinheim, died on his way back from Jerusalem in 1064 (Kos 244; Kosi 100). Comparable tragedy is retold in folk romance in a story entitled "Pilgrim to St. James in Compostela," published as part of a collection of Slovenian folk songs (Štrekelj, vol. 3, 75; Grafenauer 348). There are several other matters emphasized in other folk songs, for example, the necessary equipment of a Compostela pilgrim—shoes, trousers, shirt, waistcoat, coat, hat, and pilgrim's staff; and descriptions of St. James preaching the gospel in Spain and others (Štrekelj, vol. 1, 551; vol. 3, 795).

Not only have the footprints of pilgrimaging to Santiago de Compostela paved their way through folk song, but they have also been evoked in other genres of literature. For example, France Prešeren, a leading name of the Slovene literary canon, dedicated one of his sonnets to Matevž Langus, a contemporary painter, that also depicted the poet's beloved Julija Primic. In the poem, Prešeren compares his longing for Julija, a longing that forces him to visit the painter's house to admire her portrait, to a pilgrim's zeal for seeing the images of life in paradise depicted in different shrines—Rome, Compostela, Padua, Lussari, Trsat, and Maria Zell (Prešeren 108). Moving further through Slovene artistic invention, two additional footprints are of special interest for this discussion, a tale and an opera. In the Janez Jalen's tale, *Marko the Shepherd* (Slv. *Ovčar Marko*), first published in 1929, one of the most prominent side characters—a kind of an angel guardian, friend and counselor to the main protagonist—is a Compostela pilgrim called Jok. The topics of pilgrimage to Compostela also found their way to an opera entitled *Tajda*, describing Slovene pilgrims embarking on the ship, the Santa Fe. The opera was composed after the libretto *Compostela Pilgrims* (Slv. *Kompostelski romarji*), written by Slovene writer Ivan Pregelj, and was first performed in 1927 in Ljubljana.

Among more ancient footprints, we should mention numerous sculptures and paintings of the saint and of related legends that appear in frescoes, on canvas, altars and banners. The saint is usually depicted as a pilgrim with a pilgrim staff, calabash, wearing a wide-brimmed hat, sometimes even as an apostle, but on the pulpit of the church of St. James in Hraše also as the *Moor-slayer* (sp. *Matamoros*)—in the local context, a victor over the Turks—riding on horse-back with a banner. Also very interesting are the varied depictions of the legend that appear in the Church of St. Leonard in Bodešče, the Church of St. James in Petelinc and in Church of St. Martin in Hajdina, in which St. James rescues an unjustly condemned and hanged young man. On the frescoes in Bodešče we see a young man hanging and beside him a figure with a pilgrim's hat and shell, and in the second picture, figures sitting around the table at dinner with the bottle of wine, wine cups, and a plate with chickens that are about to rise and fly away. According to art historian Josip Dostal, it depicts the famous *Legend of a Cock and a Hen*, documented by Lucius Marineus of Sicily (35).

Besides these distinguished and popular traces, we should not over-look educational records, for example a description of a pilgrimage to Compostela by the priest, and himself a Compostela pilgrim, Jožef Lavtižar, published in the yearly bulletin of the Hermagoras Society (Slv. *Mohorjeva družba*) in 1909 (40–43). It is important to note that the Hermagoras Society is the oldest Slovenian publishing house, which was founded in 1851 and played a tremendous role in increasing literacy within the territory of present-day Slovenia in the second half of the 19th century. It has a Catholic (but not overly clerical) orientation, publishing books aimed at the general public. In 1891 it had more than 50,000 members ("O nas") and we can assume that more than fifty thousand subscribers and their household or family members read Josip Lavtižar's itinerary of his pilgrimage to Santiago de Compostela in 1905. He introduces the article with the following verse: "You are also known, Compostela, in Slovenian lands, a traveler from Carniola testifies to this" (40). At the beginning of the article he describes the manners and customs of pilgrims in former times:

> Anyone who intended to make a pilgrimage to Compostela prepared himself as if going to Eternity.... How much danger there is on (such) a journey! The high Pyrenean passes, wild Basque landscapes, and snowy Cantabrian mountains to be crossed! Lonely woods here, torrential rivers there; here hills, there endless valleys [Lavtižar 40].

He continues with the explanation that nowadays (in his time, i.e., at the beginning of 20th century) this is no longer a case, as he (himself) made a pilgrimage to Compostela quite comfortably by train in 1905. Lavtižar concludes, with no moral judgment, that nowadays everyone can reach Compostela with little trouble, by train or steamer: "No one goes on foot anymore on this long journey; so you don't need two pairs of boots, as it used to be" (43). We could not help but imagine how surprised he would be to see numerous Carniola pilgrims from the 21st century, living in the era of increased transport possibilities, walking to Santiago de Compostela on foot. It looks like walking in previous centuries was regarded mainly as a means of transport while nowadays the social role of this physical activity has changed. Pilgrimage and a new Western(ised) enthusiasm for walking has somehow overlapped, just as pilgrimage has also overlapped with other, more local and nationally charged issues. But that is another story.

Vignette 2: Society of Friends of the Way of St. James in Slovenia

It was a bright sunny day in September when we visited the home of Marjeta and Metodij Rigler, the first two documented Slovenians to have walked the Camino in a modern context[6] and the founders of the Society of Friends of the Way of St. James in Slovenia; a devout Christian couple in their late seventies living in Ljubljana. Approaching their house by bike we immediately noticed from a distance iconic yellow signs on their house, first painted along the present-day French Camino by Elias Valiña Sampedro around 1980. As we arrived, one of the society members was on her way out, chatting with Marjeta about future pilgrim hikes in Slovenia. Marjeta explained to this lady that they would not join this pilgrimage, as her husband would be having an operation. As she further emphasized, members of the society are nowadays mostly retired and this creates certain problems, mostly health-related issues, knowledge of the English language and other expertise needed to apply for funding. Once indoors, we noticed numerous traces of the Camino: a map of European Caminos leading to Santiago de Compostela, yellow shells painted on small stones, books and other small objects pertaining to the Camino. As the sole Slovenian society related to the Camino they also issue pilgrim passports in the Slovenian language, designed and prepared by the Society. "Several people told me, that we, the Slovenians, have the most beautiful passport of all European countries!," emphasized Marjeta (Rigler and Rigler, Personal interview). We were given one, issued with the consecutive number 730 for 2019 and embellished with photos of St. James statues from Slovenia. Standing there, in the middle of their house, it felt like "o camiño empeza agora."[7]

The Camino is a life project for Marjeta and Metodij Rigler, a third age project, which they started immediately after going into retirement, although Marjeta has had aspirations for traveling and tour organizing since high school. In the period of Yugoslavia (1945–1991)[8] they also undertook several pilgrimages by bus, organized by a local parish church. In 1999, in their first year of retirement, they both undertook the French Way on foot and a year later, they established the Society of Friends of the Way of St. James in Slovenia. As Marjeta, "a family initiator of Camino endeavors" explained to us and as they wrote in their book, they completed the Camino on foot for three reasons; they did it for themselves, for the family and for the homeland. When they returned from Spain, they started to actively work on the third reason by reviving accounts of the Camino in the context of Slovenia. This was also the main reason for them establishing the Society itself. Together with other Society members, they started a quest for St. James vestiges—churches, poems and frescos. The breakthrough in their search was, as they emphasized (Personal interview), a guidebook sent to them from France by their daughter, the *Guide European des Chemins de Compostelle* by Jean Bourdarias and Michel Wasielewski and published by the Cultural Routes Program of the Council of Europe in 2002, in which they found indices for a medieval pilgrimage route leading across Slovenia—from Zagreb (in Croatia) across Ljubljana and toward Trieste (374–383).

In the years that followed, members of the Society of Friends of the Way of St. James have done an enormous job in locating, cleaning and marking the Slovenian Camino, as commonly known these days. They have released several guide books, focusing either on the main route from Zagreb to Trieste (Rigler and Rigler, *Kje so tiste stezice*) or on the two northern local branches (*Bom grmovje posekal*; *Bom naredil stezice*), and organized numerous group pilgrimages. In establishing a footpath map of the Slovenian Camino they either followed literature concerning medieval pilgrim routes in Europe (e.g., Bourdarias and Wasielewski 374–383) or they drew up new routes connecting churches dedicated to St. James. These routes, as described on the Society's website, serve not so much as routes leading to Santiago, although they do connect to other Santiago trails, but they have almost an introverted logic of "getting to know our own country":

> sixty-seven churches dedicated to St. James are unique monuments related to medieval pilgrimages as well the worship of St. James in our country. The purpose of the Society is to restore the pilgrimage routes that passed through Slovenia…. In other words; the path of St. James will be like the trunk of a tree, stretching branches and leaves to our villages and hills, winding through hidden valleys, and through St. James' path we will learn about our history, culture, art, people. All this knowledge will be slowly shared with pilgrims and travelers from other countries [Popotnik].

Marking the route itself was not an easy job, as Metodij explained. First, he visited a former president of the Slovenian Academy of Sciences and Arts from whom he obtained a letter of support. With this letter he contacted every Slovene municipality through which the Slovenian Camino was marked, asking for permission to place yellow signs and shells in those public spaces. This was, as Metodij recalled, a real Way of the Cross. Marjeta and Metodij believe that the route they marked could be a successful tourist product, however they are not interested in commercializing, neither do they have strength to apply for funds to maintain the Slovenian Camino. They feel that the majority of EU funds for the Camino were already distributed to other European Union countries during the 1980s, when Slovenia was still part of Yugoslavia and, in their view, at that time, nobody cared about the Camino anyway. But they also emphasize that they are very happy that people in Slovenia have adopted the Slovenian Camino and also acknowledge the help of numerous individuals and enthusiasts in maintaining the route (Rigler and Rigler, Personal interview). The route has somehow started to breathe on its own and according to posts in one of the Slovenian Facebook groups dedicated to the Camino ("Pot Svetega Jakoba"), it looks like the trail is already well trodden, maybe not so much for religious reasons but more due to the fact that hiking as well as mountaineering and skiing are important leisure activities in Slovenia (Kotnik 56–78).

Following Rigler viewpoint, we can understand that the initial idea for the Slovenian Camino was not born as a top-down project, but as a bottom-up effort, related to a few specific enthusiasts and members of the Society. Their aspirations were mainly related to religious motives, individual desires for hiking as well as with strong, patriotic feelings. The first membership applications to the Society were signed at the top of Slovenia's highest mountain, Mt. Triglav, a strong national symbol featured on the Slovenian national flag (Rigler and Rigler, Personal interview). The Slovenian Camino has been widely accepted in Slovenia, and this can be further linked to the fact that mountain and outdoor sports such as skiing, mountaineering, climbing or just walking are extremely popular in the country and are also linked to the national identity (Doupona Topič and Coakley 371–389; Kotnik 56–78). At the same time, the Slovenian Camino also somehow naturally and harmoniously fits within a European context as emphasized on the society's website:

> This year, when Slovenia joins the European Union, the friends and members of the Society will symbolically enter the European Union along the paths of the medieval St. James Route. Slovenian territory will no longer be divided by borders and St. James churches, built by our ancestors, living in our ethnic territory, where the Slovenian language was spoken and is still spoken, will welcome us all [Popotnik].

Different political periods are linked with different borders and ideologies and it seems like the Camino fits well with Europe, erasing some of the previous borders and strengthening other ones.

Vignette 3: Mind Routes: Books, Movies and Facebook Groups

In order to understand the modern resurgence of the grand medieval pilgrimage to Santiago de Compostela, we also have to take books, movies, Facebook groups and other Internet platforms and tools into consideration, which are nowadays (such) an important part of the Camino in any local setting. As emphasized by Nancy Frey, one of the most profound changes on the Camino in the last twenty years is how it has incorporated new media technology at the level of infrastructure, planning and contact, but also on the experience of being a pilgrim. The merging of local, national, regional and global levels—facilitated by a growing book industry and new media technology—is another aspect important to understand the Camino in the context of late modernity. While the rise of the Internet has dramatically impacted how people have engaged with the Camino since 2000 (Frey), books and movies have also had, and still have their share, paving the way for aspiring hopefuls to undertake the Camino since the first modern guidebook was published in 1985 (English translation in 1992) by Elias Valiña Sampedro. Valiña Sampedro was a pastor at O Cebreiro in Lugo (Galicia) who completed his Ph.D. on the subject of the Camino at the University of Salamanca and engaged in reviving, cleaning and marking the present-day French Camino. Although he was a Camino pioneer, a man who started painting the iconic yellow arrows along the Camino, his book has never been translated into the Slovene language and is in fact little known even in other Slavic countries since it has only been translated into English, French and German and later overshadowed by the numerous other guidebooks that begin to flourish after 1990.[9]

The first two books about the Camino in Slovene were a travelogue by the previously mentioned couple, Marjeta and Metodij Rigler, entitled *Blessed Are the Poor: Pilgrimage on the Path of St. James to Compostela* (Slv. *Blagor vama uboga reveža: Romanje po poti svetega Jakoba v Kompostelo* [2000]) and a novel by Shirley MacLaine entitled *The Camino: A Journey of the Spirit*, translated into Slovene (*Camino: Po stezi zvezd*) in 2001. Although both books describe the same French Way, they actually paved two quite different mind routes as the titles suggest. The first was self-published by a Slovenian couple with a Christian religious background who undertook the pilgrimage to Santiago de Compostela in 1999 and a year later wrote the book as well as establishing the first Society of Friends of the Way of St. James in Slovenia. The second was written by an American actress with a strong interest in new-age spirituality and published by *Založba Obzorja*, a well-established Slovene publishing house.

From 2000 till 2019, over the past twenty years, more than forty books and movies on the Camino have been published in the Slovenian language. These include novels (5), travelogues (32), guidebooks (8) and movies (2). Twelve of these works were self-published, while others (31) were released by publishing houses—predominantly by smaller, privately-owned publishing houses where the authors were often also the (co)owners. With the exception of few books, it appears that these publishing projects have been driven by personal interest—a case of financially non-ambitious projects and publishing one's own experiences for a relatively small readership. There is also a great difference between the first and the second decade regarding the quantity of books published. In the first decade, only seven different books were printed (three reprints) and only nine identified authors, mainly Slovenians, with the exception of Shirley MacLaine. Over the next decade, the numbers increase drastically producing thirty-nine books (six reprints) and thirty-four authors.

Another interesting aspect of the topic is revealed by considering the lending figures[10] for books and films about the Camino in Slovenian libraries. The first one *The Camino—From Slavery to Freedom* (Slv. *Camino: Od suženjstva do svobode*) (1982 loans) was written by Petra Škarja, an entrepreneur, personal-development lecturer and a writer of self-help business books, published in 2017 (reprint in 2019), from her own publishing house. The second, entitled *Vulnerable: Stories from St. James Route* (Slv. *Ranljiva: Zgodbe z Jakobove poti*) (1963 loans) is a self-published book (in 2016, reprint in 2017), is catalogued under the category of spiritual, self-help books. It was written by a lecturer, yoga and meditation teacher, Tjaši Artnik Knibbe, who undertook the Camino after a family loss. The third one is entitled *Camino* (1121 loans) and is the self-published (in 2016) debut of Snežana Brumec, an economist and a member of a literary society in Celje. The fourth, *Camino: My Solitary Path or Purification of Body and Soul in a Feminine Way* (Slv. *Camino: Moja samotna pot ali čiščenje duše in telesa po žensko*) (1023 loans) is also a debut, published in 2009 by barrister and notary, Staša Lepej Bašelj by a small publishing house otherwise focused on schoolbooks. The fifth book, *From Nova Gorica to Compostela* (Slv. *Od Nove Gorice do Kompostele*) (788 loans) is a travelogue, written by Nace Novak, first published in 2004 and reprinted in 2008.[11] What one notices when going through these five books is that the first two can be linked to the so-called self-help genre, offering the readers a means to overcome crisis, while the remaining three can be characterized as travelogues focusing more on personal experiences along the journey.

Among books and films translated into the Slovenian language, the top five lent out in 2018 and 2019 were: *Two Steps Forward* (Slv. *Dva koraka naprej*) (3641 loans) by Australian couple Graeme Simsion and Anne Buist (first published 2017; 2018 in Slovene); Shirley MacLaine's *The Camino: A Journey of the Spirit* (1059 loans) (first published 2000; 2001 and 2007 in Slovene), which have all played an important role in broadening the Camino's popularity; *I'll Push You: A Journey of 500 Miles, Two Best Friends, and One Wheelchair* (Slv. *Nikoli vama ne bo uspelo! 800-kilometrsko romanje v Kompostelo, dva prijatelja in en invalidski voziček*) (1059 loans), the debut by two Americans, Patrick Gray and Justin Skeesuck (first published in 2017; 2018 in Slovene); Paulo Coelho's book, *The Pilgrimage: A Contemporary Quest for Ancient Wisdom* (Slv. *Magov dnevnik*) (874 loans) (first published in1987; 2012 in Slovene); and *The Santiago Pilgrimage: Walking the Immortal Way* (Slv. *Večna Jakobova pot: Nisem se ji mogel upreti*) (771 loans) by French doctor, human rights activist and novelist, and former ambassador of France to Senegal, Jean-Christophe Rufin (first published in French in 2014; 2015 in Slovene).

There are two Slovenian Facebook groups related to the Camino. The first group, *The St. James Route—Camino Slovenia* (Slv. *Pot Svetega Jakoba—Camino Slovenija*) is a public group with 3649 members and formed on 3 May 2013 ("Pot Svetega Jakoba"). The second one *The St. James Route—Camino Slovenia 2* (Slv. *Pot Svetega Jakoba—Camino Slovenija 2*) is a closed one with 419 members formed on 21 February 2019 ("Pot Svetega Jakoba-Camino Slovenija 2"). We were not accepted to the closed one, so we followed the public group, where one has access to very practical information, advice or questions about the Camino with posts by individual who have already accomplished it and also from those who are thinking to do so. There are several clusters of information available within this Facebook group: practical information, postings from the Camino hikers (the majority relating to Santiago de Compostela or Finisterre, announcements of a successful walking or cycling journeys), paid advertisements for hiking equipment or Camino tourist travel packages, announcements about public lectures on the Camino in Slovenia, posts from hikers who have undertaken other "Camino" routes in Europe (e.g., in Poland, Croatia, Hungary) or other known hiking tours (e.g., Appalachian Trail, Pacific Crest Trail), questions prior to hiking or pertaining to travel arrangements; posts about the Slovenian Camino route, books (exchanges of reading lists), announcements about religious events and seminars pertaining to walking and pilgrimage. However, the majority of information relates to practical information (asking for or giving advice) and posts from hikes (photos with short comments usually marked by hiking days—e.g., day 8) with an increasing number of posts related to Slovenian Camino over the last few years. As far as practical information is concerned, readers can get very concrete and detailed descriptions of the current situation on the Camino ("Pot Svetega Jakoba").

By following the Facebook posts on one hand, we notice that the Slovenian future or virtual pilgrim is mainly interested in practical information regarding transport and accommodation while the sole physical preparation (training, things to take…) is not at the core of their interest. On the other, an analysis of books shows a strong interest in new-age, self-help books related to the Camino among the Slovene speaking readers.

Conclusion: Shall We Start?

But where shall we start? Here, there or everywhere? Following the footprints of the Camino in a specific local setting feels like pushing different sites and times into the same frame and later reading them together. And this in itself is a dangerous endeavor. Some things fit together, while others need to be understood separately in their own specific contexts. The phenomenon of the Camino and that of the Santiago de Compostela shrine are related, but they are not the same; walking and pilgrimage share strong connections but they might as well be separate. As Slovenian parish priest Jožef Lavtižar wrote only half a century before Elias Valiña Sampedro started to paint yellow arrows aimed at walkers on the present-day French Camino, "No one walks on foot anymore on this long journey" (43). And even though by the end things do get mixed and blurred—the past does overlap with the present and the future; local merges with national and global—there are several specificities that can be told from the perspective of "the here and now."

According to the statistics of the Pilgrim's Reception Office in Santiago de Compostela, in 2006, 140 pilgrims carrying a Slovene passport received the final stamp of the Cathedral of Santiago on the *credenciales de peregrino* (pilgrim's credentials); in 2009 there were 357 Slovene pilgrims returning home with the "Compostela" and in 2018, 708 "Compostelas" roamed back to Slovenia ("Statistics"). What this simple statistic tells us is that the Camino is becoming increasingly popular in Slovenia, and by putting this piece of information together with the fact that hiking and mountain sports are traditionally popular in the country and are linked with the national identity (Topič, Coakley 2010, Kotnik 2007) we might say that the Camino as a contemporary phenomenon has fallen on fertile grounds. It also seems to have been very easily adopted by people (religious or otherwise, with strong national feelings or without) already equipped with a lot of practical knowledge on walking and mountaineering—few questions asked on the Facebook group were about walking, or preparation for walking the Camino. In the Slovenian context, these are obvious things learned in primary school or even earlier.

Following the story of the Society of Friends of the Way of St. James another footprint can be brought into the framework of the Camino. Marjeta and Metodij Rigler completed their pilgrimages well before "the Camino fever," by bus and in the political context of Yugoslavia. After completing their pilgrimage to Santiago and later determining the Slovenian Camino, it does seem that their motives were primarily religious and patriotic but also related to their pleasure of hiking and traveling. The initial idea for the Slovenian Camino was not a top-down effort but a bottom-up idea related to a specific segment of Slovene society, part of the post–World War II generation who did not feel comfortable in the previous political regime and finally felt at ease in the new born state of Slovenia. Younger generations, from different families, easily and quickly adopted their train of thought and the Camino (both Slovenian and transnational) is already well trodden by Slovenians, if not for religious or/and national pride, then certainly for recreational and/or personal self-development aspirations. That most book lending on the Camino in Slovenian libraries is related to personal development speaks to this point. Specifically, the book by Shirley MacLaine is still one of the most lent books on the Camino in Slovenia, while books by the three most lent Slovenian authors writing about the Camino are catalogued in COBISS.SI library system under the category of spiritual, self-help books. Together with visual anthropologist Tommi Mendel, who compared a young pilgrim walking the French Camino and a backpacking tourist visit to Indonesia, we might ask ourselves—is the link between religious pilgrimage and present-day Slovene endeavors a weak one after all?

It is so easy to draw a clear distinction between now and then, between here and there. But for the concluding remark we might also consider some similarities, following a Slovenian example. Count Ulrich II of Celje made his pilgrimage by horse with a wish to become a knight, but also for political and religious purposes. Even the Slovenian parish priest, Jožef Lavtižar, didn't go on foot, making his pilgrimage for religious purposes but also in order to write about it, to inform the numerous readers of the Hermagoras Society publishing house. He wrote about previous pilgrims from Carniola and emphasized how, in past times, "anyone who intended to make a pilgrimage to Compostela, prepared himself as if going to the Eternity" (40), an observation that could—on a smaller scale—apply to any journey and yet it relates to specific historical circumstances when transportation infrastructure was different and journeys were consequently longer and more unpredictable. It also relates to the individual who articulated these words—a priest—and resonates strongly on a personal level when one reads it quietly and with attention, a fact that should not be overlooked. Furthermore, the Rigler couple undertook their Camino journey for religious and patriotic purposes, also paving the way for other walkers and pilgrims to follow in their initial footsteps but were also inspired by other ideas. What the other ideas of those numerous Slovenian citizens walking the Camino are, has yet to be revealed. If we borrow here from Zygmunt Bauman's metaphors for the postmodern life strategies ("From Pilgrim" 18–37), it seems they might not be so locally specific. By referring to, or undertaking the Camino they/we might all be striving to overcome a postmodern restlessness, trying to assure an orderly, determined, predictable and ensured perspective that brings meaning to life through wandering and transforming it into "the track leading to the finishing line where the meaning resides. This 'bringing in' of meaning has been called 'identity-building'" (Bauman "From Pilgrim" 22).

Following all these different, yet related motives, maybe there is, after all, a right way to start reflecting on the Camino. A plural one. A friend once asked us, "What about you, if you would undertake a Camino, what would your expectations and hopes be?" Considering our different family backgrounds, one coming from a Catholic family and other being a descendent of conscious Yugoslavs and communists, we would probably list several different but also several similar aspirations, though surely there would be a plurality of reasons reflecting past, present (and future) contexts that we are part of. Among them also a simple curiosity, an urge for exploration. Let us end with a quote from Thomas Stearns Eliot's poem *Little Gidding,*

> We shall not cease from exploration
> And the end of all our exploring
> Will be to arrive where we started
> And know the place for the first time.

Notes

1. Older sources (folk songs, poems, tales, chronicles) talk about "pilgrimage to (Santiago de) Compostela" while contemporary sources (web pages, travelogues) mostly use the word Camino which does relate primarily to the pilgrim way(s) to Santiago de Compostela but (also) has other connotations related to hiking, new-age, popular books and movies or more generally to contemporary pilgrimage on-foot.

2. Specifically, in 1985 Santiago de Compostela's Old Town was inscribed on the UNESCO World Heritage List; in 1987, the Santiago de Compostela Pilgrim Route became the first "Cultural Route" certified by the newly-launched program of the Council of Europe; in 1993, UNESCO awarded World Heritage status to the pilgrimage route to Santiago de Compostela (only the part known as the French Way (Sánchez-Carretero 142)); and in 2000 the city was proclaimed a European City of Culture.

3. COBISS represents an organizational model of joining libraries into a (Slovenian) national library information system with a shared cataloguing.

4. The Institute of Information Science (IZUM) is a public institution established by the Government of the Republic of Slovenia as an information infrastructural service for Slovenian science, culture and education.

5. We use the term global modernity as a descriptor referring to time-space compression through modern communication and infrastructure technology following several authors such as Giddens, Bauman (*Liquid Modernity*), and Sheller and Urry.

6. Data refers to the statistics of completed "credenciales", a modern version of the "documents of safe conduct" which were given to medieval pilgrims. Specifically, during their visit to the Pilgrim's Office in Santiago de Compostela, Metodij and Marjeta Rigler were informed that they were the first two Slovenians obtaining the "credencial" according to their statistical data (Rigler and Rigler, Personal interview).

7. The Camino starts now (trans. from Galician).

8. The Socialist Federal Republic of Yugoslavia (SFRY), also known as Yugoslavia, existed from its foundation in the aftermath of World War II until its dissolution in 1992 amid the Yugoslav Wars.

9. Several authors who had researched and written about pilgrimages to Santiago de Compostela before Valiña's guidebook should also be mentioned. A transcription of the *Codex Calixtinus* by Walter Muir Whitehill in the early 1930s is very important, aiding several researchers who had no prior access to the *Liber Sancti Jacobi* manuscript (Gulish 33). Even more significant was Walter Starkie's *The Road to Santiago* (1957), a book which ushered in a new age of pilgrimage and reinvented the Route of the Milky Way, as many travelers now know it (Gulish 34). Another important element in the preservation of Santiago de Compostela—though mostly through Spanish iconography—was its promotion by General Francisco Franco. Namely, the traditional Catholic Spain of the early twentieth century felt itself threatened by the forces of modernization and Franco used the symbolism of Spain's past and medieval pilgrimage to Santiago de Compostela to restore national Catholicism. Paradoxically, however, during his leadership the Camino de Santiago experienced low periods of interest. Its true revival began in an increasingly secular society of the 1980s. In addition to the previously mentioned top-down recognition of UNESCO and the Council of Europe (cf. endnote no. 2) and Valiña's endeavors, one of the draws to the popularization of Santiago de Compostela and the Camino, especially among the Catholic youth of the Western world, was Pope John Paul II's visit to the shrine in the Holy Year of 1982 (Gulish 69–71).

10. Book lending figures for 2018 and 2019 are extracted from COBISS.SI system (cf. *Knjižnično nadomestilo*).

11. As a feuilleton, Novak's text was previously published in the local newspaper *Novi glas* in 2002.

Works Cited

Artnik-Knibbe, Tjaši. *Ranljiva: Zgodbe Z Jakobove poti (El Camino de Santiago): 850 km dolge poti prisotnosti, prebujenosti in miline*. 2016. Remco Knibbe. 2017.

Bambi, Gianluca, and Matteo Barbari, editors. *The European Pilgrimage Routes for Promoting Sustainable and Quality Tourism in Rural Areas*. Firenze University Press, 2015.

Bauman, Zygmunt. "From Pilgrim to Tourist—or a Short History of Identity." *Questions of Cultural Identity*, edited by Stuarts Hall and Paul du Gay, Sage, 1996, Sage, pp. 18–36.

_____. *Liquid Modernity*. Cambridge, Polity Press, 2000.

Beck, Ulrich. *Risk Society: Towards a New Modernity*. Sage, 1992.

Bourdarias, Jean, and Michel Wasielewski. *Guide Européen des Chemins de Compostelle*. Sarment Editions du Jubilé, 2002.

Brumec, Snežana. *Camino*. Slovenske Konjice, self-publishing, 2016.

"COBISS.net." *COBISS.net*, IZUM, www.cobiss.net/si/. Accessed 28 September. 2019.

Coelho, Paulo. *Magov dnevnik*. Tržič, Učila International, 2012.

Dostal, Josip. "Slike V Bodeščah in legenda sv. Jakoba." *Izvestja Muzejskega Društva Za Kranjsko*, vol. 19, 1909, pp. 31–36.

Doupona Topič, Mojca, and Jay Coakley. "Complicating the Relationship Between Sport and National Identity: The Case of Post-Socialist Slovenia." *Sociology of Sport Journal*, vol. 27, no. 4, 2010, pp. 371–389.

Eade, John, and Mario Katić. *Pilgrimage, Politics and Place Making in Eastern Europe: Crossing the Borders*. Ashgate, 2014.

Eliot, Thomas Stearns. "Little Gidding." *T.S. Eliot's "Little Gidding,"* www.columbia.edu/itc/history/winter/w3206/edit/tseliotlittlegidding.html/. Accessed 29 September. 2019.

Estevez, Emilio, director. *The Way*. Filmax, 2010.

Frey, Nancy. "The Smart Camino: Pilgrimage in the Internet Age." Annual General Meeting of the Confraternity of St James, 28 January 2017, London. Keynote Address.

"Galicia." *Online Etymology Dictionary*. www.etymonline.com/word/galicia/. Accessed 27 September 2019.

Giddens, Anthony. *Modernity and Self-Identity: Self and Society in the Late Modern Age*. Polity Press, 1991.

Grafenauer, Ivan. "Slovenska narodna romanca o romarju sv. Jakoba Komposteljskega." *Dom in Svet*, vol. 50, no. 7, 1938, pp. 338–348.

Gray, Patrick, and Skeesuck, Justin. *Nikoli vama ne bo uspelo! 800-kilometrsko romanje v Kompostelo, dva prijatelja in en invalidski voziček*. Družina, 2018.

Gulish, Rachael Jean. *The Rediscovery of Galicia in the Revival of the Camino de Santiago: Changing Images of Galicia in Modern Pilgrim Accounts*. 2011. Ohio State University. Ph.D. dissertation.

Izum. "Institut Informacijskih Znanosti." *IZUM*, www.izum.si/. Accessed 28 September. 2019.

"Jakobova pot Slovenija." *Jakobova pot Slovenija—Camino*, Društvo prijateljev poti sv. Jakoba v Sloveniji, 25 Januar 2018, www.jakobova-pot.si/. Accessed 25 September. 2019.

Jakop, Dolores. "Pot Svetega Jakoba-Camino Slovenija." *Pot Svetega Jakoba-Camino Slovenija Public Group*, 16 April 2019, www.facebook.com/groups/579584288729233/. Accessed 27 September. 2019.

Jalen, Janez. *Ovčar Marko*. 1929. Mladinska knjiga, 1988.

Jevnikar, Ivo. "Približati lepote romarskih poti." *Družina*, 3 August 2008, druzina.si/ICD/spletnastran.nsf/clanek/57-31-CerkevDoma-1/. Accessed 25 September. 2019.

Knjižnično nadomestilo, IZUM, plus.cobiss.si/kn/2019/. Accessed 28 September. 2019.

Kos, France. *Gradivo za zgodovino slovencev v srednjem veku*. Vol. 3, Katoliška tiskarna, 1911.

Kosi, Miha. *Potujoči srednji vek: Cesta, popotnik in promet na Slovenskem med antiko in 16. stoletjem*. ZRC SAZU, Založba ZRC, 1998.

Kotnik, Vlado. "Skiing Nation: Towards an Anthropology of Slovenian's National Sport." *Studies in Ethnicity and Nationalism*, vol. 7, no. 2, 2007, pp. 56–78.

Krajevni leksikon Dravske banovine: Krajevni repertorij z uradnimi, topografskimi, zemljepisnimitr, zgodovinskimi, kulturnimi, gospodarskimi in tujskoprometnimi podatki vseh krajev dravske banovine. Uprava Krajevnega leksikona Dravske banovine, 1937.

Lavtižar, Josip. "Kompostela." *Koledar Družbe sv. mohorja za leto 1909*, 1909, pp. 40–43.

Lepej Bašelj, Staša. *Camino: Moja samotna pot ali čiščenje duše in telesa po žensko*. Jutro, 2009.

MacLaine, Shirley. *The Camino: A Journey of the Spirit*. Pocket Books, 2000.

_____. *Camino: Po stezi zvezd*. 2001. Maribor, Obzorja. 2007.

Mendel, Tommi. *Common Roads—Pilgrimage and Backpacking in the 21st Century*. 2013. University of Zürich, the Swiss National Science Foundation, Ph.D. dissertation.

Mlinar, Janez. *Podobe Celjskih grofov v narativnih virih*. Oddelek za zgodovino Filozofske fakultete. 2005.

Novak, Nace. "Camino Frances: Od Nove Gorice do Santiaga." *Novi Glas* [Gorizia/Gorica], 31 October 2002, p.15.

_____. *Camino: Od Nove Gorice do Kompostele*. 2004. Gorica, Zadruga Goriška Mohorjeva. 2008.

"O Nas." Mohorjeva.org, Celjska Mohorjeva Družba, 27 March 2019, www.mohorjeva.org/o-nas./ Accessed 27 September. 2019.

Parežnik, Kristjan. "Zgodovina." *Krajevna Skupnost Galicija*, 2007–2011, www.galicija.si/index.php?stran=zgodovina/. Accessed 25 September. 2019.

Popotnik. "Jakobova Pot Slovenija." *Jakobova Pot Slovenija*, Društvo Prijateljev Poti Sv. Jakoba v Sloveniji, 20 February 2013, www.jakobova-pot.si/zgodovina/camino/. Accessed 20 September. 2019.

"Pot Svetega Jakoba-Camino Slovenija." *Pot Svetega Jakoba-Camino Slovenija Public Group*, www.facebook.com/groups/579584288729233/. Accessed 28 September. 2019.

"Pot Svetega Jakoba-Camino Slovenija 2." *Pot Svetega Jakoba-Camino Slovenija 2 Public Group*, https://www.facebook.com/groups/557884901379968/. Accessed 28 September 2019.

Pregelj, Ivan. "Kompostelski romarji." *Zbrano Delo*. Vol. 2. Maribor, Litera, 2005, pp. 381–448.

Prešeren, France. "Marskteri romar gre…" *Pesmi*. Mladinska knjiga, 1981, p. 108.

Rigler, Marjeta, and Metodij Rigler. *Blagor vama uboga reveža: Romanje po poti svetega Jakoba v Kompostelo*. Self-publishing, 2000.

_____. *Bom grmovje posekal, travice požel: Vodnik po gorenjski veji Jakobove poti.* Self-publishing, 2015.

_____. *Bom naredil stezice, ki so včasih bile: Vodnik po prekmursko-štajerski veji Jakobove poti.* Self-publishing, 2017.

_____. *Kje so tiste stezice, ki so včasih bile? Vodnik po slovenskem Caminu.* Self-publishing, 2010.

_____. Personal interview. 15 September 2019.

Rossell, Cayetano, editor. *Título: Crónicas de Los Reyes de Castilla, desde Don Alfonso el Sabio hasta los católicos Don Fernando y Doña Isabel.* Vol. 2. Madrid, M. Rivadeneyra, 1875–1878. eBook edition (Valladolid, Junta de Castilla y León, Consejería de Cultura y Turismo) bibliotecadigital.jcyl.es/es/consulta/registro.cmd?id=8333.

Rufin, Jean-Christophe. *Večna Jakobova pot: Nisem se ji mogel upreti.* Modrijan, 2015.

Sánchez-Carretero, Christina. "Heritage Regimes and the Camino de Santiago: Gaps and Logics." *Heritage Regimes and the State*, edited by Regina F. Bendix et al., Göttingen, Universitätverlag, 2012, pp. 141–155.

Sheller, Mimi, and John Urry. "The New Mobilities Paradigm." *Environment and Planning A: Economy and Space*, vol. 38, no. 2, Feb. 2006, pp. 207–226.

Simsion, Graeme C., and Anne Buist. *Dva Koraka Naprej.* Dob, Miš, 2018.

Škarja, Petra. *Camino: Od suženjstva do svobode.* 2017. Novo mesto, 5KA Izobraževanja. 2019.

Starkie, Walter. *The Road to Santiago: Pilgrims of St. James.* John Murray, 1957.

"Statistics." *Pilgrim's Reception Office*, Cathedral of Santiago, 2019, oficinadelperegrino.com/en/statistics/. Accessed 2 October. 2019.

Štrekelj, Karel, editor. *Slovenske narodne pesmi.* Slovenska matica, 1895–1923.

Trstenjak, Davorin. "Raziskavanja na polji staroslovanske mythologie." *Letopis Matice slovenske*, edited by Janez Bleiweis. Slovenska matica, 1870, p. 25.

Valiña Sampedro, Elias. *El Camino de Santiago: Estudio Histórico-jurídico.* Madrid, CSIC, 1971. *The Pilgrims Guide to the Camino de Santiago.* Galaxia, 1992.

Voje, Ignacij. "Romanje Ulrika II Celjskega v Kompostelo k Sv. Jakobu." *Zgodovisnki* časopis, vol. 3, 1984, pp. 225–230.

Welz, Gisela. "A Common Cultural Basis for a European Demos? Heritage Making and Participatory Memory Practices in Europe." Poem Opening Conference—Participatory Memory Practices: Connectivities, Empowerment, and Recognition of Cultural Heritages in Mediatized Memory Ecologies, 13 December 2018, University of Hamburg, Hamburg. Keynote lecture. www.poem-horizon.eu/keynotes/.

Yamashita, Shinji et al., editors. *The Making of Anthropology in East and Southern Asia.* Berghahn Books, 2004.

Acknowledgment

This essay was written in the framework of the program P5–0408 and financed by the Slovenian Research Agency.

About the Contributors

Joanne **Benham Rennick** is a social theorist and interdisciplinary scholar with research publications on modernization, globalization, social economy, international development, and post-secondary education. She was an advisor and grant writer for Jacoba Atlas' documentary film *One Path, Many Ways: The Camino Documentary* (2010–2014). She holds tenure in the Global Studies Department at Wilfrid Laurier University in Canada.

José **Domínguez-Búrdalo** received a Ph.D. in philosophy (romance languages) at Johns Hopkins University (2002). He is a professor of Spanish culture at Miami University (Ohio). He has published in several areas, including on Unamuno, Juan Goytisolo, Spanish Africanist cinema under Franco, Cervantes' *Novelas ejemplares* and on soccer. He has directed a Study Abroad program in Asturias (Spain) since 2011. A crucial part of that experience is centered on the Santiago de Compostela, which is also the basis for his documentary *Itinera*.

Maryjane **Dunn** is an associate professor of Spanish at Henderson State University, Arkansas. She has followed the pilgrimage to Santiago de Compostela both personally (first walking the *Camino francés* in 1979 as an undergraduate) and professionally in her scholarly work. Her published works have focused on pilgrimage studies and literary depictions of pilgrimage by 19th-century women writers. She also translated Books I, II, and III of the medieval *Codex Calixtinus* into English.

Annie **Hesp** is an advanced instructor at Virginia Tech. In addition to courses on the Camino de Santiago, she teaches on language, literature, medieval Spanish, and pedagogy. Her primary area of research is literary and filmic representations of the Camino de Santiago. She is also interested in other long distant pilgrimages and cultural rituals of pilgrim life such as tattoos. Every year, she leads a group of undergraduate students on a study abroad program hiking the Camino.

Terry **Inglese** is a senior researcher and lecturer. She holds a Ph.D. in education from the Università della Svizzera Italiana, Lugano and the University of Santa Barbara, California, and an MBA from the FHNW School of Business—Institute for Information Systems and the Edinburgh Business School at the Heriot Watt University of Scotland.

Špela **Ledinek Lozej** completed a Ph.D. in ethnology at the University of Ljubljana in 2012. She has been working at the Institute of Slovenian Ethnology at the Research Centre of the Slovenian Academy of Sciences and Arts since 2000—first as a junior researcher and then as a project manager and research fellow. Between

2016 and 2017 she was a research fellow at the University of Udine. Her main research interests are material culture, livelihood strategies, mountain regions and borderlands, pilgrimage and heritage.

Anne **McConnell** is a professor in the English Department at West Virginia State University. She teaches world literature, literary theory, and writing. Her first book, *Approaching Disappearance*, was published by Dalkey Archive Press in 2013. Her scholarly work focuses on contemporary literature and critical writing from France, Latin America, and the United States.

Nicol **Nixon Augusté** is a professor of English at the Savannah College of Art and Design and an American Academy in Rome Affiliated Fellowship recipient. Her interests include women and theology, rhetoric and composition, and Native American studies. She has published in *Catholic Medical Quarterly UK, The Encyclopedia of Psychology and Religion, The Encyclopedia of Women in World Religions*, and *The Tau*. Her book, *Rome's Female Saints: A Poetic Pilgrimage to the Eternal City*, has been awarded Imprimatur status.

Kip **Redick** is a professor and the chair of the Department of Philosophy and Religion at Christopher Newport University. His professional interests include pilgrimage studies, spiritual journey, spirituality of place, aesthetics, media ecology; visual, religious, and environmental rhetoric; and film studies. His specific research interest centers on the study of wilderness trails as sites of spiritual journey.

Nataša **Rogelja Caf** completed a Ph.D. in social anthropology at the Postgraduate School of the Humanities in Ljubljana in 2005. From 1998 to 2005 she worked as a junior researcher at the Centre for Mediterranean Studies. She has been working as Research Fellow at the Slovenian Migration Institute at the Research Centre of the Slovenian Academy of Sciences and Arts since 2011, where she mostly deals with lifestyle migrations, mobility studies, tourism and heritage.

Danielle **Terceiro** is a former lawyer who changed her focus from antitrust law to the close analysis of literature and is a high school English teacher in western Sydney. In 2016, she completed an MA in children's literature at Macquarie University, Sydney, with a research thesis that examined the depiction of felt experience in graphic memoirs.

Javier **Torre Aguado** is a professor of Spanish literature and cultural studies at the University of Denver. He is a specialist in contemporary Spanish literature, with a focus on narratives of travel and exploration. He has published numerous articles in this field, as well as two books: *Volver para contarlo: Temas y tendencias en la narrativa española de viajes del siglo XX* (2019), and *Diario de la expedición Domínguez-Escalante por el Oeste Americano (Nuevo México, Colorado, Utah, Arizona)* (2016).

Tiffany Gagliardi **Trotman** is an associate professor of Spanish at the University of Otago Dunedin in New Zealand. She is the author of *Eduardo Mendoza's Crime Novels: The Function of Carnivalesque Discourse in Post-Franco Spain, 1979–2001* (2009) and the editor of *The Changing Spanish Family: Essays on New Views in Literature, Cinema and Theatre* (2011). In addition, she has published articles and chapters on various contemporary Spanish writers including Lucía Etxebarria, Carlos Ruiz-Zafón, Antonio Gala and Eduardo Mendoza.

Index

Numbers in *bold italics* indicate pages with illustrations